A CULINARY TRAVELLER IN TUSCANY

✦

A CULINARY TRAVELLER IN
TUSCANY

Exploring & Eating off the Beaten Track

BETH ELON

THE LITTLE BOOKROOM ✦ NEW YORK

© 2006 Beth Elon

Book design: Louise Fili Ltd

ISBN-13: 978-1-892145-36-9
ISBN-10: 1-892145-36-7

Printed in the United States of America

Library of Congress Cataloging-in-Publication Data

Elon, Beth.
A culinary traveller in Tuscany / by Beth Elon.
p. cm.
1. Cookery, Italian—Tuscan style. 2. Food—Italian—Tuscany. I. Title.
TX723.2.T86E57 2006
641.5945'5—dc22
2005027780

Published by The Little Bookroom
1755 Broadway, Fifth floor, New York NY 10019
(212) 293-1643 Fax (212) 333-5374
editorial@littlebookroom.com
www.littlebookroom.com

FOR TRISTAN
who will grow in these places I love so well

ACKNOWLEDGEMENTS

I would like to thank the many people who have helped me in countless ways to delve more deeply into the ways of Tuscans and their culture. The restaurateurs I write about have been generous, both with their time and recipes. My many friends and neighbors have shown me the way to both beautiful sites in Tuscany and its food. To the various local vendors and producers of the products of Tuscany who have clarified local traditions and specialties for me, I offer my thanks as well. Among them are Sonia Balducci in Montecatini, Sauro Signori in Pistoia, Nando Quattrone and Daniela Zamorra in Filattiera, and Rosetta Petra in Lamporecchio.

A special grateful acknowledgement to Daniella DeNur and Yossi Riback who discussed the concept of the book with me before it even began. Marta Braun read the manuscript as I wrote, offering suggestions and corrections that were helpful indeed. Amos Elon read the entire manuscript and, as always, was invaluable in his support and critical attention. Mari Roberts in London was the first to actually carefully edit the manuscript for my British publisher, Transworld.

There cannot be a more tasteful, caring, and meticulous editor in New York than Angela Hederman, my publisher, editor, and now good friend. Her attention to detail—and to my terrible Italian language spelling—has saved my credibility. Needless to say, whatever errors remain are mine. My thanks too to Nadia Aguiar for filling in so many important spaces. Agent Abner Stein in London and his office staff brought the book to the attention of the English-language publishing world, and I am grateful.

Many other friends have helped me to discover Tuscany's rural traditions and joined me in my travels. Among them are Lina Ercolessi, Paola Canepari, Luciano and Vanna Disperati, Miranda and Paolo Giuliani, Gabriella Mazzoni, Massimo and Giovanna Duranti, Ghiberto Piccini, Sussi Pundik, Michal Pundik-Sagi, Lior Sagi, Clarissa Pryce-Jones, Penny Fantacci, Adrianna Milla, Silvia Servi, Ingrid Harbeck, Paul Gervais, Gil Cohen, Michael Schluter, Milly Passigli, Nehama and Peter Hillman, Ellen Blair, Tobia and Melina Milla-Moss, Amit Matarasso, and Anna Lisa Tempestini.

My thanks too to the helpful people at Slow Food Italy who care so much about reviving and maintaining the genuine quality of traditional food: Nino Ricci in Florence, Walter Nunciatini in Grossetto, Franco Utili in Vicchio.

Two food writers have inspired both my feeling for food and how I would like to present it. As for so many others, Elizabeth David long ago opened my eyes and my appetite to what Mediterranean food could be. Elizabeth Rohmer's *The Tuscan Year* was a book I read only after I'd been in my own small *podere* for a number of years, and could enjoy and empathize so completely with her kitchen adventures in Val d'Orcia.

And of course my thanks and gratitude go to Amos and Danae, both of whom have encouraged me in my pursuits over the years, and without them both, I would not have known Tuscany.

CONTENTS

A PERSONAL NOTE

TUSCANY—AND ITS FOOD—CAME INTO OUR LIVES MORE THAN THIRTY YEARS AGO WHEN A CHANCE encounter in a lovely little village in the Apennine foothills led to our purchasing a small abandoned farm on its edge. It would be for many years a vacation home, and eventually became our only home as we comfortably settled into a life of Mediterranean enchantment and earthy discovery. This book is a retelling of some of my most pleasurable discoveries: the rich and diverse Tuscan landscapes, the wonder of isolated, architecturally perfect ancient hill towns, along with the culture of natural and traditional food that continues to this day in the face of modernity and fast-paced living. I've tried to combine all of these aspects in the small itineraries I've chosen here; I hope readers will find their way to their own enjoyments too.

Beyond the better known larger cities that attract ever growing hordes of tourists and souvenir and fast-food shops, Tuscany has its hundreds of small clustered hill towns, each with a singular way of doing things. Throughout the Tuscan countryside, with its lovely churches, piazzas, and ancient architecture, you'll find a rural art that is often worthy of the finest city museums. There's also a population that clings obstinately to a sensual way of life that includes an authentic experience of food as one of its most wholesome elements. No great chefs, just great tastes.

We chanced upon our little farm in 1972. On what seemed like a lonely hillside, local acquaintances led us to an old, bramble-covered, heavily-beamed ruin of a farmhouse, older even than my native United States and as much in need of repair. With the house came the obligatory farm—too much of it and seemingly abandoned—and an amazing view of vineyards and olive groves, mountains beyond, and distant medieval towns sprinkled across the landscape, a view that had not changed dramatically in hundreds of years. Looking at an old map of our village some years later, I was startled to see that pretty much everything was still as it had been in the seventeenth century.

We weren't very particular about restoration, I now regret. (Once you don't add a fireplace to your living room, it never gets done.) We just patched up the house casually, covering the stall floors with bricks, adding only bathrooms and central heating. We immediately realized that we weren't located on a lonely hillside but fortunately appended to the hillside just under the church of a small village with some 110 inhabitants. Having a village at our backs meant that we could have our little corner of privacy among vineyards, olives, and forests, yet still walk up the short path to a perfect Renaissance piazza where our neighbors welcomed summer evening breezes and the children played ball. Our daughter grew up here. The Italian language became part of her heritage. And I had an entire village of invariably kind neighbors who became friends and invited me into their kitchens to gossip and learn all about the Tuscan way with food: the combination of fresh vegetables with the wild and cultivated herbs that grew all around us, the quick and precise way in which meals were prepared, the lasting power of tradition, the festive foods that came with celebrations and the most important rituals.

The house had been lived in by tenant farmers who shared its ample spaces with livestock and farm produce. At one end was the barn where chickens, goats, pigs, and sheep had fed and slept. At the other end was the large kitchen with a huge open fireplace where the family cooked, ate, socialized, and stayed warm through the winter months. A hole in the wall next to the fireplace opened to an outside oven where the daily bread was baked, and where on festive occasions game and other succulent casseroles were slowly roasted to perfection. From the large open hood of the fireplace hung a heavy iron chain with a hook to hang the large iron pots in which food was cooked and kept warm.

Between the kitchen and the stalls was the *cantina*, where wine was made and stored. When we first saw the house, an enormous chestnut wine cask still stood in the corner. (We had to dismantle it to clear space for our dining room. Luciano Disperati, our ingenious local carpenter, whose grandfather had made the cask, turned it into a desk for my husband; he's since written several books on it.) We found large green hand-blown demijohns resting in rotting straw baskets lined up against the wall. Olive oil had been stored here too, in big-bellied terracotta jugs; alas, neither oil nor jugs had been left behind.

A hand-chiseled stone staircase, well-worn and precipitous, led to the second floor where all the rooms looked out onto the hills and the Apennine mountains beyond. As far as I could tell, the sleeping area for the family was limited to two upstairs rooms, one at each end of the house. I don't know how they did it; the last to occupy the house was a family of twelve. Between the two family rooms were open spaces for hanging and drying herbs, sausages, and other meats for eating during the winter months. Clusters of grapes would be hung here too, until Christmas, when they were sealed inside a small barrel to eventually become *vin santo*, the traditional dessert wine served with hard biscuits at the end of most meals. Our farm, I would later learn, also had some of the best fig trees of the entire village; we counted six different varieties among some thirty trees. Figs must also have been hung to dry in the open spaces of the second floor. The chestnuts that grew in our forests and the walnuts and hazelnuts from the trees around the house would all go into the same upstairs larder, as did potatoes, onions, and garlic harvested during the summer.

Our house was a *casa del pastore*, a shepherd's house. No doubt heavily scented *pecorino* cheeses—made from the milk of their sheep—had permeated the air of what would become our upstairs guest room. In a corner of this room, which lay directly over the *cantina* on the ground floor, was a trap door through which harvested grapes were thrown down each autumn into the wine cask below. We could imagine the farmer lowering himself as well, to crush the grapes with his bare feet, dancing around inside the barrel. We learned later that this would have been a dangerous practice; the poisonous fumes of the fermenting grapes could overwhelm and kill. It was more likely that large battering poles were used to crush the grapes. (Or that, like with us later on, the grapes were crushed first in large open tubs—indeed with bare feet—and only later thrown into the barrel.)

The last occupants, the Teglia family, had left some twenty years earlier, to find work in the new small industries down in the valley. Many families had abandoned their farms at the time for the same reason. Tenant farming allowed a certain frugal security but was otherwise oppressive. A farmer could not dream of bettering his lot. Age-old paternalism had shaped village life—and Italian cuisine—for centuries. Up to fifty percent of a farmer's olive oil, wine and other produce went to the *padrone*; the remaining part was consumed at home, and traded or sold in the local marketplace. When land reform came in, farmers had the opportunity—rarely taken up—to buy their farms. Making a living from a farm was a daunting prospect. And so most farmers left.

Nice things began to happen almost as soon as we arrived. I was still unpacking our bags when Giuseppina appeared, having heard about the new foreigners about to move in. She had arrived a few months earlier from Benevento, an impoverished province high into the hills above Naples, to join her sister and brother who were already improving their lives in a more prosperous Tuscany. Might I want someone to help in the house, and with the farm as well? Our meeting that first day led to a warm familial relationship that lasted more than seventeen years, until Giuseppina retired and bequeathed us her loquacious daughter-in-law.

Giussepina taught me the ways of the field, how to plant what and where. She pointed out edible wild greens, broccoli rabe and fennel, prickly nettles and borage, and showed me how to use them. She taught me how to look for *nipotella*, the wild mint that makes zucchini taste like wild mushrooms, to preserve tomatoes in used beer bottles the way they did in the poorer south, to dry and shell beans and chickpeas. As we picked green beans she would admonish me not to look wearily at the unending line awaiting, but to concentrate on the plant at hand. She insisted on planting full crops of potatoes, onions, and garlic at the right moment in order that we might store them for the winter. It did no good to point out that the market could provide me with the same things at a lower cost.

I discovered our capers during my first summer. Early one morning, around 6am, I looked out my bedroom window to discover a rather grumpy-looking old villager carefully plucking every bud from a bush on the wall below. I'd thought it was a beautiful bush, with graceful pink and white flowers, and wondered aloud to Giuseppina why he wasn't letting the flowers bloom. She explained they were capers and that it was the habit to pick clean the hardy plants each morning. Hesitant American that I was, I didn't very much want to confront even the crankiest of locals, and so took the easy way out. I got to the wall each morning by 5:30am to beat out our trespasser, and plucked enough to satisfy my new urge to live off the land, leaving plenty for the old man as well. Giuseppina taught me how to pickle the buds in our own vinegar, and I continue to make little presents of them to grateful friends each winter.

We worked and learned Tuscany together, although I was more the student, she the teacher. Together we acquired a taste for unsalted Tuscan bread. Together we distrusted a major commandment that rules the Tuscan farm: chores one does or does not do with the rising and setting of the moon. Giuseppina had not followed the moon rhythm in Benevento, nor had I in Larchmont, New York. But we both gave in, Giuseppina muttering that the moon was different here than in Benevento and I simply accepting the local lore. Since then both of us have become convinced. My first experience in being contrary began with my preserving tomatoes before the moon began to descend. It ended one night with an explosion of bottled tomatoes all over the kitchen. Apart from the fright at being woken by the explosion, the scene was one of carnage. We had to repaint.

I had so much to learn. Late in our first summer, I was sitting in the doorway of what was not yet our paved terrace when an enormous pig ran by, almost brushing my knees. My only previous encounters had been "three little pigs" kind of pigs. I screamed to my husband upstairs that we were being attacked by wild boars. At that moment a farmer and his two sons came racing around the corner of the house armed with broomsticks and pitchforks. *"Scusi, Signora,"* they apologized as they ran by, *"li voglia bene le mele in dietro la casa."* ("He loves to eat the apples behind your house.") I hurried around to the back of the house to find the pig happily munching the young fruit that had fallen from the apple tree. Emilio — he had been one of the last Teglias to live in our house and the only one still to farm nearby — prodded him home. I'd had my first experience of an enormous Italian pig. (I was to later have my share with wild boars as well, mostly competing with them and huge porcupines for delicious sweet corn I'd brought from America to plant. Needless to say, I lost.)

Signor Biondi arrived at our door not long after Giuseppina. He told us he'd been working a small piece of our land during the years the property was abandoned. Surely we wouldn't mind if he resumed planting on that insignificant corner. We knew nothing of Signor Biondi but were pleased to agree, and to know that our lower terraces would be profitably used.

As it turned out, Signor Biondi became a lot more to us than just a farmer working a piece of our land. I learned a lot from him too. He helped me to plant the essential rosemary and sage and to pick the wild sour cherries that we could preserve in *grappa*. He explained and planted *cavolo nero* (black cabbage or kale) and *bietole* (swiss chard) that are so much of the Tuscan table, and brought me artichoke plants that would give us tender baby artichokes each spring. And it was Signor Biondi who all but forced me to overcome a natural revulsion to eating adorable little furry rabbits; I could never reject the warm skinned carcass he presented me with every now and again, lovely dappled fur still clinging to its four paws. The entire Biondi family became good friends. Signora Biondi and their daughter Franca were among the first women in the village I came to know well. With them I first smelled, tasted, envied their skills, and learned to make *crostini di fegato*, *zuppa di contadini*, and so many other local special dishes.

Over the years as our relationship developed Signor Biondi tended to chores around the house that we could not do ourselves. He did it all in the old-fashioned way. Mechanized tools were not yet in regular use. Every morning before six I could hear beneath our bedroom window the swishing of his little hand-held sickle, the *falce*, as he stooped to cut vines and overgrown grass along our path. He carried the rusting little tool everywhere, tucked into his well-worn leather belt, along with a whetstone to sharpen it. The blade was worn to a width of a few centimeters. He patched it when the handle broke, welded it if the metal cracked. There was no thought of replacing it. He carried one other tool, a *zappa*, an iron-headed short hoe with which to turn the earth and dig up unwanted vegetation. Newfangled tools were not for this old curmudgeon; I expect he would not have known what to do with a mechanical pruner. The quick swish became our early morning sound much as the crowing of the nearby rooster.

Signor Biondi brought us a few liters of olive oil and wine each year; we did not ask for it, he was working our land for himself. But it was pleasant to receive what he brought, the fresh, fragrant oil especially. His wine grew better with the years, and even won a much-coveted prize as the best vintage in the village one year. We began to make our own wine and collect the olives ourselves only after Signor Biondi, at eighty-five, was no longer able to get around and we began to live here all year round.

He was a natural grump and continually warned against impending disasters, especially when things looked good, every time we hoped that we might see fruit on our trees or a good crop of vegetables. He was usually right. The fruit buds had arrived too soon; frost would kill them. Not enough rain had fallen; we could give up on beans. I later read that this was indeed the curse of Tuscany. Fernand Braudel tells us in his history of the Mediterranean that between the fourteenth and eighteenth centuries there were only eleven seasons without at least one disaster: drought or too much rain and flooding, hail, epidemics, and other horrors. Signor Biondi was often sour about Giuseppina's capabilities in the vegetable garden. She came from the south — *da giu* — where they didn't really know how to farm properly. He corrected, admonished, and grouched. It was some years before she began to fight back and defend her own way, and he finally admitted that even though she came from "down there" she was really okay. In the end they had real affection for one another, each in his or her cranky way. And I loved them both.

We slowly came to know our other neighbors too. We lived just below the church. Don Giuliano, the village priest, was attended by his bent but spry old mother, who often wandered down our path on her way to find herbs in the forest below. She'd inevitably return with various weeds methodically arranged between her fingers and explain patiently what each was for: to cure a stomach ache or cough, to help digestion, or to add a taste to the *frittata* or a soothing scent to the bath.

I remember one grim day when I arrived home to a happy Henry, our dog, tail wagging excitedly, greeting me at the door with a dead chicken he'd proudly killed and brought home for us. To my dismay, the ever-practical Giuseppina was already preparing to pluck the poor limp thing. I went off to the village to inquire vaguely if someone might be missing a chicken; in those days it was 5000 lire to reimburse a farmer. No one claimed the chicken and so Giuseppina prepared it for eating, wrapped it in newspaper, and put it into the fridge. Not long after, Don Giuliano's mother wandered by, peering here and there, obviously looking for something. "Oh Signora," I said, "is it a chicken you're missing?" We went into the house and Giuseppina brought the head up from the garbage pail and asked somewhat petulantly if this was him. "Oh indeed," she replied, and it wasn't Henry's fault at all. The chicken had escaped from the coop. And thank goodness it was Henry who had gotten it. This way she knew it was safe to eat. And so she trundled off with the day's lunch.

In the beginning our neighbors could not understand why we were here at all. Few foreigners wandered by in those days, and the villagers themselves traveled no further than the local sea coast for vacation. Why would a stranger want to settle in such an out-of-the-way small town? Many Italians were still undervaluing themselves in the aftermath of defeat in the Second World War, and couldn't understand that an American might prefer to settle into an ancient, worm-eaten farmhouse rather than enjoy the splendors of fat, rich America. It was useless to attempt to explain our admiration. We slowly learned how a small Italian village works as a social unit and extended family, people taking care of one another, nurturing the lame, succoring the bereaved, and, often as not, being mean to one another too. Most of the old families in the village are related; in fact, there are only two or three old clans in all. Small rituals, yearly festivals, church processions, are all organized within the closed circle of old-timers.

Traditional foods, their preparation, and eating, are a large part of life and all its rituals. Planning and carrying out various public *feste* during the year is a major task for the village women. The parties happen, mostly in summer months, in the piazza. For each *festa*, the men roast the meat and grill the steaks, the women prepare the rest of the meal: the *antipasti*, soups and bread salads, side dishes and desserts. Over the years I've been there to offer help, but usually local tradition faces me stonily, rigidly. I'm allowed to watch and taste, but not actually to cook. The expression, *"non si fa cosi"* ("that's not how it's done") meets any innovation I might suggest. Every time I've tried to chop something differently or recommend the slightest variation or even stick my fingers into the dough, there it is: *"Non si fa cosi."*

On Ferragosto (Assumption Day), the August 15 holiday, an informal picnic happens on the piazza. Everyone brings something. My hummus — a mash of chickpeas, garlic, olive oil, and salt—has become part of the local lore. I knew that Tuscans savor a salad of chickpeas in a dressing of olive oil, garlic, and salt. My mash, I claimed, was the same thing, just prepared differently, a new sort of *crostini* topping. When I brought it to the picnic, only a few courageous souls were even ready to taste it. The most complimentary comment was *"hmm, interessante."* Mostly I just heard *"cosa sarebbe?"* "What in heaven's name is it?" Same ingredients, but not the same at all.

Making fresh pasta was something I needed to learn although it remains a challenge. When I heard that Luciano Disperati, our master carpenter and good friend, made fresh pasta for Sunday lunch, I asked him if I could come and watch. I had to see if it was as easy as he assured me it was.

One of the most traditional fresh pasta dishes here is *tortellini in brodo*, little meat-stuffed rings in broth, often served on festive occasions, especially at Christmas time. This was to be the dish on the Sunday I joined

Luciano and his wife Vanna for pasta-making. Vanna greeted me at the door at 9am and took me down to their bright kitchen. Luciano was already busy laying out the ingredients. First thing was to prepare the dough, which would rest while they worked in tandem to prepare the filling. Into the food processor went one and one-fourth cups of plain white flour, a pinch (½ teaspoon) of salt, three fresh eggs, and a tablespoon of olive oil. The processor took less than two minutes to form a solid paste. Luciano scraped it all out and worked it some more on the marble tabletop over a dusting of flour for another five minutes. Then Vanna covered it with a cloth to lie quietly while they prepared the filling.

The filling was three ounces of prosciutto (with its fat), three ounces of *mortadella* sausage, and another three ounces of grated Parmesan. We weighed it as we went, but that was mostly for me; normally they would go *al occhio*, by eye. The ingredients went into the food processor with a grinding of nutmeg and an egg. The result was a delicious mass, a grainy paste.

Luciano began to roll out the pasta. First he dusted the marble tabletop with some more flour. He worked with his own hand-fashioned rolling pin, a thick round piece of wood about a foot and a half long. His method seemed easier than any hand-cranked or electric pasta machine. He simply rolled here and there, stretching the sheet out, adding more flour. Every now and again, he rolled up the dough on the rolling pin and flipped it over to its other side. He continued working in this way for about fifteen minutes, until the large thin sheet of pasta was almost as wide as the working space, a full three feet long and about two feet wide.

Tortellini are little discs of dough, stuffed and folded in half, then pulled round your second finger and pinched to close, ending up as funny-looking fat little rings. To prepare them, Luciano used a glass of about five centimeters in diameter to cut discs from the dough. Vanna put half a teaspoon of filling on each. We all folded them and pulled them the appropriate finger to close the circle, leaving a little flap to stick up. Within minutes we had more than a hundred, enough to generously serve about ten. They went into a home-made meat broth that Vanna had prepared earlier. There was some leftover dough, and that was quickly rolled out and sliced into thin *tagliatelle*, enough for another meal. We were finished within an hour. An invaluable lesson was over, and eventually I became almost as adept as Luciano.

Preserving olives in the Tuscan way was another lesson picked up from village friends. Olives here are soaked for fifty days in water that's changed daily and then pickled in an elusive combination of spices that can include cinnamon, cloves, nutmeg, pimiento, anise, and other flavorings. Such spices — that most certainly found their way along the Silk Road into Italy — flavor almost everything preserved in Tuscany, vegetables as well as olives.

Summertime activities in the village piazza, as everywhere in Tuscany, are diverse, ranging from band concerts, operatic offerings, art exhibitions, and local theater performances to just having fun. On the last Saturday in July is a big planned party, with almost two hundred paying guests helping to finance other events. The lovely small square is filled with colorful tables with a long buffet of savory local dishes down the middle. Demand has grown over the years; reservations must be made early. The meal itself has become more elaborate, and more elegantly served too. Now we have rented linen tablecloths rather than paper sheets, cloth napkins, and real cutlery has replaced the plastic. The atmosphere is festive, the piazza dramatically illuminated. The meal itself is entirely made by the villagers, preparations go on for days in many kitchens and the final assembly takes place in the old crest-encrusted Palazzo Pretorio that fronts the square. Different *crostini* toppings are smeared onto sliced baguettes and placed on large platters. *Ribolitta* (well-flavored bread soup) and *panzanella* (bread salad) arrive, along with cold meats to slice and tasty side dishes to spoon onto large platters. The proudest display is collected in a back room: a vast assortment of desserts, cakes, and fruit tarts, creams, different versions of the acclaimed *torta della nonna* (grandmother's cake, a rich layered cream cake dotted with pine nuts). Every housewife in town made her own favorite.

The men grill the sausages, pork chops, and chicken over a large fire behind the *palazzo*, just opposite the church. Those who aren't preparing the food lay the tables, precisely and decorously. Much attention goes into the flower arrangements for the tables, and how the service is laid and the napkins folded. The little piazza becomes an elegant outdoor salon. A local band arrives just before the guests, and sets up on the grassy patch along the broad side of the church. After dinner the large buffet table is moved away to make room for dancing, traditional dancing mostly.

When it's all over, the clean-up begins, tables and chairs are gathered, tableware divided for washing up at home. The piazza is left spotless, ready for churchgoers the next morning. The following evening is for *avanzi*, leftovers, shared by everyone who's helped.

Like most foreign newcomers to Tuscany, we became enormously proud of our homemade wine, and are now almost the only wine-producing family around. Our Italian neighbors turned long ago to buy at the local *cantina*, where inexpensive wine can be bought by the demijohn for bottling at home. It was Signor Biondi who kept us at it. He never ceased trimming the vines to make wine at the end of September. A few bottles always awaited us when we arrived the following summer. When Signor Biondi could no longer do it, we continued. Now we have Stefano. The demographic nature of our village—as in all of Italy, indeed Europe—has changed over the years. (African, Vietnamese, and eastern European children have joined the games on the piazza.) Stefano arrived with his wife Flora and two lively daughters—Giulia and Melena—from Albania a few years ago, and live in the small *dependance* that adjoins our house. They tend the dogs when we're away (as we do theirs when they are off somewhere), plant and weed the *orto* (vegetable garden), and keep the produce coming for all of us. Stefano also tends the grapes and the olives, and we all join to make the wine and collect the olives that go for pressing at the local cooperative mill.

My favorite festivities are the ones occasioned by the new wine and freshly pressed olive oil. At *vendemmia*, the grape harvest, in late September, we invite friends to help pick the grapes and I prepare a hearty and festive Tuscan lunch. I remember *vendemmie* from years back, real feasts with a lot of drinking and too much eating. We do it more simply. With help from friends it doesn't take more than a few hours to cut and gather all our grapes. A few years ago Signor Biondi was still crushing the grapes with his bare feet in large plastic tubs. Now we have an aged hand-cranking press that does it just as well. The process is simple. Everything—crushed grapes, seeds, juice—is dumped into the *botte*, these days no longer a chestnut barrel but a large fiberglass vat. The fermenting juice separates from the dregs and, after a week, when the boiling stops, is decanted into demijohns. We take a sampling over to the local *cantina* for analysis; if the alcohol content reaches eleven percent, we don't have to add anything. If it's less, we add a bit of *mosto*, a heavier wine, usually from the south, to give it a bit more alcohol content as well as body and taste. Nothing else ever goes in; no preservatives or other enhancers. We transfer the wine from demijohn to demijohn a couple of times during the winter, to drain off the sediment but don't otherwise pay it much attention until we bottle the following spring. It may not be a fine Chianti but we never wake up next morning with a headache.

Making olive oil is even less of a science than wine-making. I've tasted better oils and worse. One thing is certain: fresh olive oil that you—or a friend—have made is nothing like the stuff you buy in bottles, no matter how expensive and *extravergine* it claims to be. I love the ritual that goes along with making oil. If the smell of fermenting figs fallen from the trees is my September and the odor of burning charcoal the first sign of winter, November brings the overwhelming aroma of crushed olives at the *frantoio*, the mill where we bring our olives to be ground into oil. I loved it even more when our *frantoio* was still an old mill powered by the river next to it. The olives were crushed as they had been for centuries, by two massive revolving grindstones. The oil oozed out through pads of felt squeezed by a giant screw. A big open fireplace in a large beamed room was available; while we waited our turn we could prepare the meal that ritually went along with olive pressing. Friends were invited to gather at the long chestnut table. The air was rich with smells of centuries of oil. Carafes of your own oil, still warm and bubbling from the press, arrived at regular intervals.

The traditional *frantoio* meal always began with a simple *fett'unta*, a thick slice of farm bread gently toasted on the open fire and saturated with the new thick golden-green oil. Everything that followed demanded yet another topping of the fresh oil: the *farinata*, a bean and kale soup thickened with *polenta*, salt cod—*baccala*—and boiled potatoes, grilled chicken, meats and sausages, roast potatoes, salad with a dressing of only salt and fresh oil. To finish was the traditional chestnut flour cake e *castagnaccia*—made with rosemary, pine nuts, a little sugar and, of course, more fresh oil. It was heavenly.

Our *frantoio* moved some fifteen years ago to a modern cement block enclosure, a cold affair. In the beginning it smelled only of cement. Over the years the centrifugal extraction—now through big stainless steel processors —has brought rich aromas to the new place too. The nostalgia evoking old machines are displayed like museum pieces, along with a few ancient terracotta vats that manage a bit of atmosphere. Your olives are weighed, then dumped into a dark opening in the floor. After a lot of button pushing, in about ten minutes the oil begins slowly to pour out through a spout. It's certainly more efficient but I still miss the old press. (Today some mills even feature machines that separate out the pits before beginning to crush the olives; this break from the past I've so far refused to consider.) The amount of acidity in the oil is measured immediately; if we get no more than two percent acidity, it's a good year. Most years ours measures less than one percent.

In the new mill a large side room still has its open fireplace but the long tables are covered with plastic tablecloths. Elaborate meals are rare nowadays. Our festive supper has become more of a tasting, a light meal of *fett'unta* and sausages, with lots of bread and wine to wash it all down. No longer do lots of friends join in, just a few neighbors, Stefano, Flora, the girls, and us. I still think of it as tradition.

Such have been my particular adventures in Tuscany. I hope the traveller will partake of some of our pleasures in the ten itineraries that follow. The restaurants I've chosen all serve traditional food. You can count on a good meal in any of them. Their cooks have generously shared recipes with me. Nothing has been altered or changed, not even ingredients that might be difficult to come by. Careful substitutes can certainly be made. I've tried all their recipes at home; those included in the book have succeeded well, with friends, family, and other prejudiced critics. Most often they are dishes of local tradition. Occasionally there's something innovative; I've included those when they've been interesting and good.

The greatest legacy of the old tenant-farming system is what is now —all too fashionably—called the *cucina povera*, the poor kitchen. *Cucina povera* is a misnomer. Tuscan food may be simple but it isn't poor. It can be amazingly imaginative, occasionally even innovative, and always based on the freshest local produce. This cooking is still well available in rural *trattorie* and unpretentious restaurants throughout the region. It is the basis for this book.

CHAPTER 1

The Lunigiana and the Mountains of Carrara

MYSTERY, LEGEND, AND A TOUCH OF PAGANISM ENVELOP THIS MOST NORTHWESTERN AREA OF Tuscany in and around the Magra valley, giving its craggy mountains and looming castle ruins the feeling of an Italian Land of Dracula. Even its name—which translates loosely as Valley of the Moon—has a slightly ominous cast. An assortment of local legends evokes witches, ghosts, and goblins that inhabit moonless nights, wander about castles, and hang from lonely trees. Spirits of the medieval ruling counts Malaspina still haunt evocatively named towns such as Fosdinovo, Bagnone, Fivizzano, Licciana Nardi, Filattiera, Minucciano, Filetto, and Pontremoli.

Tuscan names often seem designed to flex power or ward off the evil eye, especially those beginning with *mal*, which means "bad" or "evil." The name of the man in charge of restoring our house was Malforte, or "evil strength." The name is quite popular in these parts. Evil he certainly wasn't, but strong, yes. We still encounter names like Malatesta ("evil head"). Maltagliati ("badly cut") designates the brand name of a well-known local pasta. It also happens to be the name of a local dressmaker. I once even met a lawyer in Pistoia called Malconsiglio ("bad advice").

Malaspina, the name of the leading noble family of the Lunigiana during the Middle Ages, means "evil thorn," a particularly nasty surname allowing for all kinds of interpretation. In fact, the family had two branches, locally known as the Malaspina *secca*—the dry thorn, or bad Malaspina—and the Malaspina *fiorita*, the flowering thorn or good branch. Dante, who spent some time with the Malaspina *secca*, locked them into his Purgatory. The flowering Malaspina could be pretty awful, too; a ruling count in Filattiera—his castle still sits in the main square—shot an unsuspecting suitor coming to woo his daughter.

A werewolf is said to terrorize the old *borgo* in Pontremoli. The ghost of a maiden abused by Francesco Malaspina plays practical jokes in an old family fortress that is now a school in Mulazzo. On the road to Villafranca — no one knows exactly where — goblins and witches are said to dance around in a mysterious oak. The most famous spirit is that of the young Marchesa Malaspina of Fosdinovo, who haplessly fell in love with a stable hand and was imprisoned by her father in a windowless room of the castle. Under a full moon her longhaired ghost is still said to wander about the *castello* in a floating white gown. Such are some of the macabre old tales of the Lunigiana.

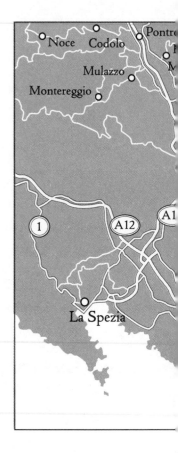

The Lunigiana is actually a lovely small mountainous corner of Tuscany, touching upon Liguria along the coast, Emilia in the north, and the Garfagnana to the east. The food here is often different from the rest of Italy, tasty dishes you won't find anywhere else. For a long time, from the tenth century on, the Lunigiana was the northern gateway to Tuscany and Italy's south. Pilgrims passed through here along the Francigena, the main route from France, on their way to Rome, pausing to build churches and hospices. The church grew here on the ruins of a pagan past. Ancient stone pagan icons continue to be dug out from under old Romanesque churches; pagan legend still mingles with church tradition.

The Lunigiana includes some of the most unspoiled landscapes of the region, the Zeri valley and the foothills of the Apuan Alps. In recent years, castle ruins have been turned into museums that give a real feel of the place and its past. In Pontremoli and Villafranca they are well worth a visit. The ancient castle in Pontremoli (see page 28) displays extraordinary stele dug up in various parts of the Lunigiana. Interestingly enough, most of the figures have moon-shaped heads that resemble the geographical shape of the Lunigiana itself, and from whence comes the name Luni. In Villafranca, an old water mill has been turned into an ethnological historical museum (see page 31). Popular tradition throughout the Lunigiana intermingles fes-

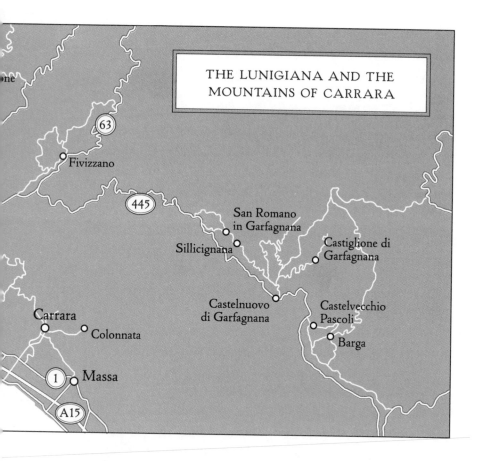

THE LUNIGIANA AND THE
MOUNTAINS OF CARRARA

tivals, amulets, and popular superstitions with a devotion that reaches back to a pre-Christian religious past.

There are several ways to approach the Lunigiana. When time is of no import, the most dramatic approach is over the Passo del Cerreto from Lucca and the Garfagnana, down the mountain through the Apuan Alps, where one never loses the dramatic view of the cold white marble mountains of Carrara. The nicest way to reach the pass is a small road that leads off from the Garfagnana main road between Castelnuovo and Castelvecchio. A lovely winding old way takes you past two pretty hill towns — Sillicagnana and San Romano — and under the fortress of Verrucola, which stands on a high hill defending the entire valley. From below, it looks like a piece of the Great Wall of China. Continue along this road into the Lunigiana, down to Fivizzano, an old Medici town and today a mountain summer resort. In the restaurant of an old inn, Il Giardinetto (see page 37), in Fivizzano, you'll find some fine traditional fare of the Lunigiana. From here you descend into the valley of the Lunigiana.

A more comprehensive way to see much of the Lunigiana is to exit the Cisa Pass autostrada between La Spezia and Parma at Pontremoli, and travel the main road down through Filattiera and Villafranca to Aulla (or reverse, exiting at Aulla and heading up to Pontremoli). Detours along the way take you to some impressive hill towns and imposing castle ruins.

Leaving the *autostrada* at Pontremoli, a small side trip before heading into the town will take you into the Zeri valley, an unspoiled landscape with vast vistas of the Apuan Alps and luscious green nearby hills. Among the shepherds' huts and pastures, you'll come upon a little town called Noce, a tiny center of old stone houses with ragged slate roofs that might have been fashioned by elves. It is totally harmonious. The sound of a rushing river below enhances an eerie quiet. This is poor land, characteristically independent and proud, known for an indigenous white sheep named after it, the Zerasca, which looks something like a cross between a small llama and a goat. A local adage tells us of the Zerasca that the people of the valley "eat its bread and clothe themselves with its skin." You can circle the entire area and return on a different road to Pontremoli.

Pontremoli is actually a peninsula, snuggled in between the Magra and Verde rivers. Two ancient walking bridges span them, once the only way to approach the town. Today there's a modern bridge joining both sides, from which you drive up the Via Cavour to reach Piazza del Duomo and limited parking. From the piazza it's a short walk to Da Bussë (see page 32), one of the most welcoming restaurants of the Lunigiana.

Pontremoli has been an important strategic market town since feudal times, under the patronage of one feudal family after another. In the seventeenth century it became part of the republic of Genoa. It is a noble little city, interesting and pretty, with baroque palaces and churches, and a castle ruin overlooking it all. The Castello del Piagnaro was never one of the Malaspina fortresses; rather it was built sometime in the ninth and tenth centuries, and later reinforced to bar the way—unsuccessfully—of northern armies passing through. Today the climb up to the castle and its archeological museum is a splendid trudge through an ancient past (Tel. 0187-831-439; summer, open daily 9am–1pm and 2:30pm–4:30pm; winter, closed Monday). The old stone houses are supported by ancient arches that stretch from house to house across the narrow road. The crest, at the gateway to the museum, affords nice views of the town below. Just look straight ahead, avoiding the popular housing estates and the monster of an *autostrada* looming over the landscape to the right. The way into this small museum that houses some of the important ancient finds of the area can be a bit slippery on wet days; take care.

The big cathedral, or *duomo*, on the main square is a gaudy rococo seventeenth-century splendor, with gilded chandeliers and candelabras in sharp contrast to the austere Romanesque churches elsewhere in the Lunigiana. It was built, a notice tells us, "as a sumptuous noble temple, capable of holding as many people as possible." Just off Piazza del Duomo, in the heart of old Pontremoli, you can find some of the area's food specialties at Salumeria Angella. Owner Andrea Guiduglia has his own laboratory to season and age his pork products. Especially good are the *filletto*, paper-thin slices cut from the leanest part of the pork, the undersized *mortadella*, and the dried *spalla* (pork shoulder). They are all seasonal products, not always available.

The road from Pontremoli to Aulla brings you soon to Filattiera. Just before the town you'll come upon one of the loveliest Romanesque churches in Tuscany, the Pieve di Sorano, sitting quietly on the edge of an old cemetery. It's a monumental granite-gray complex of a church, built over an old pagan temple. Pre-Christian idols and urns have recently been excavated. The inside is as simple and neat as the outer complex itself.

Filattiera calls itself the gate to the pilgrim's road; during the sixteenth century the little town was a major power in the area. In the cobblestoned *borgo*, three main roads lead from the piazza and its perfectly proportioned fifteenth-century mini-castle of the "flowering" (i.e. good) Malaspinas. This was where the aforementioned "good" Malaspina shot his daughter's suitor coming to claim her hand. The young *principessa*'s tears are said still to flow down the wall into a carved basin. There is a handsome round bell tower in Filattiera, with a terrace on top, from which approaching enemies, as well as more amenable pilgrim groups, could be seen afar. At the bottom of the town, the perfect Romanesque chapel, San Giorgio, is well worth a visit. The Ospedale di San Giacomo is another old building, built to house pilgrims arriving along the Francigena on their way to Rome.

Filattiera, like so many small Tuscan towns, celebrates its food and other traditional pleasures during the summer months with a local *sagra* or *festa*. The *festa* here is appropriately called a festival of *La Fame e la Sete* (Hunger and Thirst). It takes place the first four days of July every year. The entire town busies itself in preparation and execution. I once persuaded some friends to join me at the festival in order that we might taste just about everything offered. We came early. The smell of meats grilling on a large open wood fire at the entrance to town was already in the air. The beautiful little village square, filled with tables, was alive with what one friend likened to hobbits, dozens of small children in bright t-shirts preparing to serve all comers. Filattiera is a small place. Most of the villagers were either busy cooking at home for the event or getting ready to serve some particular dish. Local specialties included a fritter of zucchini flowers, a light pancake of chestnut flour topped with the freshest *ricotta* cheese, pastas, and fried little fresh anchovies. Freshly made local bread, called *tigelle*, was ready, waiting to be eaten while still warm.

Maria Angela Pagani had invited me into her kitchen to prepare with her a Lunigiana favorite: vegetable pie. The Filattiera version was filled with grated zucchini, green onions, potatoes, chopped chard, and a lot of grated cheese. In simpler days it used to be a hardened goat cheese; today she uses the more elegant Parmesan. The pie was made with the simplest of pastries surrounding the vegetables, top and bottom. Maria Angela worked quickly and efficiently, making it all seem effortless. It was a dish she made in one form or another almost every day, she told us, especially during seasons when fresh vegetables are available in her kitchen garden. The pie was delicious. It was a perfect lesson: an ingenious dish of the so-called *cucina povera*, or "the poor man's kitchen." The pie developed over the years to become a sophisticated, authentic delicacy (see Maria Angela's recipe page 45).

A small detour along the road between Filattiera and Villafranca leads to the little medieval hamlet of Bagnone, a harmonious cluster of granite houses sculpted out of an almost perpendicular hillside. One comes upon it through the gracious portal of the lower town. As you drive through the arch, the town on the hill sits directly before you. At the very top is the ever-present castle, and from its terrace, you can look down at the entire valley and the mountains beyond. Along the road to Bagnone, a kilometer or so from the main road between Filattiera and Villafranca, there's a very pleasant garden restaurant, Gavarini (see page 46), around a bend in the small nondescript town called Mocrone.

Villafranca in Lunigiana is a valley town almost destroyed during the Second World War; the ruin of yet another Malaspina castle dominates it. Villafranca was often recorded by pilgrims passing through in past times. The area ethnological museum is here, a good introduction to the culture and ethnology of the Lunigiana, its Christian and pagan past, and its symbols and charms against illness, danger, and the ever threatening risks of bad harvest. Amulets against "the evil eye" abound. (Ethnological Museum of the Lunigiana, Via Ponte Vecchio, Tel. 0187-493-417; summer, open daily 4pm–7pm; winter, open 9am–noon and 3pm–6pm; closed Monday.)

Other towns off the main road to wander through include Filetto, an ancient little walled *borgo* with a single main street ending in old arches on both ends; the remains of a castle form part of the surrounding wall. Go by foot along the main street and you'll note a miniature urban plan, with a well-designed piazza in the middle. Here, too, a fine festival takes place every August, usually the second week. The local population dresses in costumes of past centuries; food specialties and a medieval artisan market fill the streets.

Mulazzo is off the north/south axis. To reach it from Villafranca you pass under the *autostrada* that cuts through the Lunigiana. Here is yet another Malaspina castle — now a school — more notable because Dante Alighieri passed part of his exile here working on *The Divine Comedy*. The Malaspina here were of the *secca* branch. One Mulazzo Malaspina, Alessandro, was a well-known seventeenth-century scientist and explorer. The Spanish claim, as they do with Christopher Columbus, that he was one of them.

A bit further up the same road is totally isolated old Montereggio, seemingly tucked away in nowhere, but strangely enough bearing street and piazza names of the greats of modern Italian publishing: Mondadori, Rizzoli, Einaudi. In this little mountain village during the sixteenth century, a great Lunigiana cultural tradition of book selling was born. Somehow, villagers here took on the role of itinerant booksellers, and from Montereggio went on to become major publishers and booksellers all over Europe. One of Italy's major literary prizes — the Premio Bancarella — is awarded here.

Aulla, at the southern end of the Tuscan Lunigiana, has always been a transit point, mostly for pilgrims and armies passing through. It boasts the obligatory Malaspina castle but otherwise little else. From Aulla you can travel over the mountains to Fosdinovo, where the most complete and imposing Malaspina castle sits on a hill ruling the entire landscape. It is, in fact, still the summer home of the counts Malaspina. The castle, with many of its ancient rooms still intact, may be visited by appointment (Tel. 0187-68891). The ancient town ambles down from the castle. From Fosdinovo there is another spectacular mountain road down to Carrara.

It's a moot point as to whether the twin towns of Massa and Carrara, south of Aulla, are part of the Lunigiana. When one thinks of the Lunigiana, these two towns don't come to mind, and yet Massa has the biggest Malaspina castle of all Lunigiana. Carrara has its great marble mountain looming over the town to the east. Drive through the center of Carrara and up the mountain, eight kilometers through cascading white marble, to some of the oldest quarries. Here Michelangelo personally supervised the cutting of the blocks he needed for his sculptures. Each sculpture meant months of scouring the quarries for the perfect block. The marble for "David," the "Pieta," "Nicodemus," "Moses" and other major pieces came from here. The close-up view of the spectacular mountain begins soon after you leave Carrara. The vista opens. The marble mountain lies just opposite. You can visit the quarries from which sculptors sent the great blocks down to the sea on carts pulled by up to twenty oxen. Loaded onto barges, the blocks were carried along the coast to the mouth of the Arno and from there to Florence. From the Lungarno in Florence, teams of laborers carted them off to the nearby studio.

From the quarries, continue on up to the almost hidden little hamlet of Colonnata. Quarry workers have lived here for centuries, nourished by a local specialty, *lardo di Colonnata*, the seasoned and aged lard of Colonnata. Almost unknown outside of here for centuries, this delicious fat has been discovered by food lovers in recent years, and it's now cherished all over Europe. The town has thrived on its new notoriety; in recent years, the little piazza of Colonnata has been smartly paved in decorated marble slabs. Near the square a small staircase leads onto a theatrical setting that affords a breathtaking view of the marble mountain opposite; the little terrace also includes a rather startling modern marble tribute to the quarry workers of past centuries.

SPECIALTIES OF THE LUNIGIANA

LARDO DI COLONNATA IS ONLY ONE OF THE VERY SPECIAL FOODS OF THIS AREA. THE LUNIGIANA IS probably the most autonomous of Tuscan areas in how it eats. Its specialties are mostly unknown elsewhere in Tuscany. One most notable dish is *testeroli al pesto*, the particular pasta of the area eaten in the familiar basil-based sauce. It's not really a pasta, but more like a quickly baked *crepe* that is then sliced into little squares and boiled, drained, and smothered in the special *pesto* of Lunigiana.

Testeroli take their name from the pan in which the first baking happens, the *testo*, a large round baking dish with a tightly fitting domed cover. I've seen them mostly in copper or even tin; the original *testi* were of earthenware. I searched vainly in shops for a *testo* — even an old one — all over the Lunigiana; it seems to be a utensil of the past although I did see one or another in almost every restaurant and home I happened upon. *Testeroli* are still made in the old way; in the Lunigiana the finished product can be bought in every grocery or bread shop.

The *testo* was the major cooking utensil of the farmhouse. It could be used to make *crescente*, the round loaf of Lunigiana (bread is salted here, unlike in other parts of Tuscany), the large vegetable pies so typical of the area, and various chestnut flour flatbreads and cakes. All were cooked in the ashes of the big open fireplace; both the plate and cover maintain a uniform heat.

The *testo* actually came into use long ago with shepherds and woodsmen who went off for long periods to live in huts in arable grazing land or forests. The *testo* they took with them cooked a splendid variety of dishes from the simple provisions they could muster.

As in other mountainous regions of Tuscany, chestnuts and chestnut flour have been basic sustenance throughout Lunigiana's history. It is estimated that two-thirds of the daily intake of calories once came from chestnuts. In our own days of more easily milled wheat and corn, chestnut flour has become something of a luxury. In the Lunigiana, the simplest preparation is called a *pattona* — *polenta* made with chestnut flour cooked to a soft paste in salted water, mixed with milk, and served as an accompaniment to roasts. *Panigacci* are "wet bread," baked with the same mixture.

There's also a fine oversized bean here, tasty and tender, its local cult status a testament to the value Tuscans invest in their beans. This particular bean doesn't get much further than the hills of the Lunigiana. I discovered it quite by accident. A waiter in Fivizzano mentioned that a famous local bean came from the village of Bigliolo, on the way from Fivizzano to Aulla. My husband is a bean-lover; a search for the village was irresistible. Unfortunately, the small road that was marked for Bigliolo seemed to lead nowhere. I stopped at the first cluster of houses where few people were in evidence. It was Bigliolo. An open doorway led me into a wine storeroom and a family absorbed in the monthly transfer of their new wine from one demijohn to another. When I asked about the bean, they looked perplexed. Then one of the women ignited with a spark of recognition. A farmer just down the road might have the bean, she said. It was more than just down the road, but we did find Luigi Perdrelli, his wife Giulia, and the bean, along with some young farm lamb that Giulia was chopping into cuts for the Easter market. There was also a slew of farm animals and some splendid olive oil. We went off with a package of the little-known Bigliolo bean along with some very tender lamb. The bean was perfect in a *farro* soup. I'm still looking for another reputedly fine bean in the Lunigiana, *fagioli con il grembiule* — "beans with a vest." It grows in the Zeri valley, but we've not yet found it.

The real specialty of the Zeri valley is the aboriginal Zerasca baby lamb that is raised only in this small valley northwest of Pontremoli. The little animal is almost unknown elsewhere in Italy, and probably the world as well. It pastures during the entire year, its milk going only to feed its young, giving it a particular soft and delicate flavor. Ask for it when you're in a Lunigiana restaurant; I found it in Mocrone, at Gavarini (page 46). (The lamb we brought home from Bigliolo was tender and tasty, but not Zerasca.)

Lunigiana is also special territory for beekeepers. For more than five hundred years they have been producing honey in the same valley woods between the Apuan Alps and the Apennines, an area with low humidity and lots of varied wildflowers for bees to suckle. Acacia and chestnut honey from the Lunigiana are among the most desirable in Tuscany.

Vegetable tarts, so ubiquitous in the Lunigiana, come in many variations according to local whim and season. They are a specialty that you won't find elsewhere in Tuscany except perhaps in the nearby Garfagnana. A product of the farm kitchen, they encase a variety of vegetables in simple pastry. The vegetables that go into the tart come right from the garden, mostly potatoes, Swiss chard, onions, cabbage, and kale in the winter and, in the summer, a greater variety that includes zucchini, spinach, and wild asparagus. In some towns cheeses are added, in others not. The choice of cheese also varies from town to town; originally it was strictly the cheese of the local sheep, *ricotta* and aged *pecorino*. In Pontremoli tarts, you'll still find *ricotta* cheese. Everywhere the tarts are delicious local favorites, home and restaurant staples throughout the area. I've included a number of recipes from various restaurants. Those with only vegetables and some grated cheese are the lightest; those with *ricotta* are richer. But each reflects the particular taste of the area.

Stuffed baked vegetables are another dish of the Lunigiana. This, too, was traditionally a way of extending the seasonal provision into a main course. In the fall there are wild mushroom caps, in winter, cabbage leaves and onions; spring and summer bring zucchini and their flowers, peppers, eggplant, and Swiss chard. The stuffing is without meat, usually of bread-crumbs mixed with a flavorful combination of garlic, herbs, grated sheep cheese, and soft *ricotta*, with eggs to hold it together.

As I mentioned above, marble white *lardo di Colonnata*—slices of pork fat deliciously seasoned and aged—has turned the little town above Carrara into a place of culinary pilgrimage. Once the hearty lunch of the quarry workers—Colonnata was their home—this little slab of shiny white pork fat has become a delicacy. Its fame, and Colonnata's fortune, arrived in a backhanded way. Few had heard of *lardo* before someone suggested —probably in Brussels—to outlaw it, not only in Italy but throughout the European Community. As with non-pasteurized French cheeses, San Daniele prosciutto, and other treasures of gastronomic Europe, an uproar ensued. *Lardo* became the center of a controversy that spread through Europe, with all the ensuing attention. The ruling was rescinded. The best result is that now we're all craving and enjoying *lardo di Colonnata*.

My first experience with the seasoned pork fat came some years ago, before all the controversy, at a dinner party in Lucca. A great hunk was sitting in the middle of the table. I couldn't believe that we were expected to eat this slab of fat. "Taste it," urged a friend, as he carefully sliced a paper-thin sliver and wrapped it around a piece of toast. I did, not without trepidation, and instantly became a *lardo* fan. Since the uproar, the little quarry workers' town has turned from marble to *lardo*. The original two *lardo* producers in Colonnata have expanded to include almost all the other families in the little village. Thousands arrive for the *Sagra di Lardo*, celebrated here in mid-August.

The pig itself doesn't come from Colonnata, or even nearby. Great hunks of fresh pork back fat arrive from elsewhere, mostly from Parma. It is the seasoning and the unusual method of aging it in heavy marble vats that make it so special.

Traditionally the quarry workers of Colonnata went off on winter mornings carrying their lunch: some *lardo*, a sliver of preserved tomato, and a crust of bread to ward off the chill of the stone with calories. It is a tradition that dates back to the eleventh century. Pigs were raised here then, skinny and underfed. No longer. The fat now comes from rich pigs, and much more is produced. It is heavily seasoned in layers of salt and a great number of herbs and spices that includes black pepper, rosemary, garlic, chopped sage, oregano, cinnamon, coriander seeds, nutmeg, and anise. Once seasoned and layered, it is bathed in a water and salt solution, covered, and allowed to age for a minimum of six months.

The end product resembles a slim block of streaked white stone. It's sliced paper-thin, and wrapped around a slice of toast that has been brushed with olive oil, and heated gently to make the most delectable little *bruschetta* imaginable.

TYPICAL RESTAURANTS
& THEIR RECIPES

FIVIZZANO

IL GIARDINETTO
Via Roma 155, Fivizzano • Tel. 0585-92060
Open daily, except Monday, for lunch and dinner. Priced moderately.

Walk up the stairs at this charming little hotel and you feel as though you've entered someone's parlor. But for the extraordinary odors emanating from the nearby kitchen, the dining room at Il Giardinetto could be somewhere in England. It's a family home from the early twentieth century; stained-glass doors lead into the gracious old wood-paneled dining room, complete with the urn of silk flowers that sits at one end, and the various family portraits and drawings that cover the walls.

Il Giardinetto is owned by the Mercadini family. The grandparents of the current Mercadinis opened the restaurant some eighty years ago. With each generation the place has expanded a bit, and it is today a decent-sized hotel. The same traditional kitchen still serves the dishes of all those years ago.

You'll find many of Lunigiana's traditional dishes at this little mountain hotel. *Testeroli al pesto* is the traditional starter, after some local salami and prosciutto that comes with preserved vegetables. If a vegetable tart has been made in the morning, that's on the menu as well. Lamb is served with *polenta incatenata*, "polenta in chains." A specialty of the house is *bomba di riso*, the festive rice dish of the Lunigiana. It can be ordered in advance. It's a celebration, a true bomb: a large mold of deliciously flavored rice filled with game birds (pigeon or quail), sausages, various cuts of veal, and innards.

Wild berries from the surrounding mountains are always on the menu, fresh during the summer, preserved during other seasons. House specialty is *semi-freddo di myrtille*, a soft ice cream mold with wild blueberries.

Testeroli with Pesto
TESTEROLI CON PESTO

⬤

Serves 6

Testeroli are rarely made at home these days. They are available everywhere in the Lunigiana, either fresh or in vacuum packs, from the local grocer. There are those who claim this as the first Italian pasta; archaeological discoveries lend credence to the theory. The traditional method of cooking, in the covered *testo*, required no turning; this method does. Use the largest frying pan available.

FOR THE TESTEROLI:

3½ cups flour

About 2½ cups water

Salt

1 tablespoon extra virgin olive oil, plus additional for frying

½ raw potato

FOR THE PESTO:

2 cups fresh basil leaves

2 tablespoons pine nuts

2 garlic cloves, crushed

½ teaspoon salt, or more to taste

½ cup grated aged *pecorino*

¼ cup grated Parmesan

¾ cup extra virgin olive oil

Make the batter by putting the flour into a bowl and slowly adding the water, mixing all the while, to make a thick batter that can be poured. Add a pinch of salt and the tablespoon of olive oil, and mix again.

Cut a small potato in half, dip the cut side in some olive oil, and use it to oil a large frying pan. Heat the pan, and pour in just enough batter to cover the bottom of the pan and make a disk about ¼ inch thick. Lower the heat, cover the pan for about 2 minutes. Turn the *testerolo* over and cook for another 2 minutes. Repeat to use all the batter.

Roll up each *testerolo* (to save space) and allow to cool. They will keep like this, wrapped and refrigerated, for several days. To prepare, cut each disk into diamond shapes or squares of about 2 inches, and toss into boiling water to cook for another few minutes. Drain and serve with a thick sauce of *pesto*.

To make the *pesto*, combine all the ingredients in a blender or food processor and process to a smooth consistency. The *pesto* should be thick but not pasty. Add a bit more oil if necessary.

Polenta "in Chains"

POLENTA INCATENATA

Serves 6

When I asked my young host at Il Giardinetto why this substantial dish was called "chained," he wasn't too sure; perhaps it was such a heavy bundle that it could be tied. (Or, as someone else in the Lunigiana has suggested, the beans are enchained by the *polenta*.) It's heavy, but very tasty.

1½ cups dried *borlotti* or cranberry beans
1 small bunch kale leaves, large ribs removed, and well chopped
10 cups water
1 teaspoon salt
½ cup extra virgin olive oil
3 cups *polenta**
Grated Parmesan or grated aged *pecorino* at table

Soak the beans overnight. Drain and put into a large pot with the water. Bring to a boil, lower the flame, and cook at a simmer until almost tender. Add the salt, kale, and olive oil, and slowly pour in the *polenta*, a handful at a time, stirring constantly to prevent lumps from forming. When all the *polenta* has been added, turn up the fire a bit and cook until thick and smooth, about 45 minutes. Serve with lots of grated cheese at table.
*If you are using instant polenta, allow the beans to cook until soft and tender before adding the polenta.

PONTREMOLI

———— ❖ ————

DA BUSSË

Piazza Duomo 31, Pontremoli • Tel. 0187-831-371

Open daily for lunch; on Saturday and Sunday also open for dinner. Closed
Friday and first three weeks of July. Priced moderately.
Reservations recommended.

Talking about food with Antonetta Bertocchi at Da Bussë is great fun, a
pleasure surpassed only by the eating. She practically fondles the *pesto* that
will accompany her *testaroli*. She pounds the fragrant basil by hand, with just
the right amount of garlic. Perfectly aged *pecorino* comes next, and finally a
precise amount of fresh olive oil from a nearby mill, "never any other."

She spoons out a taste of her soothing *salsa verde* that goes with the
special young beef *bollito* served daily at Da Bussë. In the winter she adds
a *cotechino*, a sausage-like stuffed shin of pork, to the *bollito*. She manages
it all by herself in a sparse, well-organized kitchen. But for a simple mixer,
the small space is unencumbered by machines. The great earthenware casserole she uses for most of her dishes sits on the old stove. She talks with
a mother's love about the ingredients she handles, giving a taste here, a
demonstration there.

Antonetta plans her menu as you might at home. On the front door is
a sign announcing "we serve no *funghi* here." When I asked her why, she
told me it just isn't her thing. She plans her menus the evening before; wild
mushrooms are not something she can plan for the next day, so she just
doesn't serve them.

Testeroli and *bollito* are always on the menu, as are traditional vegetable
pies, delicately stuffed cabbage leaves and, on Wednesdays and Saturdays
—market days in Pontremoli—Da Bussë's famous *la zuppa*, a soupy *ragù*
served over the thinnest slice of *pagniaccio*, a local, lightly-salted bread. The
stew is topped with a grating of aged *pecorino*.

The restaurant is open only for lunch during the week, but its small
stand-up bar becomes a kind of men's club at dusk. The men stop by
after work for their evening glass of wine. No food is served at this hour,
but the talk seems mostly about it. Inquire of a particular dish and they'll

know everything about it, and talk with great lust about the preparation of *testeroli* and the meats that go into a *bollito*.

The restaurant consists of four small appealing rooms, with walls frescoed in gentle floral patterns by Antonetta's sister-in-law. Da Bussë has been in the family for years. It was begun by Antonetta's father in 1930, with her mother as cook. Today Antonetta and her sister, who helps out with the serving, continue the traditions of their parents.

RECIPES FROM DA BUSSË

Stuffed Cabbage
CAVOLO RIPIENO

Serves 6

FOR THE CABBAGE:
1 Savoy cabbage
2 pounds Swiss chard, with hard white core removed
1 bunch parsley leaves
½ clove garlic
1 cup *ricotta*
2 eggs
2 large handfuls grated Parmesan
Salt and freshly ground pepper
Extra virgin olive oil

FOR THE SAUCE:
2 cloves garlic
1 bunch parsley leaves
2 tablespoons extra virgin olive oil
1 large can (1 lb. 12 oz.) Italian plum tomatoes, drained and chopped
About 1 cup meat broth

Carefully separate the cabbage leaves. Chop 2 or 3 of the outer leaves finely, together with the chard, parsley, and garlic. Salt and drain in a colander. Boil the remaining cabbage leaves for 5 minutes and drain in another colander.

Squeeze dry the chopped vegetables, and add the *ricotta*, eggs, and

Parmesan. Season with salt and pepper and mix well. Dry the cabbage leaves and place a tablespoon of filling into each. Fold each stuffed leaf into a loose bundle and tuck them all together, into a well-oiled ovenproof casserole, with the seam facing down.

To make the sauce, chop the garlic and parsley together and sauté in the oil in a pan large enough to hold the entire sauce. When the oil around the garlic begins to bubble, add the tomatoes and cook over a medium heat until the sauce thickens, about 10 minutes. Pour the sauce over the cabbage, add enough meat broth to cover, and simmer over a low flame for 1 to 1½ hours. Serve warm.

Swiss Chard or Spinach Pie
TORTA DI VERDURE

Serves 8 as main course; 10 as a first course

For this and the following pie, you'll need a large (14–16 inches) round pan. I use a *paella* pan.

FOR THE PASTRY:
3½ cups flour
Salt
2 tablespoons extra virgin olive oil, plus additional for brushing the pastry
Warm water

FOR THE FILLING:
3 pounds Swiss chard or spinach
2 eggs
2 big handfuls grated Parmesan
1 cup *ricotta*
Salt and freshly ground pepper
1 large handful breadcrumbs
Extra virgin olive oil

Preheat the oven to 350 degrees.

Wash the chard or spinach and chop into thin strips. Salt well, place in a colander, and allow to sit for at least an hour. Squeeze out the water, put back in the colander, and let it sit some more. Squeeze again as hard as possible.

Place the chard in a large bowl, add the eggs, the Parmesan, the ricotta, lots of freshly ground pepper, salt, and mix well.

To make the dough, put the flour and a good pinch of salt in a mound on a working surface, make a hole in the middle, and add the oil. Slowly add warm water, working the flour into it until the dough has reached a consistency that is soft but malleable, and easy to roll out. Divide into two balls. Flour a work surface and gently roll out one ball into a paper-thin round. Oil the pan well, and place the pastry in the pan.

Fill the pan with the vegetables and spread evenly. Roll the second ball into another paper-thin round and cover. Brush the top with olive oil and bake for about an hour. Serve warm. Leftovers can be heated and served again.

Rice and Onion Pie
TORTA DI RISO E CIPOLLE

Serves 10

This is another perfect example of the inventiveness of the so-called *cucina povera.*

Pastry *(see recipe page 34)*
3 pounds yellow onions
Coarse salt
1 cup rice
1 cup *ricotta*
2 big handfuls grated Parmesan
3 eggs, beaten
Salt and freshly ground pepper
2 tablespoons extra virgin olive oil, plus additional for brushing the pastry

Preheat the oven to 350 degrees.

Prepare the pastry dough as for the recipe above.

For the filling, slice the onions, not too thinly, sprinkle well with the salt, and place in a colander for about an hour to drain off their bitter juices.

Squeeze the water out of the onions, wash, and squeeze dry again, this time in a kitchen towel.

In a large bowl, mix the rice with the onions. Add the *ricotta* and Parmesan, mix well, and mix in the beaten eggs. Add salt if needed and lots of black pepper.

Roll out the pastry dough and fill with the onion mixture. Brush the top with olive oil and cook for about an hour.

Piquant Green Sauce for Bollito
SALSA VERDE

Makes about 1 cup

1 thick slice country bread
Red wine vinegar
1 large bunch parsley leaves
3 hardboiled eggs
5 anchovy fillets, washed
2 tablespoons capers under vinegar, drained and washed
Salt and freshly ground pepper
About ¾ cup extra virgin olive oil

Completely moisten the bread with the vinegar. Meanwhile, chop the parsley leaves, together with the hardboiled eggs, anchovies, and capers. Squeeze the bread dry and crumble it into the sauce. Add freshly ground pepper and salt to taste, and cover with olive oil. The sauce can be stored in the refrigerator for several days.

FILATTIERA

———— ❂ ————

Maria Angela Pagani's Vegetable Pie
TORTA DI ERBE

❁

Serves 8 generously

This is a recipe that I watched Maria Angela Pagani prepare in her Filattiera home. The vegetables came from her garden that morning. She makes
the tart in a large (16 inch) pan; I've prepared it in a large *paella* pan that's
a bit smaller.

FOR THE PASTRY:
3½ cups white flour
1 tablespoon salt
Water
4 tablespoons extra virgin olive oil

FOR THE FILLING:
5 medium zucchini
1 bunch Swiss chard
6 large green onions
3 large potatoes, peeled and grated
1¼ cups grated Parmesan
Salt

Preheat the oven to 400 degrees.

To make the dough, put the flour into a bowl with about a tablespoon
of salt and 2 tablespoons of the olive oil and add water slowly, working it
into the flour. When it reaches a sticky but firm consistency, start to work it
into a pastry, kneading and adding additional flour as necessary. Work the
dough for about 5 minutes, until it has some elasticity.

Grate the zucchini into a colander, chop the chard, and add it. Mix well
with a good amount of salt, and leave for an hour or 2 to eliminate as much
water as possible. Into another colander, grate the onions. Chop in as much
of the green part as is fresh. Salt well and leave to drain.

Wash the grated vegetables well and squeeze out as much water as possible. Mix them all together. Add the potatoes, the Parmesan, and the remaining oil and mix well. Add salt to taste.

Roll out the dough into two very thin disks, one a bit larger than the other. Line a large baking pan with parchment paper, place the larger disk of dough on the bottom, and fill it with the vegetable mixture. Place the smaller disk on top and fold the edges of the bottom disk over the top pastry, sealing the tart. With wet hands, slap the top all over. With a fork, prick holes all over the top.

Bake the tart for about 40 minutes, until the top is slightly brown and the vegetables cooked. Serve hot or warm. If there are leftovers, heat them again before serving.

MOCRONE

GAVARINI

Via Alberico Benedicenti, off the road to Bagnone, between Filattiera and Villafranca, at Mocrone • Tel. 0187-493-115

Open daily for lunch and dinner; closed Wednesday. In August, open every day. Closed February. Priced moderately. Reservations recommended, especially in summer months.

The little town of Mocrone lies just off the main provincial road between Filattiera and Villafranca. Turn at the sign to Bagnone, and you'll soon see a sign on the left for Mocrone and the restaurant Gavarini. Follow the road around (it becomes frighteningly narrow) and on the small Piazza Benedicenti, you'll find the small inauspicious entrance to Gavarini, a large and welcoming restaurant with an adjacent garden for summer dining.

Even in winter it's a cheery room. Large picture windows framed with sheer orange draperies look out to the garden beyond. Gavarini has been a family restaurant for four generations. It is currently run by Nadia Folloni, her husband Pierangelo, and their son Fabio. Nadia's grandmother actually turned her popular little bread *forno* into the restaurant. It was expanded by her mother Elvezia. The menu hasn't really varied since. It is seasonal and features specialties of the region: *testeroli* with *pesto*, vegetable pies, *farro* soups, and chestnut flour pasta. *Sgabei*, little quickly fried puffs of bread filled with bits of *ragù*, are served with the *antipasto*. A favorite *antipasto* is the *torta di cipolle*, a thin pastry with lots of fresh onions sliced right into it. Twenty-two vegetables go into the *minestra di verdure*—vegetable soup —in a six-hour preparation. *Chicchere della nonna* are pinky sized *gnocchi*, swimming in a tomato cream sauce. A *bomba di riso* is the festive dish of the region and must be pre-ordered. I first tasted the notable lamb of the Zeri valley here; it was tender and succulent. Lamb chops are always on the menu; sometimes an entire crown is as well. The dessert not to miss is *pasticcio della nonna*, a combination of crumbled amaretto cookies with whipped cream and melted chocolate on top.

The restaurant has recently expanded into a small guest house and has added an atmospheric wine bar, where a different menu is offered. There you'll find a good selection of cheese and wines from all over Italy.

Fried Bread

SGABEI

Makes about 30 rolls

3½ cups white flour
1 tablespoon yeast
1 teaspoon salt
About 1 cup water
Vegetable or peanut oil for frying
Ricotta or other soft cheese

Mix the flour, yeast, and salt and add enough water to make a soft dough. Place in a warm place to rise for an hour. Roll out into a thickness of about ½ inch, and cut into strips about 1½ inches wide and 2 inches long.

Heat about 2½ inches of vegetable or peanut oil in a heavy pan. Throw in the strips, and fry until golden and puffed up. Drain onto a paper towel and serve hot, broken open and spread with any number of fillings. I like them best with *ricotta* or another soft white cheese.

Polenta and Onion Tart

TORTA DI POLENTA E CIPOLLE

Serves 6-8

4 large white onions, thinly sliced
1½ cups *polenta* (not instant)
½ cup white flour
½ cup grated Parmesan
1 teaspoon salt
2 or more cups milk
2 tablespoons extra virgin olive oil, plus additional for oiling the pan
Salt and freshly ground pepper

Preheat the oven to 350 degrees.

Put the sliced onions in a large bowl, with cold water to cover, for about an hour. Drain and dry the onions, pressing out the liquid in a dry cloth. Mix well the *polenta*, flour, Parmesan, and salt, and add the milk and oil to make a fairly thin batter. Add the onions and mix well. Season to taste. Line a large jellyroll pan with baking paper, oil lightly, and pour in the batter. Spread evenly, and bake until golden and firm, about an hour. Cut into squares and serve.

Winter Vegetable Tart

TORTA D'INVERNO

Serves 6-8

This is another version of the Lunigiana tart.

FOR THE PASTRY:
3½ cups flour
2 tablespoons olive oil
Salt
Water

1 pound Swiss chard (or borage, if available)
2 leeks, finely chopped
2 potatoes, peeled and cubed
¾ cup extra virgin olive oil, plus additional to drizzle over the crust
1½ cups grated Parmesan

Preheat the oven to 400 degrees.

Make a simple pastry by mixing together the flour, olive oil, salt, and enough water to make a dough that can be easily rolled out. Let rest while you prepare the filling.

To make the filling, wash and salt the chard or borage and drain in a colander for half an hour to release its water. Squeeze well to remove as much water as possible. Chop and place in a bowl. Add the leeks, potatoes, oil, and cheese, and mix well.

Oil a large rectangular jelly roll pan. Roll out the dough so that it is large enough to cover the bottom of the pan with some dough left over the edges to fold back over the vegetables (the top crust doesn't have to entirely cover the vegetables). Place the dough in the pan, fill with the prepared vegetables, and fold over the dough to form the top crust. Prick a few holes in the crust with a fork and drizzle with additional olive oil.

Bake for 30 to 40 minutes, until the top is golden.

COLONNATA

RISTORANTE VENANZIO

Piazza Palestro 3, Colonnata • Tel. 0585-758-062; Fax 0585-758-033

Open every day, for lunch and dinner, during the summer; in winter, closed Thursday and Sunday evening. Also closed from Christmas Eve through January 10. Prices, excluding wine, are moderate, including the menu degustazione. Reservations recommended, and necessary during the summer months, especially August.

Venanzio was the first owner of this little gem of a restaurant on the main piazza of Colonnata. Thirty years ago, quarry workers would end their days with a drink and something to eat here. Two long-time employees took it over a few years ago. They kept the name. Rather than workers, today owners and managers of the great quarries arrive with their foreign business associates — buyers and agents — for a lunch that's a touch more sophisticated.

Although he is still in his twenties, Chef Alessio Lucchetti has been working in the kitchen for more than twelve years. He began to work summers for Venanzio while still in hotel school in nearby Massa. Roberto Ferlini, the genial manager and host, has been at Venanzio's for twenty years. He works the *lardo*, seasons and stores it in the marble vat. He has become a master of the art. Restaurateurs from all over Europe, and even, surreptitiously, from the United States — where it is indeed prohibited — come to buy chunks of *lardo* from him. He delights in discussing the process of aging it, and showing off the marble vat in which it soaks up all the goodness. He's also developed a seasoned *carpaccio* of beef that's put into the seasoning for a week or so. The restaurant is still pretty much a family affair; Roberto's wife Anna is in the kitchen with Alessio — she makes the light delectable pasta — while Alessio's fiancée Pamela is out in front with Roberto.

This is a restaurant where I'd go for the *menu degustazione*, a taste of everything. The great variety and taste of all the starters makes it hard to choose; it's easier to choose them all. There is, to begin with, the paper-thin slices of *lardo* served on warmed, almost toasted, bread. From there, go on to delicate stuffed zucchini flowers and the *torta di zucchini* and the simple platter of single-layered *melanzane alla parmigiana*. Pasta arrives next, *ravioli* stuffed with meat and Swiss chard, enhanced with a bit of chopped fried *lardo*, and topped with a fresh tomato sauce. Another pasta is *lasagnetta*, thick green noodles made with borage — a wild green much used in the northern Tuscan home kitchen — and served, in fall and winter, with a sauce of wild mushrooms. Main courses include a rabbit, boned and stuffed with *lardo*, or a guinea hen stuffed and served with a truffle sauce (black in the early fall, white when they come into season later).

Desserts are the only thing that come out of the freezer; Alessio and Roberto boast that almost everything in their little out-of-the-way restaurant — save the *lardo* — is absolutely fresh, brought up to Colonnata in the morning to cook for lunch. They live down the mountain in Carrara, so it's less of a feat than it might seem. But I liked especially when Roberto told me that they make their own olive oil. This is not olive country — it's much too high — so Roberto buys his olives from a farmer he knows in nearby Lucca and takes them to the *frantoio* to be crushed into oil. He wants to know the oil he's serving.

The desserts are good. My favorite ending to the meal is a local cheese, *pecorino*, that's also been aged in a marble vat and is served with a candied fruit mustard. Other desserts are seasonal; there's a coconut or chocolate mousse served with fresh fruit sauce or an apple tart made with Calvados. Others are made according to the whim of the day.

RECIPES FROM RISTORANTE VENANZIO

Ravioli in Fresh Tomato Sauce
RAVIOLI CON SALSA POMODORO

Serves 6-8

FOR THE FILLING:
5 pounds Swiss chard
2 fresh ripe tomatoes
3½ ounces *lardo di Colonnata* (or solid lard), finely chopped
1 tablespoons extra virgin olive oil
1 onion, finely chopped
4 cloves garlic, minced
2 pounds mixed chopped meat, including beef, pork, and veal
Salt and freshly ground pepper

FOR THE PASTA:
3½ cups flour
4 eggs
1 teaspoon extra virgin olive oil
Salt

FOR THE SAUCE:
4 pounds tomatoes
2 tablespoons extra virgin olive oil

2 tablespoons butter
About 1 cup grated Parmesan

To prepare the filling, cook the chard until tender, squeeze dry, chop, and set aside. Chop two of the tomatoes and set aside. Fry the lard in a tablespoon of oil, and add the onion and garlic. As the lard becomes crisp, add the chopped meat and let it brown. When the meat has lost its color, add squeezed chard and the two chopped tomatoes. Add salt and pepper to taste, cook for another few minutes, and set aside.

Prepare the pasta by mixing together the flour, eggs, olive oil, and salt. Knead well and roll out thinly, using a pasta maker if available, into strips about 2½ inches wide. Place teaspoons of filling along each strip, leaving 2 inches between each teaspoonful. Cover with another strip of pasta, and cut, with a *ravioli* cutter, into squares. Separate, making sure each square is sealed.

To make the sauce, drop the remaining tomatoes into boiling water until their skins are loosened. Drain, skin, squeeze out the juice, chop the tomato flesh, and sauté gently in 2 tablespoons butter and 2 tablespoons olive oil.

Drop the *ravioli* into a big wide pot of boiling salted water. When they are cooked through, remove with a slotted spoon onto a serving dish, pour over the tomato sauce, and sprinkle with Parmesan.

Stuffed Zucchini Flowers
FIORI DI ZUCCHINI RIPIENI

Makes about 30 flowers

These are about the most delicate stuffed flowers I've tasted.

FOR THE FILLING:
3½ ounces cooked ham, chopped into tiny cubes
1½ cups *ricotta*
2 eggs, beaten
3 tablespoons grated Parmesan
Salt
Nutmeg

30 zucchini flowers
½ cup vegetable broth
2 pounds tomatoes, juice and seeds squeezed out, and chopped

Preheat the oven to 450 degrees.

To make the filling, mix the chopped ham with the *ricotta* and eggs. Fold in the Parmesan and add salt and a good grating of nutmeg.

Carefully open the flowers along the side without breaking them completely, and break off and remove the yellow pistil. Oil a baking dish large enough to hold the flowers side by side. Spoon a teaspoon of the filling into each flower, and close it into an envelope, first the sides and then folding over the top. As you work, lay the flowers in the baking dish.

Pour the broth over the flowers, add the tomatoes, and bake for no longer than 10 minutes, until the broth begins to bubble. It is important not to overcook the flowers; you don't want to cook the filling. Remove gently and serve.

CHAPTER 2

Valle del Serchio and the Garfagnana

THE GARFAGNANA, ALWAYS A FASCINATING PLACE WITH ITS IMPRESSIVE CASTLE RUINS AND PRECIP-itous hills, has lately become especially inviting for food lovers. In this area north of Lucca, the sweet plump *farro* and coarse savory *polenta* made from overlarge corn kernels have brought the area well-deserved celebrity. In the past, both *farro* and *polenta* were poor man's food, the area less alluring to the outsider.

The Garfagnana lies in the wildest part of the Apuan Alps; old fortified towns hang over narrow valleys, skinny roads wriggle their ways up through seemingly unsurpassable mountains. A few hundred years ago, the area was little more than a strategic passage, continually occupied by overbearing outsiders, robber barons, bandits, and mercenaries — a gloomy place. The poet Ludvico Ariosto, a fifteenth-century governor of the area, wrote rather grimly about "tears, voices and life in the cold white marble mountains of Castiglione…(where) man wins over death and disarms it."

These days the fifty-kilometer excursion into the forests and hills along the Serchio river that meanders down from the Apuan Alps to Lucca is a lot more enticing. Agriculture and small industry along the Serchio have given the area a new prosperity. Nowadays the roads are decent. It's a special pleasure to head up from Lucca along the twisting riverbank road that slowly winds into the hills. The magnificent marble mountains to the rear of Carrara suddenly emerge looking like pure snow. The softer Apennine hills curve off forever in the other direction. Within this endless forest of great green chestnuts, oaks, and pines, lie not only castles and fortress towns, but a little-known wealth of local produce as well.

Its intimidating landscape kept the Garfagnana poor and isolated. Until Italian unity in the nineteenth century, the area was controlled at varying times by the warring lords of Ferrara, Florence, and Lucca. Their castles

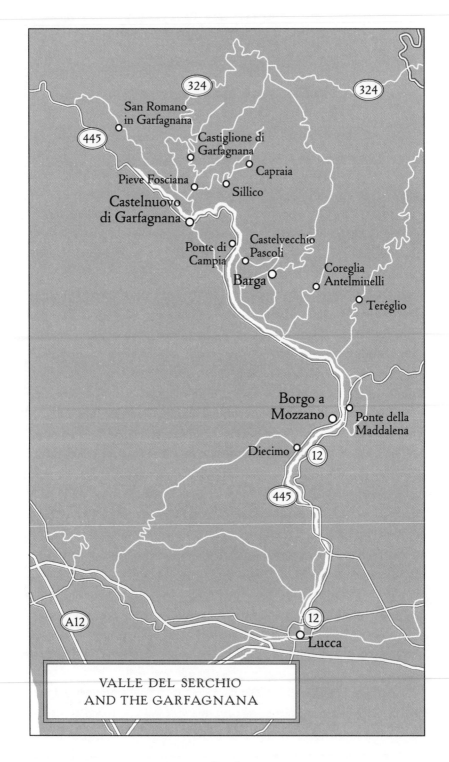

324

San Romano
in Garfagnana

445

Castiglione di
Garfagnana

Capraia

Pieve Fosciana

Sillico

Castelnuovo
di Garfagnana

Ponte di
Campia

Castelvecchio
Pascoli

Barga

Coreglia
Antelminelli

Teréglio

324

Borgo a
Mozzano

Ponte della
Maddalena

Diecimo

12

445

A12

12

Lucca

VALLE DEL SERCHIO
AND THE GARFAGNANA

and fortresses are still there, marking the landscape, etched into the towns. Armies passing through picked up their fighters from available mercenaries along the way, and armaments too.

The right-hand side of the river Serchio is the best way to travel up the valley from Lucca (even though signs point to a bridge crossing at Ponte Moriano). On the other side, you may encounter annoying truck traffic to and from the many paper factories and other industrial plants that have sprung up indiscriminately in recent years.

As you travel up, a first worthwhile detour is at Borgo a Mozzano, and the Church of Santa Maria Assunta in Diecino. Cross the river at the bridge indicating Borgo a Mozzano and head back toward Lucca for a few kilometers on the other side; you'll note a sign to the church on the right-hand side of the road. Follow the signs that bring you to Santa Maria Assunta, sitting on its unassuming site since the sixth century. What you actually see is the finished twelfth-century church. Its massive bell tower is one of the most impressive of the area. The simple, harmonious Romanesque church, like so many others you encounter in this area, is built of soft, seemingly pliable *pietra serena* — a deep gray travertine stone with a particular depth and beauty. Most are graced within by marble and wood sculptures of the primitive early Gothic style that is pervasive here. The Diecino church is a perfect example. Inside — along with an early Roman sarcophagus found nearby — is a collection of early medieval wall sculptures. My favorite is *"re pippino,"* a seemingly headless horseman. There's another of the Prophet Isaiah, looking sternly medieval.

(It's a matter of chance to find any particular country church open during lunch hour, or even open at all. If you find a church closed, there's usually a house nearby where you can find someone with a key; if the church is big enough as an attraction, you'll find it open even at lunchtime. Usually country churches close between 12 noon and 3. Alas, there's no way to check beforehand.)

Travel back to the right side of the river at Borgo a Mozzano. Just past the town — where a very pleasant meal can be had at Osteria I Macelli (see page 65) — you'll soon be struck by the sight of an unusually high-arching walking bridge. It is the Ponte della Maddalena, better known as the Devil's Bridge. A feat of fourteenth-century engineering, it spans the river in three gracefully asymmetrical arches. A first sighting takes the breath away. On a sunny day the arches are perfectly reflected in the river making three shimmering diminishing circles. At night, it's smartly lit. There are a few parking places, and a walk over the bridge is a heady experience.

It's here, at the Devil's Bridge that the flat Valle del Serchio begins to edge up into the Garfagnana. A few kilometers further on, a leisurely detour takes you up through nine kilometers of curved mountain road to Tereglio, a remarkably long and narrow little town, built along a steep ridge that falls off into deep gullies on both sides. I discovered Tereglio some years ago with Giovanna and Massimo Durante, Luccan friends who owned several decrepit houses and were slowly, almost brick by brick, putting together a little inn — La Fagiana — no doubt in the hope that visitors who had come so far, so high up the steep mountain, might want to spend the night, and indeed they do. Hundreds arrived for the festive opening to celebrate the new inn and enjoy the rich offering of Garfagnana special dishes, thick *farro* and bean soup, savory sausages, *polenta* and *funghi*, and more. The inn — during its season from May through October — is as popular as its owners (Tel. 0583-762-179).

Tereglio may strike you as one of the most unusual mountain villages you've ever seen. Once a remote mining town, it consists of a single, long, narrow lane. The meandering pedestrian walk of several kilometers begins and ends with two portals, built centuries ago to protect the place. Ancient stone houses line the way, effectively blocking a view of what lies behind them. A lovely surprise waits just beyond the halfway point. The street curves gently down to an ancient rounded staircase. Directly below is the graceful red-tiled roof of the medieval church of Santa Maria Assunta fronting a little piazza. Looking down at the church and over the rooftop at the surrounding mountains, you might believe you've reached heaven. The silence is penetrable, the feeling awe-inspiring.

From Tereglio you can follow a rather long and tortuous narrow road to another mountain town, Coreglia Antelminelli. Look right as you enter the town; there's a little ninth-century church of San Martino, a squat three-aisled rectangle. A strange lopsidedness adds to its harmony. On one of the main squares of the town, there's a delicious life-sized statue of Mario Pisani, a *figurinaio* or figure-maker who sculpted portraits in plaster of Paris that give Coreglia its bit of notice: from here spread the popular art of making *gesso* figures, little white plaster shapes to paint and decorate. A small museum nearby is dedicated to the art (Museo della Figurina di Gesso e dell'emigrazione, Via del Mangano 17, Tel. 0583-78082; June–September, Monday–Friday 9:30am–12:30pm, Sundays and holidays 10am–1pm and 3pm–6pm; October–May, 9:30am–12:30pm; closed Sunday and holidays).

The sculpture of figure-maker Mario is smartly dressed, ready to emigrate (which he did) in a suit and little cap, standing determinedly with a rather Egyptian-looking cat sitting on one shoulder and two saintly heads held in the other arm.

Nearby there's a little inn called L'Arcile (see page 67), which, during wild mushroom season, can sate you with a full meal of *funghi*. *Farro* dishes are also a specialty.

From Coreglia, an almost untraveled mountain road leads you down to Barga and its majestic cathedral. This approach is special in that you come upon the majestic dome from above. Barga's cathedral, a grand travertine-faced structure, dominates its surroundings. It sits at the top of the old town, its large porch grandly overlooking the landscape of rooftops and the dramatic mountains beyond. The cathedral was badly damaged in an earthquake in 1897 and later impeccably restored. The impressive statuary inside survived intact. Most remarkable is the thirteenth-century Romanesque pulpit by the Lombard sculptor Guido Bigarelli, held securely in place by two serene lions.

On the road north from Barga to Castelnuovo di Garfagnana, you pass through Castelvecchio Pascoli, named after a beloved nineteenth-century poet who enjoyed life here a good deal more than Ariosto. His home has become a museum. (Casa Museo Pascoli, Via Caprona 4, Tel. 0583-766-147; October–March, open Tuesday 2pm–5:15pm; Wednesday–Sunday 9:30am–1pm and 2:30pm–5:15pm; April–September, Tuesday 3:30pm–6:45pm, Wednesday–Sunday 10:30am–1pm and 3pm–6:45pm; closed Christmas).

Canti di Castelvecchio (Songs of Castelvecchio) evoke the landscape and aura of the Garfagnana:

Al mia cantuccio, donde non sento
Se non le reste brusir del grano

Il suon dell'ore viene con vento
Dal non veduto borgo montano

(In my corner I hear nothing
But the rustle of the bearded grains.
The ringing of the hour comes with the wind
That sees not the mountain town.)

Ariosto, author of Italy's great classic *Orlando Furioso*, may have been a better poet, but Pascoli was well enough thought of to have the town named after him. Osteria al Ritrovo del Platano (see page 70), an evocative restaurant directly on the road, is filled with Pascoli memorabilia. The poet breakfasted here daily with his host, present owner Gabriele de Prato's grandfather.

As the road winds gently up to Castelnuovo, the Apuan Alps emerge more and more dramatically, a scene marked as well by distant spires and castle ruins. The hub of activity that is Castelnuovo di Garfagnana comes almost as a surprise. Here is the small capital of the Garfagnana, and as you arrive at its main crossroad, a fortress built by the Este dukes of Ferrara appears on the left. Inside the city walls, there is a simple Romanesque cathedral to visit. It has the usual travertine *pietra serena* façade, and an impressive thirteenth-century crucifix inside. Thursday morning is market day here; the town bustles with shoppers and visitors from all over the Garfagnana. At the edge of the market, along the main road, look for the overwhelming food shop, L'Aia di Piero. It is crammed with every sort of specialty that the Garfagnana has to offer: breads, stone-ground grains, chestnut flours and *polenta*, preserved vegetables, jams, honeys, *farro* tarts, and cheeses from goats and sheep grazing in the hills above. Around the corner is Andrea Bertucci's Il Vecchio Mulino (see page 73), a little bar and lunch stop that overflows on every wall with specialties, wines, olive oils, photographs, posters, and everything else that speaks of Garfagnana.

From Castelnuovo, the road continues up toward Castiglione di Garfagnana. The mountains on both sides take on an awesome beauty as you climb. If there is time, a small road on the right leads to Sillico, an ancient Garfagnana hill town with a local *trattoria*—Locanda Belvedere (Tel. 0583-662-173)—whose terrace affords some of the most spectacular views of the surrounding landscape. Drive beyond Sillico to Pieve Capraia where you'll find the lonely little church of Santa Maria. It sits in the middle of a wood. A few stones are all that's left of the castle that once stood here. The church and its little stone house adjoining became a settlement of hermitic monks; today it emanates a timeless serenity, the quiet broken only by a melodic rushing of the river below. The church gives you a surprising example of arts of earlier times: several stunning large hand-painted Florentine wood-carved frames of the fifteenth century.

A short drive brings you back to the main road and on to Pieve Fosciana where there is yet another simple beautiful church, San Giovanni Battista. The façade is of the usual soft gray stone, but the imposing tower was created not from *pietra serena*, but from the ancient building stones of a nearby fortress ruin. Inside is a lovely Annunciation by Luca della Robbia. At Pieve there is also the ancient water-driven mill where chestnut flour and *polenta* are still stone-ground. You must call first if you wish to visit (Tel. 0583-666-095). At Pieve, you'll also find Il Pozzo (see page 78), one of the finest restaurants of the area.

The road from Pieve Fosciana continues up the mountain to Castiglione di Garfagnana, a great fortress with ramparts and watchtowers presiding over the surrounding landscape. Take the "new gate" in, walk up the ancient street to the left along the wall to find the handsomest little church of them all, Chiesa di San Michele with its sculpted twelfth-century façade of layered *pietra serena* and pink marble.

SPECIALTIES OF VALLE DEL SERCHIO
AND THE GARFAGNANA

❖

LIFE WAS HARD IN THE GARFAGNANA. EACH RULER IN HIS TURN EXTRACTED HEAVY TAXES FROM the local population, and as a bonus forced them to keep up the defenses within the territory as well. The food specialties are those of the poor and all the more interesting because of the area's isolation.

Farro is a good example. When we first arrived here, few had even heard of it. Now *farro* is being exported in greater and greater quantities. It is a hearty grain, similar to the spelt or emmer mentioned in the Bible, and given as a yearly tithe to the Roman emperors. *Farro* has been found in Etruscan tombs, but was not so long ago all but lost to the West. Were it not for a few hardy farmers of the Garfagnana, who grew it in this amenable soil, mostly as animal feed, the grain might have been lost to us completely. In this small corner of Tuscany, this mother of all grains has been resuscitated and refined to its current plump and crunchy desirable sweetness.

These days *farro* has come back into fashion. Visitors to local *trattorie* in Lucca, impressed with its earthy taste and ability to retain both shape and firm bite when cooked, carried it to the world. Garfagnana farmers took advantage of this new interest, and developed a solid export trade. *Farro* is also grown in mountain areas elsewhere in Tuscany, but the soil in the Garfagnana seems to favor it best. A puréed bean soup, in which *farro* has been cooked, is best eaten here, made with an intensely flavored bean that also has been grown for a long time in the Garfagnana. The bean is called *gialliorini*, after its yellow color and small shape.

While these mountains nurture a good amount of *funghi porcini*, game, and wild berries, other interesting food products have found their way into domestic production. Early on, the farmers of the Garfagnana discovered their mineral-laden earth was perfect for the growing of grains. Alongside *farro*, a very special corn — *granturco di Garfagnana* — is grown here to produce savory *polenta* and cornbread. The long skinny cob of this special corn was brought from the Americas in the sixteenth century and, with a certain pride, is called *otto file di Garfagnana*, "the eight rows of Garfagnana," because of its eight rows of large hard kernels rather than the usual twelve or thirteen. It is not a corn that one wants to nibble; the kernels can break a tooth. But ground into *polenta*, or into flour for bread, it produces a robustly flavored product.

As in other mountainous areas of Tuscany, the ubiquitous chestnut forests were once a primary means of sustenance. You can still find stone-grinding chestnut flour mills on private farms. Constant threat of war—right up until the Second World War—kept sending the local population into the forests to eke out sustenance from chestnuts. Blight after the war temporarily cut off the supply, but chestnuts are now again collected in large quantities to be roasted, boiled, and turned into flour for breads and cakes. The flour is known as *farina dolce* (sweet flour), and combined with normal grain for bread. Small pancakes called *frittelle* or *necci*, served with fresh *ricotta*, are a favorite finish to a winter meal. While chestnuts are also roasted over an open fire, Tuscans seem to prefer them boiled in either milk or water flavored with fennel until they are soft and the meat can just be squeezed out.

Often stone-ground chestnut, *farro*, or *otto file* flours are added to wheat flour to make a variety of other breads that in the past helped to make precious wheat go further. Mashed potatoes are often added as well, to give longer life to the loaf. Each kind of bread is delicious, and each is eaten with different specialties. Pasta too is made from *farro* and chestnut flour. In this non-wine-producing area, the local alcohol is a tasty *farro* beer.

The *salumi* or cold cuts of the region are diverse and spicy, going well with the different breads. The most noteworthy is the *biroldo della Garfagnana*, made with what the local population calls "the least noble parts of the pork"—head, heart, lungs, and tongue, all cooked together for hours and spiced generously with cloves and anise, cinnamon and nutmeg, a few wild fennel seeds, salt, and pepper. Blood holds the ingredients together as they are packed into the stomach lining of the beast. It sounds awful, but it's quite delicious when seasoned, aged, sliced, and eaten on a slab of one of the rough local breads, especially bread made with chestnut flour. The most elegant sausage is *mondiola*, made with the choicest pork meat, seasoned with laurel, stuffed into a broad intestinal sac, and folded in half to make a big round sausage tied with a laurel twig. The home-cured prosciutto of the area—*prosciutto bazzone*—is made from fat old pigs raised on wheat, corn, whey, and, in the last months, chestnuts; it tastes of all of them. Spiced well, *prosciutto bazzone* is more savory and succulent than the elegant prosciutto of Parma and San Daniele. I recently tried a newly concocted sausage called *linchetto*, made of beef that has been aged wrapped in a coat of dried *funghi porcini* that imbues the meat with the heavy musty perfume of the dried mushroom. All the *salumi* are made in an acclaimed artisan *norcineria*—maker of pork products—in Ghivizzano, just before Barga on the road up to Castelnuovo. If you'd like to see them at work, call Rolando Belandi at L'Antica Norcineria (Tel. 0583-77008).

The cheeses of the Garfagnana come from both sheep and cows that graze in the highest mountain pastures. The most favored *pecorino*, or sheep's cheese, ripens firmly for six months to a year in a wrapping of straw. The most valued cow's cheese, *vacea*, comes from cattle that graze above 1500 meters, on the highest peaks of the Apuan Alps. *Vacea* is available only from September through May, but another fine cow's cheese—*vaccino Bertami*—is more available and pleasingly eaten with fresh marmalade or one of the fine local honeys.

TYPICAL RESTAURANTS
& THEIR RECIPES

BORGO A MOZZANO

OSTERIA I MACELLI

Via di Cerreto, Borgo a Mozzano • Tel. 0583-88700
*Open daily for lunch and dinner; closed Sunday. Prices inexpensive to moderate
for a full meal, including antipasto, pasta, main course, and desert, including a
Chianti house wine. Reservations recommended, especially weekends.*

Osteria I Macelli sits behind the old main street of Borgo a Mozzano
above the municipal parking lot, in a bright yellow building that was once a
slaughterhouse and is now one of the more enticing restaurants of the area.
Owners Patrizio DeServi and Alberto Lina returned to Borgo a Mozzano
some time ago after years spent making New York City a better place to
eat. Patrizio is a pastry specialist (and owns a delectable pastry shop —
DeServi — in Fornaci di Barga, on the road to Barga); Alberto knows
wines. The confidence that the two acquired in New York is evident from
the well-placed tables, the knowledgeable waiter, and the freshness of every
dish. Opened in 2002, Osteria I Macelli has become a popular eating place
at lunchtime for local business people. In the evening, white tablecloths are
laid and a more elaborate menu is offered.

Specialties include the *salumi* — cold cuts — of Lucca and Garfagnana,
as well as local soups — a light vegetable *zuppa alla frantoiana* is peerless,
another *passato di verdure* that adds various grains is especially good. The
freshly made *ravioli* tastes as though it's been made for you. Main courses
are unusually varied. Rather than the normal list of grilled meats, you'll find
wild boar or venison stewed in an olive-laden sauce, beef simmered in Chianti, and roast baby veal in a milk sauce. And because Patrizio is a pastry
chef, a list of delicious desserts is offered.

The menu changes by the day, and at lunch is written on a blackboard
in each of the restaurant's two pleasant rooms. You can also buy Lucchese

olive oil here, but the house wine is from Chianti. All this goodness is remarkably inexpensive.

RECIPES FROM OSTERIA I MACELLI

Mixed Vegetable Custard
SFORMATO DI VERDURE MISTE

Serves 6

2 carrots
1 cup fresh young green beans
2 zucchini
2 carrots
1 onion
1 leek
2 tablespoons extra virgin olive oil
Breadcrumbs
2 cups Béchamel sauce
3 eggs
½ cup grated Parmesan
Salt and freshly ground pepper
Good grating of nutmeg

Preheat the oven to 350 degrees.

Chop the vegetables into bite-sized pieces and cook gently in 2 tablespoons olive oil and water to cover. When the water has all but evaporated, add a handful of breadcrumbs to absorb the remaining liquid. Remove from heat. Make the sauce, then beat the eggs with the Parmesan and mix with the Béchamel. Add the vegetables, salt, pepper, and nutmeg. Mix well and put into a deep baking dish. Cover with more breadcrumbs and bake for about 30-40 minutes, until the custard is firm and the top golden.

Beef Braised in Wine
BRASATO AL CHIANTI

❖

Serves 6

1 sprig rosemary
2 sprigs sage
3 cloves garlic
Salt and freshly ground pepper
2 pounds top round or roast beef
2 carrots, thinly sliced
2 stalks celery, thinly sliced
1 large onion, halved and thinly sliced
2 tablespoons extra virgin olive oil
1 bottle Chianti

Chop the rosemary, sage, and garlic, and place in a mortar or food processor with about a teaspoon of salt and a teaspoon of pepper. Pound or grind finely together into a paste. Rub the entire roast with the mixture.

Put the sliced vegetables together with the olive oil into a large heavy pot, and sauté gently in the olive oil until they are soft and aromatic, about 10 minutes. Add the beef to the pot and, over a lively flame, brown on all sides. Pour the wine over the meat, and bring to a boil. Lower the flame to a bare simmer, and cook for 2 to 2½ hours, until the wine has reduced to a thick sauce and the meat is well cooked. Allow to rest, and serve in fairly thin slices with the sauce.

COREGLIA ANTELMINELLI

L'ARCILE

Opposite the duomo, Coreglia Antelminelli • Tel. 0583-78401
Open every day during the year, lunch and dinner. Priced moderately.

L'Arcile's restaurant (it's also an inexpensive inn) sits on a flower-filled terrace just opposite Coreglia's main church. The bell tower looming over the narrow street below is in close view as you dine.

Owner and chef Giustina Paladini didn't have much patience when we chatted about authentic traditional food in the Garfagnana. I'd eaten several meals at L'Arcile, and they were all notable for a strict adherence to local products and traditions. I was pretty sure she'd open up with some enthusiastic response. But it wasn't to be. It was full season, and she was probably too tired from running her quirky little nest of rooms she calls a *pensione*. Or maybe because she was up to her elbows in newly-gathered *porcini* mushrooms preparing an all-*funghi* dinner for forty-five diners from Lucca who were traveling up to Coreglia for her special meal. When I asked her about traditions and finding genuine food, she snorted. "Who cares about tradition anymore? All kids want today are pizzas and McDonald's. No one cares about whether foreign *funghi* [i.e., mostly Croatian] invade our markets. They all come from somewhere else, and nobody cares." She continued to rail against what she calls the loss of tradition. My protests went unheeded. How was it that she was still serving only the most local of products to her guests? Why would they come all the way up from Lucca for *funghi* from the nearby woods? Wasn't it local *farro* that made her seafood salad so special?

At this, she grunted a small assent and agreed she was just too tired to be agreeable. She did look a bit sweaty. I asked her what her all-*porcini* meal would consist of. I'd just eaten her salad of fresh grated *funghi* and Parmesan dressed with balsamic vinegar and olive oil that she'd served on a thin slice of *bresaola*—dried beef—that certainly would be a part of such a dinner. What else? For antipasto, there'd be the addition of *crostini di funghi*, small toasts with chopped sautéed mushrooms. For *primi*, or first courses, *malfatti*, an oven dish of *funghi* and *ricotta*; *zuppa*, a cream of mushroom soup; and *pappardelle di funghi*, wide homemade pasta with *funghi trifolati*; or chopped mushrooms in a garlic, oil, and parsley sauce. She'd then serve another *funghi* dish I'd enjoyed at L'Arcile: slices of large *porcini* caps dipped in a batter of *polenta* and flour, quickly fried in olive oil, and served with a large slab of gently aged pecorino. All this was a "light" version of her all-*funghi* meals; another might include large meat-stuffed and baked mushroom caps or a main course of wild boar with *funghi*. Giustina prepares such a meal only on order, for at least five diners. But she is happy to spend her day preparing it during the months when *porcini* arrive daily from the woods, from the last days of August through November.

There are plenty of non-mushroom dishes at L'Arcile, depending on the season. The tomato *bruschetta* has a touch of balsamic vinegar along with the usual coating of extra virgin olive oil; the *farro* and seafood salad is a staple when there's time and good seafood around. Homemade *ricotta* and spinach-filled *tortelli* are rustic and served with large sage leaves fried crisp in olive oil. A walnut sauce covers freshly made *tagliatelle*.

Her meat courses are the usual grilled and roasted meats, with game added when it's available. Desserts are varied; the most "typical" would be something she claims the young don't care about anymore: *frittelle di castagne*—fried chestnut flour fritters with a topping of *ricotta*.

RECIPE FROM L'ARCILE

Farro and Seafood Salad
INSALATA DI FARRO E FRUTTI DI MARE

Serves 6

1 cup *farro*
Juice of ½ lemon
5 ounces small shrimp, peeled and deveined
5 ounces calamari, thinly sliced
1 pound mussels, scrubbed and bearded
1 pound clams, scrubbed
½ cup white wine
1 tablespoon plus ½ cup extra virgin olive oil
12 large crayfish
1 bunch parsley leaves, chopped finely
¼ cup balsamic vinegar
Salt and freshly ground pepper
1 bunch arugula

Cook the *farro*, drain, and run under cold water. Douse with the lemon juice and set aside.

Prepare the seafood. Chop each shrimp into 3 pieces and cook in boiling salted water for about 2 minutes. Remove and cook the calamari in the same water for 5 minutes. Drain and add to the shrimp. Steam the mussels and clams in the white wine, with about a tablespoon of olive oil. When they are open, remove from the liquid, cool, and shell. Discard any that have not opened.

Boil the crayfish in a pot of boiling salted water for 5 minutes. Drain and set aside.

Mix the *farro* with the shrimp, calamari, mussels, clams, and parsley. Add the vinegar and oil, and mix well. Taste and add salt and lots of pepper.

Chop the arugula and spread over a large platter. Spoon over the *farro* salad, and place the crayfish on top, two crayfish for each serving.

PONTE DI CAMPIA

OSTERIA AL RITROVO DEL PLATANO
Ponte di Campia • Tel. 0583-766-039
Open daily for lunch and dinner; closed Wednesday. A meal, not including wine, is inexpensive. Reservations recommended for dinner and on weekends.

At a turn in the road, between Castelvecchio Pascoli and Castelnuovo Garfagnana, just over the bridge called Ponte di Campia, you'll bump into Al Ritrovo del Platano, the oldest inn in the area. Two large plane trees (*platoni*) sitting in front and the name of the *trattoria* clearly painted on the outer front wall indicate you are there.

The interior of Al Ritrovo del Platano is dedicated to poet Giovanni Pascoli, who was one of its first habitués in the nineteenth century. The small bar/*trattoria* is cluttered with memorabilia, its walls covered with large photographs and manuscripts. Interesting old wooden farm machinery takes up a good amount of floor space.

The *trattoria* has passed from generation to generation. Owner Gabriele de Prato's father, Luigi, and mother, Maria Grazia, are still cooking, although the restaurant now belongs to the younger generation. Maria Grazia is there first every morning preparing the various breads and pasta. The food hasn't changed much here since Pascoli ordered *ravioli* and fresh river trout for lunch. Gabriele and his wife Michele are enormously proud of their ties to the local food and literary culture and a way of life that becomes obvious the minute you begin to order.

Homemade pastas at Al Ritrovo del Platano are made witih a well-kneaded whole-wheat dough called *grano torrenova*, another venerable old grain special to the Garfagnana. The pasta, *granscuro*, is thicker and chewier than normal pasta, with a heartier flavor. The *tortellaccio* of *granscuro* is a single large *ravioli*, filled and sauced with wild *funghi porcini*, a specialty of the restaurant and heavy with earthy tastes.

Two thick soups also show off local products. Both the *passato di fagioli* and the *minestrone di farro* are made with the seemingly skinless *giallorini* beans special to the area.

Like so many small *trattorie* of Tuscany, the first courses are the most interesting. My choice for a main course would be a local river trout dish that dates back to the time of Pascoli, *trota marinata del Corsonna*. It's best in spring and fall, when fresh trout fishing is permitted and the trout comes not from a fish farm, but from the heights of the river Serchio before it gets to all the paper plants in the valley. Another interesting main course is a platter called *pascoliano*, a selection of local cheeses and cold cuts served with a variety of breads that Gabriele's mother bakes each day at the restaurant. There is chestnut flour or *farro* bread, local *biroldo* sausages, and other samples of Garfagnana cold cuts. Sweets in winter include chestnut flour *crepes* with a topping of *ricotta*.

On Sundays a fried roll is added to the offerings, usually for a take-out lunch bought at the front bar. It is lightly crisp outside, with a soft dough filling, something like a puffed-up *foccaccia*. It serves perfectly for any of the sausage or cheese fillings on hand.

At Easter time you'll find a special sort of dry cake, the *panettone Pasimata*.

Gabriele de Prato's zest for old food traditions of the Garfagnana has been joined by his new passion for recreating the wine that was once made here. He began the first new commercial vineyard of the area, with its premier vintage in the year 2000. Melograno is not yet widely available, but if you find it, it's the perfect accompaniment to a meal at Al Ritrovo del Platano.

Trout with Rosemary and Wine
TROTA MARINATA DEL CORSONNA

FOR EACH SERVING:
1 fresh trout, weighing about ¾ pound
1 sprig rosemary
1 clove garlic
2 tablespoons extra virgin olive oil
1 glass white wine
Juice of ½ lemon
Salt and freshly ground pepper

Clean and wash the trout. Chop together the rosemary and garlic. Heat the oil in a pan large enough to hold the entire fish, add the rosemary and garlic and then the trout. Brown the trout for a minute, and gently turn, taking care not to break the fish. Add salt and pepper to taste.

Add the lemon juice and then the wine. If necessary, add a bit of water toward the end of the cooking, which should be no longer than 5 minutes. It is served at al Ritrovo del Platano at room temperature, with the soft *polenta* of the Garfagnana, but can be served with boiled potatoes and fresh vegetables as well.

Easter Cake
PANETTONE PASIMATA

1 tablespoon anise seeds
1 tablespoon yeast
Pinch of salt
Grated peel of 1 lemon
Grated peel of 1 orange
5 cups white flour
8 eggs, divided
1¼ cups sugar, divided
1 tablespoon vermouth

¾ cup butter, plus enough to butter the pan
1 packed cup currants or small black raisins
4 tablespoons extra virgin olive oil

Preheat the oven to 325 degrees.

Soak the anise seeds for 20 minutes. Dissolve the yeast in 1¼ cups of warm water. Add the salt, the drained anise seeds, the lemon and orange peels, and enough flour to make a soft dough. Leave the dough to rise in a warm place for 2 hours.

Add 4 eggs, ⅓ of the sugar, and a tablespoon of vermouth and mix. Sprinkle over a layer of flour and allow to rest in a warm place for an hour.

Add the remaining ingredients. The dough should be soft and sticky. Pour into a buttered 8 inch springform baking pan and leave to rise in a warm place for another ¾ of an hour. Bake for 50 minutes, until the cake has reached a deep brown and the odor wafts through the house. Remove from oven, and allow the cake to rest for 5 minutes before removing the sides of the pan.

The cake is eaten during the Easter period, and, in a closed sack, can last for more than a week. It is served with a glass of *vin santo*.

CASTELNUOVO DI GARFAGNANA

IL VECCHIO MULINO

Via Vittorio Emanuele 12, Castelnuovo di Garfagnana • Tel. 0583-62192
Open from early lunch through dinner. Closed Mondays. Inexpensive, depending upon how much you eat and drink. No reservations are necessary; if the single large table inside is filled, there are tables outside. One may also stand.

You'll find the perfect choice of local products at this small inauspicious bar/*osteria* at the entrance to Castelnuovo di Garfagnana. Owner Andrea Bertucci is called the Indiana Jones of the Garfagnana, not out of a particular quest for tombs or holy grails but for his excavating of food traditions and local produce. A good sampling of what he has uncovered lies on the shelves at Il Vecchio Mulino. The place is packed with jars, bottles, and dry goods, a cluttered *Wunderkammer* of Garfagnana delights.

Meals are local cheeses and cold cuts served on wooden plates, along with tarts and other specialties of the Garfagnana. The major attraction is from Emilia: a huge *mortadella* sausage, looking like a ballistic missile and weighing more than 400 pounds upon arrival, lying on its own fitted table next to the hams and sausages in a corner of the tavern. Slice by slice, it lasts about three months. Directly next to it sits a large *prosciutto Bazzone*, the succulent fat prosciutto of the area, its juices almost dripping.

To all who have encountered him, Andrea is the guiding light of the Garfagnana culinary experience and his little *osteria* provides samplings of all the specialties he has uncovered. He serves no hot food—a lukewarm *farro* and bean soup, or the very Luccan spring soup called *garmugia*, is about as hot as it gets—but rather an assemblage of Garfagnana specialties that he has collected from small farmers and bakers, meat curers and cheese makers. The sampling of what the Garfagnana means to its food lovers arrives at the table on a thick wooden board.

On the board, you'll find *lardo di Garfagnana*, a thin slice of seasoned pork fat, a cured *carpaccio* called *manzo di pazzo* ("beef for the crazy"), various sausage samplings, and some wonderful cheeses of the Garfagnana, all accompanied by thick slabs of *farro*/potato bread.

RECIPES FROM IL VECCHIO MULINO

Andrea has more *farro* recipes than anyone I've met, and it's a pleasure to share them with other fans of this plump little grain.

Farro and Bean Soup
IL FARRO DELLA NONNA

Serves 8-10

This is a classic version of *minestra di farro*, the traditional *farro* in a bean purée. The soup tends to thicken; add water until you reach the consistency you want.

1½ cups dried *borlotti* or cranberry beans, soaked overnight

Mineral water

5 cloves garlic, divided

1 sprig fresh sage leaves

2 tablespoons extra virgin olive oil, plus additional for drizzling

1 large yellow onion, finely chopped

1 carrot, finely chopped

1 rib celery, finely chopped

4 Italian plum tomatoes, peeled and chopped

2 medium potatoes, peeled and cut into cubes

1¼ cups *farro*

2 sprigs rosemary leaves

Lots of salt and freshly ground pepper

Soak the beans overnight in mineral water. The next day, cook the soaked beans in the water in which they have been soaked, plus enough more to cover by about 2 inches. Bring to a boil, lower the flame, and cook over the lowest possible heat together with 2 cloves of garlic and a large sprig of sage. Add more water as necessary. After about 2 hours, the beans should be cooked. Keep them in their water.

Meanwhile, chop the 3 remaining garlic cloves and sauté in the olive oil in another pan. Add the onion, carrots, and celery. Cook for about 10 minutes over a low fire. Add the tomatoes and continue to cook until the tomatoes soften into the other vegetables. Add the potatoes, mix well, and cook for another few minutes. Put the contents of the pan into the cooked beans and their water, and continue to cook for another 40 minutes. Purée the entire mixture, and add enough water or stock to make a creamy thick consistency. (It must have enough liquid to allow the *farro* to cook when it is added.) Add lots of salt and pepper to taste.

Put the blended soup back into the pot. Add the *farro* and the rosemary and cook for another half hour. Allow to stand for at least an hour. If the soup becomes too thick, add some more water. Serve warm with a good dripping of fresh olive oil and a grinding of fresh pepper.

Farro Risotto
FARROTTO

⊕

Serves 2

1 cup *farro*
½ onion, thinly sliced
2 tablespoons extra virgin olive oil
Vegetable broth
1 small potato, peeled and cut into small cubes
1 carrot, cubed
3 tomatoes, skinned and chopped
½ cup grated *pecorino*

Wash and drain the *farro*. In a fireproof casserole, melt the sliced onion in the olive oil, and add the *farro*. Toast for a minute or 2. Add 2 cups of broth, salt, and freshly ground pepper, and allow to cook slowly, adding more broth as the *farro* absorbs the liquid, stirring often. After 15 minutes, add the cubed vegetables and cook slowly until they are softened, adding broth just to cover as needed. When it reaches the consistency of a *risotto*, remove it from the stove. Allow to rest for 5 minutes, and add the *pecorino* before serving.

Farro Pudding
BUDINO DI FARRO

⊕

Serves 6-8

Not too different from an English rice pudding, but rather more firm. Farro has a special nutty flavor, and retains its bite. In the Garfagnana, this mixture is also used as a filling for tarts.

2 cups *farro*
4 cups milk, divided
Pinch of salt
2 egg yolks
1 whole egg, beaten
1¼ cups sugar

⅓ cup flour
1½ cups *ricotta*, preferably sheep
2 tablespoons cherry liqueur, or *amaretto* or rum
Butter
Confectioners' sugar

Preheat the oven to 350 degrees.

Cook the *farro* in 1½ cups of gently salted milk until the milk is entirely absorbed, about 15 minutes.

In the meantime, prepare the cream by whisking the egg yolks together with the whole egg. Put the egg mixture, sugar, and flour in a large saucepan; whisk together over a low fire until the sugar begins to melt. Add the remaining milk and bring to the boiling point. Remove from flame and whisk in the *ricotta* and the liqueur. Add the *farro* and mix well.

Butter a large oval baking dish (about 13 by 8½ inches) and pour in the mixture. Bake until the top begins to brown and the pudding is firm. Sprinkle with confectioners' sugar and serve warm.

Luccan Spring Soup
GARMUGIA

❀

Serves 4

This is Lucca's welcome to spring, unknown outside of the province. I once asked a vegetable monger in a neighboring province about *garmugia* but the term was totally unknown to her. Rich with bits of spring vegetables, it's a thoroughly comforting dish for a light supper. It's usually cooked atop the stove in an earthenware pot.

3 small onions, thinly sliced
3 tablespoons extra virgin olive oil
1 ounce *pancetta*, in small cubes
¼ pound ground lean beef
1 pound fresh broad (*fava*) beans (weighed with their pods), shelled
3 fresh artichoke hearts, chopped into small cubes
¼ pound small fresh garden peas (weighed with their pods), shelled
1 small bunch asparagus, chopped

3½ cups vegetable broth (more if needed)
Butter
4 slices toasted rustic bread
Freshly ground pepper

In a deep earthenware flameproof casserole, melt the onion in the olive oil. Add the *pancetta* and ground meat. Break up the meat with a fork, and cook together for 10 minutes. Add the vegetables, mix well, and cook for 5 minutes. Add the broth and continue cooking for 20 minutes. At the end, taste for seasoning, add freshly ground pepper and a small knob of butter and serve from the casserole over a slice of toasted farm bread.

PIEVE FOSCIANA
———— ❧◉❧ ————

IL POZZO DI GIORDANO E MAURIZIO
2/A Via Europa, Pieve Fosciana • Tel. 0583-666-380
Open for lunch and dinner. Closed Wednesdays. Priced moderately.

Enter the large dining room of Il Pozzo any day after the bells strike twelve and you'll find the large rustic beamed dining room full, each table with five, six, or ten men quietly and intently finishing a meal. They are local laborers, who crowd into this restaurant every day for their main meal. Giordano Andreucci is genial host to them all. A little later, after 1pm, white collar workers from nearby banks and offices arrive, and perhaps a few women from Lucca out for an afternoon. Evenings, it's just as crowded with families and groups of friends. Il Pozzo does seem to be a local treat for everyone. During summer, there is a garden full of tables as well.

While he claims Sienese origins, Giordano's family has been in the Garfagnana for eight generations. His grandfather was a local *mugnaio*, a miller of the three main Garfagnana flours—wheat, corn, and *farro*—that have always been the staples of the area. He is the first of the family to become a proper restaurateur, deciding early on it was a decent and quick way to earn a living. He also developed a timely philosophy and determined his restaurant would maintain and revive the traditional dishes of the area. He presents them well, so well that the restaurant has been awarded a "snail" for quality/price, one of thirty-two in all of Tuscany bestowed by the fastidious Italian branch of the Slow Food organization.

Giordano's partner, Maurizio Romei, is chef at Il Pozzo. He makes his *tagliarini*, thin fresh noodles, when he arrives every morning. His truffled *tagliarini* — with local truffles — are as celestial a dish as you'll find in the more popular truffle areas of Tuscany. They are a recent luxury in the Garfagnana; in the past, truffles were never sought out; they were a delicacy that had little to do with the local taste or pocketbook. In time, as in other areas of Tuscany, the brownish truffle has become ubiquitous; its most flavorful moment is in late fall and early winter.

Antipasti include the special cured pork products of the region, the elongated, succulent prosciutto and delicately spiced *biroldo* and *mondiola* sausages, all served with a choice of the splendid breads that are so particular here. *Primi* — pastas and soups — include a *minestra di farro* and *pappardelle rustiche* of *farro* pasta sauced with a venison *ragù* that's almost sweet.

A special main course puts chestnuts and chestnut flour to good use at Il Pozzo, a roast pork loin with chestnuts and a sauce thickened by the flour. Ask also for *fagioli scoppiati*, cooked borlotti beans roasted in a hot oven until they burst.

The dessert of the house has the irresistible name *la torta squisita* ("the exquisite tart"), and is a crunchy mélange of pastry, *ricotta*, and caramelized sugar. Giordano is also a qualified sommelier; his wine selections can be well relied upon. The simple house wine is also fine.

RECIPES FROM IL POZZO DI GIORDANO E MAURIZIO

Pork Tenderloin with Chestnuts
MAIALE CON CASTAGNE

Serves 6

1 onion
1 carrot
1 rib celery
1 clove garlic
1 handful parsley leaves

2 ounces pork fat (lard), in one piece
4 tablespoons olive oil
1½ pound loin or tenderloin of pork
1 cup white wine
Meat broth if necessary
1 small tin or vacuum packed preserved cooked chestnuts
    (unsweetened), chopped
2 tablespoons butter
2 tablespoons chestnut flour

Finely chop together the onion, carrot, celery, garlic, and parsley leaves to make a *soffrito*. In a large pot with cover, combine the *soffrito* with the pork fat and olive oil and cook for a few minutes over a medium flame to soften the vegetables.

Add the meat and brown on all sides. Add the wine. Cover and cook for half an hour, adding meat broth if the meat becomes dry. Incorporate the butter into the chestnut flour and mix it, along with the chestnuts, into the broth. Cook another half an hour.

Exploded Beans
FAGIOLI SCOPPIATE

Serves 4

A curiosity more than a dish, but fun to eat. The beans burst open, get a bit crisp, and with some good olive oil and salt, make a nice side dish.

1 cup *borlotti* or cranberry beans
3 sprigs sage leaves, divided
4 garlic cloves, divided
1 sprig rosemary leaves
2 tablespoons extra virgin olive oil, plus additional at table
Salt

Preheat the oven to 450 degrees.

Soak the beans for at least 12 to 18 hours, covered with lots of cold water. With a slotted spoon remove the beans to a small pot, and add the sage, rosemary, and garlic. Cover with some of the soaking water and cook slowly over a low flame, covered, until the beans are well cooked but still whole. Add water, just to cover, as they cook. Add salt at the end of cooking, and allow to cool in their own water.

Drain the beans into a shallow pan with a few tablespoons of the water, add 2 tablespoons of oil, 2 sprigs of sage, and 2 cloves of garlic. Place in the hot oven for about 10 minutes, until the beans burst open. Salt well and serve either warm or at room temperature drizzled with olive oil.

CHAPTER 3

La Valdinievole and
Svizzera Pesciatina

THE VALDINIEVOLE, OR FOGGY VALLEY, IS A VAST
BASIN IN THE PROVINCE OF PISTOIA, PROSPEROUS,
busy, surrounded by mountains and hills. It was once a vast swampy lake
with steam fogging up the entire plain, thus perhaps giving it its name. To
the north soar the craggy Apennine Mountains. In the east lie the gentler
green hills of Monte Albano. Amid the terraced hills of olives and vineyards are small inviting hill towns called *castelli*, the former strongholds of
aristocratic families ruling over the entire wet valley. In many, you can still
see vestiges of the great castles. The young Leonardo da Vinci wandered
through these hills sketching the *castelli* and later mapped the entire valley
in an attempt to devise a water control system of the area. A copy of his map
hangs in the little Leonardo museum in Vinci.

Today, brightly refurbished old farm houses reflecting the general prosperity of the area are scattered through the hills. There's an ever increasing
international demand for good olive oil, and farms that were abandoned in
the 1960s are again thriving, many of them with foreign owners.

The Valdinievole begins in the west around Pescia, includes the once
fashionable spas of Montecatini and Monsummano Terme, the wine center
of Montecarlo and the small historic town of Fuccecchio with its lovely
old center. The *padule* (marshland) of Fuccecchio is the largest wetland in
Tuscany, all that's left of the muddy lake that was once the scene of raging
battles between the navies of Florence and Pisa. Today, the swamp is a
national park, a mecca for bird lovers and rare flora enthusiasts.

Pescia, Valdinievole's principal town tucked comfortably under its
surrounding hills, is the flower-growing center of central Italy. An eighteenth-century portal, the Florentine Gate, built by the last, rather decadent
Medici who controlled Pescia, welcomes you into an old town filled with
lovely surprises. Among them is a great oval main square, a backstage set

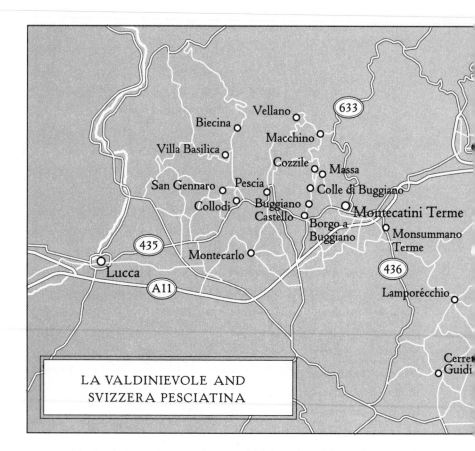

almost hidden behind the Pescia river that divides the two sections of the
old city center. An impressive thirteenth-century city hall rises at one end
of the oversized square and a little chapel crowned by a magnificent cof-
fered ceiling stands at the other. Noble buildings line both sides. The long
oval is packed every Saturday morning for the weekly market.

On the other side of the river, opposite Pescia's hospital, a dramatic
thirteenth-century painting of San Francesco hangs in the gloom of a
church of the same name; nearby is another little treasure, the tiny chapel of
the Oratorio di Sant'Antonio, where you'll find a moving twelfth-century
group of carved figures depicting the Deposition of Christ.

Pescia is also home to the wondrous display of citrus plants in the
greenhouses of Oscar Tintori. Potted, shaped lemon trees have been grown
in Tuscany since before the Medici. At Tintori you can still find enormous
pots of fruiting five-hundred-year-old trees. Once a small citrus orchard,

Tintori has become the largest exporter of ornamental citrus in Italy. They've recently inaugurated Il Giardino degli Agrumi, a landscaped hesperidarium of more than two hundred different kinds of citrus. You can visit anytime, but if you want a guided tour, check for hours (Tel. 0572-429-191; guided tour, 3,50 euros). You can also buy from a choice selection of citrus jams and citrus-based honeys, some of them unlike any I've seen elsewhere. Giorgio, son of Oscar, and his two sons are usually there to show you around.

In the heart of Pescia you'll also find the best-known *trattoria* of the area, Trattoria Cecco (see page 94), a restaurant that prides itself on offering almost exactly the same menu for the past hundred years.

From Pescia to the west along the old provincial road to Lucca are a few more surprises. Just past the turnoff to Collodi, a town to which we'll return, is a sign on the right to San Gennaro. A long stretch of tall umbrella pines and cypresses leads you to this small town, with yet another hidden treasure inside the small eleventh-century church of San Gennaro. If the church is closed ask next door for the key. Inside a wondrous Angel of the Annunciation awaits you. Only a few years ago, when it was attributed to Verrocchio, you could still freely approach, even touch the lovely sculpture. Today, it is acknowledged to be an early work of Leonardo da Vinci, thus it's gone behind glass.

From San Gennaro there's an inside road to Collodi and the place where Pinocchio was born. The castle town cascades down a mountain hillside into the Villa Garzoni, a splendid house that seems to hold the village on its back. The tales of Pinocchio were woven in the kitchen of this large villa. Today, a bustling Pinocchio tourism is the town's mainstay. The main square below the villa is filled with stalls selling Pinocchio replicas of every size and function, thousands of bright red little dolls to welcome you. Nearby is a Pinocchio theme park, unlike most in that there are no rides, but rather a landscaped series of mosaics, figures, and scenes from the original story executed by a group of Italian artists. A large whale does invite children into its mouth.

A few miles into the hills from Collodi, the road curves up to the town of Villa Basilica, a cul-de-sac ending in an odd little square that has at its heart a twelfth-century church most remarkable in its Luccan/Pisan Gothic style. Its stone is the soft gray *pietra serena*. Four tiers of columns, each column with a different capital, make it almost as imposing as Lucca's cathedral. The interior is pristine, with little ornament to mar its tranquility.

As you go back down toward Collodi, a sign will indicate a left turn for the inauspicious Trattoria Aldo (see page 97) at Biecina that offers the simple classic dishes of the area.

Return to Pescia, where, along the western bank of the Pescia river (the side with the square), a narrow valley road runs up into the lower Apennines. The hills and thick chestnut forests are known as the Svizzera Pesciatina (Pescia's Switzerland), but *le dieci castella*—a collective singular meaning ten castles—is the official and more attractive designation. Both terms describe the area well. Capping the peaks of dramatic hills, ten tiny medieval hamlets today attract few but discerning travelers. Although almost every one of the ten hamlets offers an attractive church and ancient lanes, few number more than fifty inhabitants. The Swiss essayist, Jean Sismondi, who lived in Pescia in the early nineteenth century and wrote a celebrated history of the Italian republics, apparently gave the area its Swiss nickname. The ten *castelli* better resemble remote mountain villages of Sicily, perched as they are atop each peak in the area and totally independent from one another.

Vellano is the largest, the *capoluogo* (main village) and the only one still featuring any sort of commercial life. On the main road below this medieval *borgo*, you can sit on the terrace of a little inn, Antica Locanda del Borgo (Via Matteotti 32, Tel. 0572-409-137; open daily, lunch and dinner, except Thursday), eat a fairly typical meal (try the *trippa della casa*, a saucy version of the well-known Florentine plate of tripe), and look down on the valley below. The Antica Locanda brings some life into the village with Saturday evening jam sessions and little theatrical productions both inside and on the large terrace across the way. During summer months, Vellano takes on a resort air; Italian and foreign—mostly Swiss and German—vacationers come to enjoy the breezy hills.

The road circles up to the top of the village and its medieval wall, from where you can look down at several of the other little hamlets. A tiny portal in the wall brings you into a warren of old streets and tunneled alleyways that lead into a well-preserved mini-square. The square is the heart of a chestnut festival held in the town each October.

Leaving Svizzera Pesciatina at Vellano, continue to Macchino, where a right turn takes you back toward the valley and the most inviting hill towns between Pescia and Montecatini, four little towns that remain an oasis of well guarded calm. It wasn't always so; in earlier times they were either warring with one another or caught in the crossfire of battling Luccans, Pisans, and Florentines. The Florentines won the day in the fifteenth century and the Medici took over the whole area for several hundred years. Highest of the towns is Cozzile, fronted by its remodeled old castle. Cozzile is known as "the balcony of the Valdinievole." On a clear day you can see the entire basin almost to the sea. A local saying claims that all of Tuscany sits at the foot of silent and tranquil Cozzile.

The sister village to Cozzile is Massa, with an impressive old portal leading to its eleventh-century tower and porticoed church of Santa Maria Assunta. Inside the church is a trove of precious church objects, including a lovely old wooden Madonna, and a carved inlaid wooden sacristy. A walk up through Massa's narrow streets brings you to the medieval city hall and an impressive view.

Below Massa are two hill towns, Colle di Buggiano, where you can enjoy a rustic meal at Antico Colle (see page 100) directly on the lively piazza and, just below it, Buggiano Castello, perhaps the loveliest of them all. Buggiano Castello spreads out against the hill, with a tenth-century Romanesque abbey at its top. The church is fronted by an undisturbed little Renaissance square, dominated by its Palazzo Pretorio encrusted with dozens of coats of arms. It's an idyllic playground for the children of the village. Sporadic cultural activities — plays, concerts, a traditional festive dinner — take place on the piazza. The harmony of Buggiano Castello is accentuated by the deep brick red or ochre color of so many of its homes.

Just under the old gate of Buggiano Castello is Sant'Elena restaurant and its terrace, where on a sunny Sunday afternoon, you can have an afternoon glass of wine accompanied by what owner Mario Cortesi calls his

Tuscan *merenda*—tasty *bruschette*, *crostini*, and other snacks on a pleasant terrace. It's also a nice place for a pizza or a full meal (Tel. 0572-30548; open daily except Monday, for lunch and dinner). Borgo a Buggiano, the commercial center below, was once the central meat market of Tuscany. The *mercato del bestiame* (the animal market) still carries the name, and today houses a remarkable old country store—Michelotti & Co—that not only supplies the needs of local farmers and granaries, but can provide you with some of the fine produce of the area. Their beans, lentils, and other legumes are sold from sacks and are the freshest of the season.

Just across the valley, on a small hill of its own, is the wine-growing center of Montecarlo, an imposing medieval red brick hill town with a broad main pedestrian street linking its two old gates. Montecarlo is well-known for its white wines; less known is a perfect tiny little seventeenth-century court theater—still used for summer concerts and plays—just off the main street. There are a number of impressive restaurants in Montecarlo; if you want to join local farmers for a simple meal, try Trattoria di Natale in a pine grove just under the town (Via Roggio Baldino Primo 21, Tel. 0583-286-540; open daily lunch and dinner, except Wednesday).

Nearby is Montecatini Terme, where a variety of thermal waters are proffered in a Roman-style spa filled with romantic gardens; a roving Viennese quintet strolls in the background. Montecatini has all the stylish hotels and shops that the clientele of elegant spas demand. It's also home to a compact produce marketplace, and a teeming weekly market that takes up a good portion of town every Thursday morning. The vegetable market is impressive every day, divided between wholesale suppliers and local farmers selling to local buyers.

The marketplace has the added attraction of a fine artisan pasta shop: P&P (Via Mazzini 60; Tel. 0572-773-511), named after its proprietors, Paola and Piero Zucconi (no relation to another less remarkable pasta shop called Zucconi down the street). Neither Paola nor Piero ever miss a day in their busy shop. Seven days a week they and their staff work at hand-rolling and stuffing the most melt-in-the-mouth *ravioli* and *tortelli* imaginable. The variety of fillings is vast. Beyond the usual you find fillings of truffles, *ortica*—the delicious and nutritious prickly nettles that grow wild all over Tuscany—squash, wild mushrooms, orange, artichokes, and a host of others. The shop has been in business for almost sixty years ever since

Piero's mother, Marietta Romani, began hand-rolling pastas for neighbors. Monsummano Terme is another spa next door to Montecatini Terme, less known for its waters than for the blistering thermal grottoes in the quarried mountain visible from everywhere in the valley. Just beyond Monsummano on the road to Lamporecchio and Vinci is an enticing small café and chocolate shop that is definitely worth a visit. Slitti has a fine array of handmade chocolates — sold throughout Italy and Europe — and the best coffee around. Out of a small bar that Luciano Slitti opened in 1969, the family enterprise has grown to become a major exporter of fine chocolates and coffee. Some time ago, Luciano turned over the production and distribution of products to his sons Andrea and Daniele. You'll still find Luciano manning the cash register every day. Andrea manages the production and Daniele the marketing. Daniele tells me that Slitti's chocolates contain a good deal less fat than French or Belgian chocolates. Coffee spoons and old Tuscan farm tools made from chocolate are hand-fashioned here in soft molds. If you're anywhere in the area around Easter time, don't miss the shop. The large, elaborately decorated chocolate Easter eggs are the status gift of the season, and despite their steep price manage to disappear completely before Easter Sunday (Slitti Caffe, Via Francesca Sud 1268, Tel. 0572-640240; open daily except Sunday).

It is mostly because of Slitti's fame that Monsumanno plays host to a feast of chocolate — the *Cioccolosita* — every January, a heady fair that features handmade chocolates from all over Italy.

The long low mountain of Monte Albano lies just beyond Monsumanno and completes the half-circle of hills surrounding the Valdinievole. Castle remains at Larciano overlook the valley. The nearby hill town of Lamporecchio is the home of *brigidini*, paper-thin crisp sweet biscuits that find their way to street fairs all over Italy. Along Lamporecchio's main street you'll also find a friendly restaurant — Antico Masetto (see page 102) — with a large inviting menu of local dishes.

Vinci, Leonardo's birthplace, is nearby. The best approach is from Monte Albano over a mountain road from Lamporecchio: Via Pistoiese, the old route that Leonardo undoubtedly traveled, back and forth from Vinci to Pistoia (now the provincial capital). His father had an accounting office there. Santa Maria del Pruno, a little church along the road, in Orbignano, has some lovely late fourteenth-century frescoes; one is a most unusual Madonna that has been attributed both to Giotto and the school of Donatello. Ask the keeper next door to open the church as you pass by; it's a nice surprise.

This mountain road descends to Vinci from the hills above the town. An angle of Vinci strikes you suddenly as you descend, protruding like the bow of a ship above the olive-covered landscape below. I visited Vinci in 1986, the year of the big frost, when the olives were burned black, and I remember how the little walled town stood sad but proud above the devastation around. The recovered full-blooming olive groves now look as though they'd never known disaster. Vinci has become the center of a busy well-tended Leonardo industry, with Leonardo replicas, Leonardo cafes, Leonardo restaurants, tobacco shops, and even laundries. The farmhouse where he is said to have been born is open to the public, along with two small museums that feature his inventions. The main museum—Il Museo Leonardo da Vinci—sits in the Castello Guidi, an imposing structure rising in the middle of the old town (Tel. 0571-56055; open daily 9:30am–6pm). The second, more recently opened, "*nuovo*" Museo Ideale Leonardo da Vinci, is just below, on the main street of town (Tel. 0571-56296; open daily 10am–1pm and 3pm–7pm). Both demonstrate the genius of the man, his imagination, and his contrasting dreams of advanced armaments and a better life. The more recently opened Museo Ideale also contains examples of his machines for olive pressing, wine-making, and a working rotisserie that may seem a bit archaic these days, but would have been an amazing culinary advance in the fifteenth century.

Just across the street from Museo Ideale, is the busy little restaurant Il Ristoro del Museo (see page 106), a favorite lunchtime *trattoria* of museum workers and their guests. Further on, just beyond Valdinievole into the valley of the Arno river is Cerreto Guidi, a small cluster of a town surrounding the impressive Villa Medicea of Cerreto, once a Guidi family stronghold and later—redesigned—of the Medici. Here the daughter of Cosimo I, Isabella, was strangled by her husband for an alleged infidelity. The room where it all happened is a major attraction.

Springtime and fall are the moments to sample the best of this area's specialties. Fragrant wild *porcini* mushrooms and chestnut dishes are the menu of the fall. From late September through November, the hills are packed with families out in the earliest hours of the morning to scavenge for *funghi* and castagne. *Funghi* have lately been arriving from all over Europe, but the locals wait for *nostrale* ("our own") from the nearby woods. As the season draws near and the firm dark mushrooms with their pure white flesh begin to arrive, shoppers will always ask, "but are they local?" Strangely enough, there's little cheating. It's assumed the buyer can actually see and taste the difference. We are warned away from buying from the large trucks filled with *funghi* along the main roads; who could know where they come from and who is selling them?

Large *porcini* caps are grilled like steaks; smaller ones and their stems are generally served *trifolati*, chopped and sautéed in olive oil with garlic and parsley. Chestnuts are roasted or boiled with a sprig of wild fennel, eaten whole, or squeezed from their shells. The smaller ones are ground into flour — called *farina dolce*, or sweet flour, to produce two of the favorite winter desserts: *castagnaccia*, a flat unleavened cake of chestnut flour, pine nuts, rosemary, and olive oil (which takes some getting used to); and *necci*, chestnut flour *crepes* deliciously served with a topping of fresh *ricotta*.

A very special velvety small white bean is harvested in late August and September along the Pescia river under Sorano, one of the little mountain towns of the Svizzera Pesciatina. The Sorano bean is treasured throughout Tuscany, but the harvest is small and precious. (There's such a thing as Sorano-type beans, meaning they are grown elsewhere; the real Sorano is a DOP controlled appellation.) The beans are quickly dried and quickly sold; you can find them here only from autumn through the following spring. Their notable texture results from a micro-climate in the narrow river valley; the sun reaches it only for a few hours each day, thus keeping the plants moist and cool. The beans, gently simmered, with some sage leaves, smashed garlic, and a bit of oil, feel almost skinless, and have a perfectly smooth consistency. They're eaten with just a sprinkling of salt, a fresh grinding of pepper, and a dripping of newly-pressed extra virgin olive oil, sometimes with *bottarga* (fish roe) grated over. Sorano beans are hard to come by outside of the Valdinievole and expensive when you do find them. Bean lovers should look for them in the markets here in September and October. Many restaurants in the area also serve Sorano beans and list them as such on the menu.

Springtime brings fine, fat, pale green asparagus of Pescia, served abundantly in restaurants throughout the Valdinievole. The season is short; it is worthwhile to take advantage when offered. The same is true for the local tiny spring artichokes and fresh green peas. A *risotto* with either or both, or a veal escalope under a covering of thinly sliced sautéed artichokes, makes a fine main course. The little artichokes are also served raw, with a topping of sliced Parmesan cheese, fresh olive oil, and salt, as part of an antipasto.

The small *trattorie* of the area faithfully reflect their peasant past. Beyond sheep and goats, few animals graze here; home-bred pork, rabbit, and chicken are still the main meats. The *caccia*, or hunt, in the past reserved for the rich, is more popular now. From the first days of September, when the hunting season begins, a popping of rifles spattering shot randomly into flocks of sparrows, thrush, and blackbirds is as much a weekend disturbance as the roaring of motorbikes. You won't find the shot-laden little birds — mostly thrush — on restaurant menus, but wild boar and hare are offered throughout the winter. Simple little homemade pasta squares called *maccheroni* are served with a sauce of either. Another local specialty you'll find only in the typical *trattoria* is *concia alla pesciatina*, not a dish for the weak of heart, or stomach. It is best described by its origins in the tanneries of Pescia, the *concerie*. It was a poor time, with little meat. Tannery workers, so the story goes, stripped whatever bits and pieces of meat they could find on the fresh skins, to mix with a few herbs and boil into a stew. Needless to say, the dish has been gentrified over the years; today it is made from the most edible and gelatinous parts of a beef muzzle, a savory stew cooked for hours and hours. *La concia* is a great winter favorite among local inhabitants.

Bread in the Valdinievole is a precious staple and is never thrown away. Entire winter meals are constructed from different porridge-like soups poured over a slice of day-old bread. In summer, *panzanella* — stale bread soaked in water, flavored with vinegar and extra virgin olive oil and mixed with summer vegetables—is a major *antipasto*. Corn meal, *farina giallo*, is also very much used. *La farinata*—which elsewhere in Tuscany can be a cornmeal *crepe*—is the almost regal local appellation for a favorite winter soup of kale, beans, and *polenta*. It is a dish to savor.

Like elsewhere in Tuscany, two favorite traditional Friday dishes are made from types of preserved cod: salted *baccala* and dried *stoccafisso* (stockfish), which, for hundreds of years, have been imported from Norway. They can be found side by side in local markets. (I've been told that eighty percent of the Norwegian yield each year is exported to this part of the world.) Both are well soaked before being fried or served in a tomato sauce.

Other specialties are the sweet *brigidini* of Lamporecchio, wafers that look like potato chips although they are baked, not fried. In Montecatini Terme, you'll find a similar wafer, the *cialda*, a pair of large paper-thin discs pressed together with a hazelnut paste filling. Tins of *cialda* can be bought in bars and at specialty shops throughout the spa. Both sweets have their origins oddly enough in the communion wafer.

Brigidini originated—some say as a cooking mistake—in the Convent of Santa Brigida in Lamporecchio in the sixteenth century. A nun was preparing the host for communion and somehow sugar and anise fell into the edible little wafer dough. They are still produced today in Lamporecchio, shipped fresh in cellophane wrappers all over Italy, to be sold from stands at street fairs and church festivals.

To end a meal in the Valdinievole most will choose a small glass of local *vin santo*, fortified sweet wine, dipping hard little half-moon-shaped *cantucci* into it.

TYPICAL RESTAURANTS
& THEIR RECIPES

PESCIA

TRATTORIA CECCO
Via Forti 96/98, Pescia • Tel. 0572-477-955
*Open daily for lunch and dinner; closed Monday. Moderately expensive,
depending on the choice of main course and the house wine.
Reservations recommended.*

Cecco is located between Pescia's river and its main square; one can enter from either side. Cecco has been serving the best of local food since the end of the nineteenth century, when Francesco Pacini opened a little inn of six rooms. He was the grandfather of cousins Dino and Francesco, who retired in 2005 to leave the restaurant in new local hands. Cecco is still thought of as the most reliable in the area. Such is its reputation that new owner Federico Schiavelli — himself a Pesciatino and scion of another restaurant family — is determined to maintain the tradition and standard just as it's always been.

The menu has hardly changed over the years; old dishes of the area remain as staples. Sorano beans are usually on the menu, either as a side dish with a sprinkling of fresh olive oil and salt, or as an appetizer sprinkled with grated *bottarga* or small pieces of octopus. *Bottarga* can be made from the roe of tuna or gray mullet; here it's usually that of tuna. Asparagus in season comes from a single trusty farmer, who divides it for the restaurant into bunches according to size. The slimmest go into a *tagliatelle* pasta sauce, or *risotto*; thick stalks are served either with oil and lemon dressing or with a fried egg. In fall and winter, there is fresh *tagliatelle* dressed with butter and a generous scraping of San Miniato truffles, a dish that must be one of the world's most heavenly.

The preparation of *concia alla pesciatina*, offered throughout the winter, is almost a rite. The stewing and solidification of the beef maw takes days to prepare. *Pollastrino al mattone* (*mattone* means brick in Italian) a crisp and juicy small chicken sautéed under a weight, seems to have originated at Cecco. A more recent addition—perhaps only a generation old—is *branzino sotto sale*, a fresh sea bass baked under a thick coating of coarse salt. The *branzino* is moist, succulent, and not at all salty. But Cecco does have a tendency to over salt other dishes; if you're not crazy for salty things, be sure to mention it. The chef may be in love, but he can serve up unsalted dishes as well.

Desserts are both rich and diverse. One of the more straightforward is a simple pear baked in wine and covered in caramelized sugar.

RECIPES FROM TRATTORIA CECCO

Baby Chicken under a Brick
POLLASTRINO AL MATTONE

Serves 2

This dish is traditionally cooked under the weight of a brick in a flat earthenware dish; thus the word *mattone*, but any heavy weight will do. Just make sure the pan in which the chicken is cooked is well covered, perhaps with an inverted cover or another frying pan. This will prevent fat from splattering too much.

1 small chicken, not more than 2 pounds, split and opened flat
Salt and freshly ground pepper
About 1½ cups olive oil, or enough to immerse (but not cover) the chicken
Juice of ½ lemon
½ cup white wine

Open the split chicken and flatten well with a good kitchen mallet. (Or, have your butcher do it.) The legs should be tucked in under the thigh, and the wings flattened out. Season well on both sides with salt and pepper. Heat the olive oil in a pan just large enough to hold the entire flattened chicken.

Heat the oil to sizzling hot and place the chicken, skin side up. Cover immediately with another pan filled with a weight to press the chicken even flatter. Cook in the hot oil for about 8 minutes. Remove the weight, check that the chicken has taken on a golden hue, and turn. Cook on the other side, under the weight, for another 8 minutes. Turn again, add the lemon juice and wine (this will spatter a bit), replace the weight, and cook for another 5 minutes. Remove to kitchen toweling to dry off any liquid, and serve immediately, half a chicken to each diner.

Sea Bass under Salt
BRANZINO DI MARE SOTTO SALE

Serves 2

Why this salt coating of the fish makes such a difference to the taste is difficult to understand; the bass turns out delicate and moist, in no way salty. The presentation is lovely; the golden brown crust breaks open easily and the fish is served filleted.

1 2-pound sea bass
2 sprigs fresh rosemary
Freshly ground pepper
Olive oil
1 pound coarse sea salt
1 egg, beaten
1 small wineglass white wine

Preheat the oven to 450 degrees.

Clean the fish, put the rosemary and pepper inside, and place in an oiled oval baking dish. In a large bowl, mix the salt together with the beaten egg. Coat the entire top of the fish with the salt, making a thick crust. Place in the pre-heated oven for 10 minutes, remove, and pour the wine around the fish—not on the salt. Put back in the oven and cook for another 10 minutes. By this time the salt should take on a golden color. Remove from oven and pour off any remaining liquid.

At the table, gently remove the crust in one piece (or broken, it does not matter), slip off the skin, and fillet the fish.

BIECINA

———— ❖ ————

TRATTORIA ALDO

Via delle Cartiere 175, Biecina • Tel. 0572-43008

*Open daily for lunch and dinner; closed Sunday. The restaurant serves
a simple prix fixe lunch priced at nine euros for workers from nearby
paper factories. The dinner menu offers more choices. Prices inexpensive to
moderate. Reservations recommended for dinner, and for both lunch
and dinner during the fall funghi season.*

Trattoria Aldo lies about five kilometers up into the hills above Collodi,
past the turning to Villa Basilica, in Biecina. It's one of the more popular
local restaurants, hard to find the first time you look. You reach it on an
old road that runs alongside a small runoff of the river Pescia, lined with
old Gothic ruins of once majestic paper plants. It's the largest concentra-
tion of paper producing mills in Italy from the thirteenth century on. To
the traveller's eye, the old crumbling ruins are a lot more attractive than the
modern plants behind them that function today.

Aldo's unprepossessing green neon sign reading TRATTORIA greets
you on the left. It's also a bar (Jolly Caffe, says the sign) and grocery, and
easy to pass right by in the dark. There are several entrances, and chances
are you'll walk into a noisy collection of card players in the bar. Continue
up a flight of stairs and through the kitchen that also serves as family dining
room (television blaring) into a more soothing room filled with checkered
tablecloths and family portraits. This is the domain of Mirco Flosi, owner
and cook, carrying on the family tradition of father Aldo, now ailing, and
his grandfather who started it all. His mother serves; the rest of the family helps. Mirco learned to cook growing up in the kitchen. He has never
thought to pick up anything really new. Thus the restaurant remains one of
the true *casalinga*—home cooking—locales of the area.

The very decent house wine is from a popular *cantina* in Vinci and is
served from a carafe; the bread comes from a nearby wood oven, the olive
oil is the restaurant's own, fresh and extra virgin. Dishes are simple, beginning with an *antipasto* of local prosciutto and salami and a subtle warm
mélange of vegetables in a light vinegar-oil marinade. A basket of toasted

[97]

bread comes with a garlic clove to rub the toast and a decanter of fresh olive oil with which to inundate it.

To prepare for seasons when mushrooms aren't available, Mirco dries enough *funghi* to serve the year round. Second courses include handmade thick *tortelli* stuffed with dried *funghi* and served in a sage/butter sauce, *farro* and dried *funghi risotto* (this is an area close to the *farro*-producing Garfagnana), or squares of homemade pasta called *maccheroni* served in a variety of sauces. On occasion you'll find a *maccheroni* of chestnut flour topped with a walnut sauce. Fall is the major season at Aldo's, a time when the nearby woods are filled with *porcini* and *funghi* become the prevalent dish, made in every conceivable way.

Main fall and winter courses emphasize game: wild boar in a black olive sauce, hare and venison. The best way to finish a meal at Aldo's is with the homemade little hard biscuits of Prato, *cantucci*, dipped in *vin santo*.

RECIPES FROM TRATTORIA ALDO

Mixed Marinated Vegetables
VERDURE SOTT'ACETO

◉

Makes 2 pounds, or a large jarful

This is a lovely smooth accompaniment to first courses, with just the slightest pungency. It keeps in the refrigerator for several weeks.

2 pounds (about 4 cups) mixed vegetables including cauliflower flowerets,
    celery, carrots, mushrooms, red peppers, and yellow onions
10 large whole black olives
1 hot red pepper, chopped well
1 tablespoon salt
2 cups white wine vinegar
4 cups water
1 teaspoon of mixed spices, including cinnamon, allspice, and nutmeg
Extra virgin olive oil

Thinly slice the celery, carrots, and mushrooms, and chop the remaining vegetables into small bite-sized pieces. Add the whole olives and chopped hot pepper and mix.

Bring the vinegar, water, salt, and spices to a boil. Add the vegetables, and cook for 10-15 minutes. Drain immediately and spread on a clean cloth to dry.

Put the vegetables in a large Mason jar or other glass container, and cover with olive oil. Place in the refrigerator and serve with a bit of the oil and bread to soak it up with.

Farro Risotto with Dried Mushrooms
RISOTTO DI FARRO AI FUNGHI SECCHI

Serves 6

Garfagnana *farro* is the best for this dish. It needs no soaking, cooks in 15 minutes, and turns into nice round chewy kernels that retain their firmness. (If using another *farro*, follow instructions on the package for soaking and cooking.)

2 cups *farro*
Salt
2 tablespoons butter
2 cloves garlic, chopped
2 ounces dried *porcini* mushrooms, soaked in 1 cup warm water for ½ hour
Salt and freshly ground pepper
½ cup whole milk

Put the *farro* to boil in salted water until it is cooked firm to the bite. (See above). Leave the *farro* in the water for the time being.

In a small pan, melt the garlic in the butter. Drain the mushrooms, reserving the soaking water, and add them to the pan. Add ½ cup of the soaking water, taking care not to pour in any sediment, and cook for 10 minutes. Drain the *farro* and add the mushrooms, mix well, add the milk, and mix again. Serve warm.

COLLE DI BUGGIANO

ANTICO COLLE
Piazza Cavour, Colle di Buggiano • Tel. 0572-30671
*Open daily for dinner. Closed Thursdays. During the winter, open also for
lunch on Sunday and holidays. Reservations necessary, especially for the terrace during spring and summer. Priced moderately.*

Diners from nearby Montecatini and Pescia crowd into this pleasant, very
reliable *trattoria* on the main square of picturesque Colle di Buggiano. Summer evening dining is the best, out on the lively square. Pietro Belardi and
Mila Lupori are the husband/wife team who own the place. Pietro cooks
in a small compact corner kitchen; Mila controls the dining room. Their
daughter and a few local youngsters serve. The grandchild runs around.

The menu is filled with local dishes, never grand, never complicated.
It changes somewhat from season to season. Pietro prepares some interesting traditional dishes, *ravioli* stuffed with a pear and *pecorino* paste filling—odd sounding, but delicious—and *la farinata*, the local *polenta-*
thickened bean and kale soup. *Ribollita, pappa al pomodoro, acquacotta ricca*
(a rich man's *aquacotta*, thick and different from that of other areas), and
other bread-based dishes are listed as *piatti tipici*, traditional first courses.
You can also sample each of them in a single serving. In the summer,
panzanella (bread salad) is a favorite *antipasto*. Pizza, thin and crisp, is a
staple here: there are thirty-five different kinds on the menu and a special
wood oven in the back room to bake them. During autumn, wild *porcini*
and other mushrooms arrive daily with Mila's uncle who has been out since
before dawn searching them.

Main courses include various grilled meats, sliced steak called *tagliata*
served with various toppings, Florentine-style tripe, salt cod served in a
spicy tomato sauce, and the *concia alla pesciatina* popular here. They've
recently added some traditional fresh fish dishes to the menu.

Desserts are simple. And Mila usually offers a homemade *limoncello*
that can finish off both dinner and diner.

Polenta-thickened Bean Soup

LA FARINATA

Serves 6-8

2 cups *borlotti* or cranberry beans
4 cloves garlic, divided
½ cup extra virgin olive oil, divided, plus additional at table
2 onions, halved and thinly sliced
2 ribs celery, thinly sliced
4 carrots, thinly sliced
2 bunches kale (about 20 leaves), stems removed and thinly sliced
½ small white cabbage, halved and thinly sliced
3 ripe tomatoes, or contents of 1 small tin tomatoes
1 vegetable bouillon cube or 1 teaspoon vegetable broth powder
1½ cups *polenta*
Salt and freshly ground pepper

Cook the soaked beans in a quart of water with 2 garlic cloves and a tablespoon of olive oil. Bring to a boil, immediately lower the flame, and simmer until the beans are soft. Add salt at the very end. Purée half the beans and return them to the pan with the remaining beans and their water.

In a large heavy soup pot, heat the remaining oil and add the onion and remaining 2 cloves of garlic, thinly sliced. Cook for a minute and add the celery, carrots, kale, and cabbage. Cook for 10 minutes. Add the tomatoes and simmer for another half hour.

Add purée and beans to the pot with their water. Add the broth cube or powder, mix well, and add enough water to cover by several inches. Bring to a boil, and slowly add the *polenta*, stirring constantly to prevent lumping. Continue mixing for another 20 minutes, until the soup is thick and creamy. If it becomes solid, add water. Taste for seasoning, add salt and freshly ground pepper and serve with a good dripping of olive oil.

Bread Salad

PANZANELLA

⬤

Serves 6

For this salad you must have a loaf of Tuscan-style bread that does not
dissolve into a mass when soaked but retains a grainy consistency when the
liquid is squeezed out.

1 small (1 pound) loaf of country bread, at least three days old, sliced
Red wine vinegar
3 ripe tomatoes, halved vertically and sliced into thin slivers
1 red onion, halved and thinly sliced
1 cucumber, thinly sliced
1 rib celery, thinly sliced
1 large bunch basil leaves, chopped
Salt and freshly ground pepper
½ cup extra virgin olive oil

Soak the bread for at least half an hour in water flavored with a few tablespoons of red wine vinegar. (The bread should be well moistened, but not
swimming in the water.) Meanwhile, combine the vegetables in a large bowl.
Break off pieces of the bread, squeeze all the water from each, and break
it up over the vegetables. Sprinkle the chopped basil over the top, add
salt and pepper, ¼ cup or more of vinegar and about ½ cup of oil. Mix the
entire salad well. Taste and season again, adding more vinegar or olive oil
if necessary.

LAMPORECCHIO

——— ≫❀≪ ———

ANTICO MASETTO
Via Gramsci 83, Lamporecchio • Tel. 0583-82118
Open for lunch and dinner. Closed Thursday and all of August.
Priced moderately.

A good reason to pause in Lamporecchio is a visit to this diverting little restaurant that serves some very good typical food of the region. Owner Walter Maccione named it Antico Masetto after a special character in a Boccaccio tale that takes place in Lamporecchio. In the story, Masetto, an impoverished stranger, arrives in Lamporecchio to seek a living. After an unsuccessful search, a townsman suggests Masetto play deaf and mute to plead with the nuns at the Convent of Santa Brigida for work. The nuns take him on as a gardener. As Boccaccio tells it, when the young Masetto finally departs the convent, he leaves all of the nuns in a "family way." From this tale, Antico Masetto was born in 1967. Walter is the host, his wife Sylvia the cook.

The menu is fun, filled with expressions in old Tuscan dialect. Ask for a translation. It is a characteristic menu of the area, an *antipasto* of local Tuscan prosciutto, liver *crostini*, or a savory mix of artichokes and olives from trees on the nearby hills.

Second courses are more special. *Ribollita al fraticello* (a diminutive for monk) is a savory fresh vegetable bread soup fashioned by cook Sylvia. There's also a soup of *farro* and barley in bean broth, and a tasty *risotto co'l cibreo* with artichoke pureé and chicken livers.

Daily fresh fish are also on the menu; you can even order a lobster. More typical are the charcoal-broiled Florentine (*Chianina*) beefsteak and boar with olives.

For dessert, try the delicious *tiramisu* prepared with a whipped-cream topped cappuccino instead of the usual coffee.

RECIPES FROM ANTICO MASETTO

Vegetable Bread Soup
RIBOLLITA AL FRATICELLO

Serves 6

Walter Maccione calls this a *ribollita* "in the manner of the little monk." It's more a *minestrone*, with few tastes other than vegetables cooked in their own juices and the half-puréed cooked beans added and served on toasted bread. (Traditionally *ribollita*, "twice-boiled soup," denotes a soup on the second day it is served. On the first day, it's just a bread soup, on the second day, it's either sautéed in oil for a second cooking or put into a baking dish with some oil and cheese on top and crusted for another meal; thus its name.)

1 cup dried white *cannellini* beans
2 sprigs sage
8 cups water
5 tablespoons olive oil, divided, plus additional at table
Salt and freshly ground pepper
2 leeks, thinly sliced
2 zucchini, thinly sliced
2 carrots, thinly sliced
2 potatoes, peeled, chopped into small pieces
1 bunch Swiss chard, finely chopped
5 kale leaves, ribs removed, finely chopped
½ Savoy cabbage, tough core removed and thinly sliced
1 bunch parsley
2 garlic cloves, crushed
3 large slices stale Tuscan bread, broken into large pieces
Olive oil and Parmesan at table

Soak the beans overnight. Drain, put in a pot with the water, a tablespoon of olive oil, and the sage. Cook over the lowest heat possible until the beans are soft, about 2 hours. Add salt just before the beans are finished. During the cooking keep adding water as it evaporates.

While the beans are cooking, put all the vegetables together with the remaining 4 tablespoons of olive oil into a heavy soup pot. Add a good amount of salt, and cook the vegetables slowly, covered, mixing often, until soft. This can take almost as long as the beans. Add salt to taste.

Purée half the beans in a food processor with the parsley and garlic and add the purée, the remaining beans, and their water to the cooked vegetables. Mix well, adding a bit of water if necessary. Mix again, taste for salt, and add some freshly ground pepper as well.

To serve, place a bit of toasted bread on the bottom of each soup plate and pour over the soup. Serve warm, with olive oil and Parmesan.

Chicken Liver Risotto
RISOTTO CO'I CIBREO

Serves 4

Cibreo is one of the more ancient traditional foods of Florence, a mixed stew of innards and the crest of a cock. Walter Maccione uses only chicken livers in this *risotto*. It's made with Persian basmati rice, a new addition to the Italian table.

2 tablespoons olive oil
4 chicken livers
2 cloves garlic, divided
1 anchovy fillet or 1 teaspoon anchovy paste
2 sage leaves
3 tablespoons capers
3 fresh or frozen artichoke hearts
3 tablespoons butter, divided
1-½ cups *risotto* or Persian basmati rice
1 wineglass white wine
Light vegetable stock
Salt and freshly ground pepper
Parmesan at table

In 2 tablespoons of olive oil, sauté the chicken livers with a garlic clove, the anchovy or anchovy paste, and sage, until the livers are just cooked. Add the capers and cook for another minute. Place in a food processor and blend, but not too finely. Set aside, keeping warm. The mixture should be creamy; if it feels too dry, add a bit of boiling water to the pan and mix the chopped livers into it. Add salt and pepper to taste.

Slice the artichoke hearts and cook them with another clove of garlic in a little oil. Add water to cover and cook until the water is completely gone. Purée the artichokes, return to pan, add a tablespoon of butter, and salt well. Set aside, keeping warm.

To prepare the rice, first bring the vegetable stock to a boil and keep it simmering on the stove. In another pan, melt the remaining 2 tablespoons of butter, add the rice, mix well to coat the rice with the butter, and add the wine. Allow the wine to evaporate and add boiling vegetable stock slowly, covering the rice with a bit each time as it absorbs. Do it slowly in order to make a fairly dry *risotto*.

Mix the finished *risotto* well with the puréed artichokes, add lots of salt, and freshly ground pepper, and turn into an oval serving dish. Spoon the chicken livers over and serve with lots of freshly ground Parmesan.

VINCI

IL RISTORO DEL MUSEO
Via Montalbano 9, Vinci • Tel. 0571-56516
Lunch and dinner. Closed Friday evening and Saturday lunch. Prices are moderate, including for the very decent local house wine. Best to reserve, especially during tourist season, for both for lunch and dinner.

Enter Ristoro del Museo through a small, cozy bar and plunge downstairs into a warm, colorful cellar with a terrace facing a landscape of olives and vines. The staff in this *trattoria* numbers two: Mariella Beretta, breathless hostess and waitress, and her more reticent husband, Maurizio Beretta, who mans the kitchen single-handedly. A surprising number of genuine dishes emerge from the small compact kitchen. Maurizio comes from the mountains of Sicily, but he's learned Tuscan fare well. His dishes are fairly sophisticated reflections of deep ties to both the Tuscan tradition and his own.

A mix of *crostini* appetizers (*funghi porcini*, liver paste, and a chopped topping of red *radicchio* salad and the popular sweet red Tropea onion from Puglia) come first, in "serve-yourself" little candle-heated terracotta bowls brought to the table. The *zuppa del contadino* (farmer's soup) has a wonderful overwhelming aroma of fresh thyme and rosemary. Don't miss the *tagliata* (sliced steak) topped with aromatized fresh virgin olive oil (a secret that Maurizio is not about to part with) and a vegetarian cutlet in a *porcini* sauce. Il Ristoro freezes fresh *porcini* to serve throughout the year, and it works very well; both the *funghi crostini* and the cutlet sauce have an authentic fresh — not dried — taste.

Farmer's Vegetable Soup
ZUPPA DEL CONTADINO

Serves 8

So called because it utilizes seasonal vegetables from the *orto*, this restaurant's version adds a bit of white wine to give it a touch of tang.

1 cup *borlotti* or cranberry beans, soaked overnight
1 cup white *cannellini* beans, soaked overnight
1 onion, thinly sliced
3 cloves garlic, crushed
3 tablespoons extra virgin olive oil
1 bunch kale leaves, stems removed, chopped
1 small wineglass white wine
1 pound ripe tomatoes, skinned, or canned peeled plum tomatoes
3 carrots, halved and sliced
1 rib celery, sliced
3 zucchini, sliced
1 large potato, peeled and cubed
1 cup fresh, or frozen, peas
1 large bunch fresh thyme
2 sprigs fresh rosemary
Salt and freshly ground black pepper
Grated Parmesan and extra virgin olive oil at table

Cook the soaked beans in lots of water over a low flame until done. Saving the water in which they cooked, purée half the beans, and mix them with the remaining whole beans. Set aside. Cook the onions, garlic, and olive oil over medium heat, until the onions are melted. Add the kale and cook until wilted. Add the wine, and allow to evaporate. Add the tomatoes and cook for another 10 minutes. Add the remaining vegetables and herbs, and add boiling water to cover. Taste and add a good amount of salt and pepper. Cook, partially covered, over a low fire until the vegetables are cooked, but still firm, about an hour. Serve warm with Parmesan and olive oil to drip over.

CHAPTER 4

Pistoia and its Mountains

PISTOIA, ABOUT HALF AN HOUR WEST FROM FLOR-
ENCE, IS THE SINGLE SIZEABLE CITY I'VE CHOSEN
to write about. It is a small city, filled with splendid churches and their art,
and home to one of the most delicious little marketplaces imaginable. Not
many tourists find their way here. Pistoia is also a good place from which to
head up into the foothills of the Apennine Mountains to the peaks around
Abetone, all part of Tuscany that few visitors get to.

The historic center of Pistoia — within walls that date back to Roman
times — is really a small town. A good number of imposing austere Romanesque churches contain a rare richness of pre-Renaissance sculpture. Sculptors Nicola Pisano, his son Giovanni, and a lesser-known Giovanni Pesani,
were the precursors to Renaissance sculpture much as Duccio and Giotto
were to Renaissance painting. All three are well represented here, along
with some sublime works of the earliest della Robbia studio. Pistoia's spa-
cious and harmonious cathedral square is surrounded by elegant buildings:
the small richly decorated *duomo*, the large gracious tower next to it, the
striped baptistry opposite, and the old tribunal, the Palazzo Podesta. In
the tribunal you still see the stone seats, so hard, so uncomfortable, that the
judges must have been anxious to finish the business of meting out justice
as quickly as possible. Opposite the tribunal is the austere Palazzo Pretorio, the city hall. Imagine the youthful Leonardo arriving from the hills of
Vinci to seek out his father at his Pistoia accounting office, approaching
this grand square through one of the narrow streets that still lead to it.
They're now lined with Max Mara and Luisa Spagnoli shops.

To the rear of the large square, behind the baptistry, sits the irresistible little marketplace, appropriately called Piazza della Sala, square of the
salon. In the eighth century the palace of the Lombardian governor stood
here, hence its name. A graceful, lion-topped fifteenth-century fountain —
Il Pozzino — stands in the middle. Every day the square is packed with

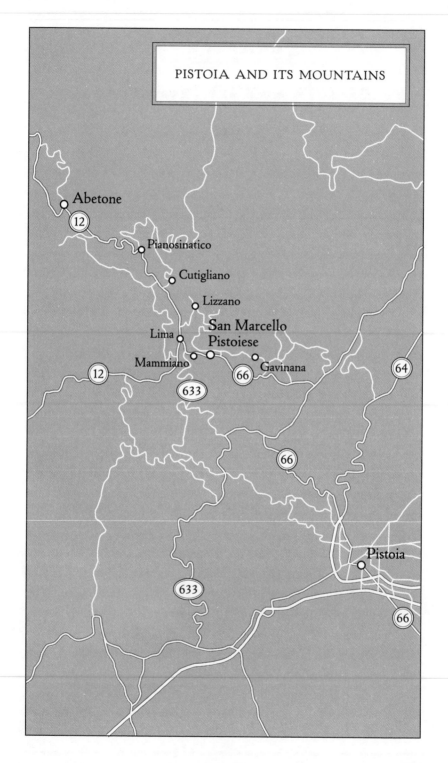

PISTOIA AND ITS MOUNTAINS

Abetone

12

Pianosinatico

Cutigliano

Lizzano

Lima

San Marcello
Pistoiese

Mammiano

12

66 Gavinana

633

64

66

633

Pistoia

66

food stands, at its edge a table laid out with fresh herbs and wild greens. On Primetta Bartolomei's little table you'll find neatly tied little bundles of oregano, lavender, thyme, and *nipotella*, a wild mint growing all over Tuscany that goes into the frying pan with *funghi*, zucchini, and other fresh vegetables. Primetta claims magic powers, and is ready to tell you how to use her greens and where they all come from.

Food and artisan shops surround the square and fill the side streets as well. On the far corner you'll find a cheese shop to dream about. Simone Bovane's Spaccio del Parmigiano (Piazza della Sala 19) has a hygienic glow, and carries a wide variety of every kind of cheese. The *pecorini* are mostly of *latte crudo* — unpasturized milk — a Pistoian specialty Simone brings to his shop from small producers all over the surrounding hills. Parmesan comes from a single producer in Emilia; the buffalo *mozzarella* is delivered daily from the south.

Near the cheese shop, notice a sign that says *Norcineria*, or pork shop. It's an old-fashioned word, once the appellation of a wandering pork butcher. In the old days, before refrigeration, the *norcino* traveled from door to door and farm to farm, slaughtering pigs and preparing them to feed a family for the year. He would salt, season, stuff, hang, and do whatever else necessary to make the meat last, readying prosciutto, *spalle* (shoulders of the pig), different sausages, livers stored in their own fat, marinated chops, and whatever else. The shop on the square sells them all.

There are also three separate bread shops on the square, each with its special breads and *focaccie*.

My favorite for all produce is Sauro Signori's open vegetable and specialty shop that faces the square. Bins of the freshest sort of seasonal vegetables are out front. Inside you'll find lots of homemade take-aways including a non-offensive collection of garlic cloves bathed in a piquant marinade, tuna-stuffed little green tomatoes and hot peppers, gourmet pastas, and, as Sauro puts it, "every fine bean" in Italy. Tuscany is bean country, and here you'll find its best and most freshly dried — no soaking needed — including Sorano, Purgatorio (not really Tuscan, these are mostly from Umbria), and Zolfino. Sauro can give you a history of every item in his packed shop.

Via del Lastrone, a short, narrow little street lined with fourteenth-century houses, leads out from Piazza della Sala. It too is filled with specialty shops, *trattorie*, pizzerias, and coffee bars. La BotteGaia (see page

120), at number 4, is a little restaurant that attracts a large lunchtime crowd and changes its menu each week. It also has a back door leading right on to Pistoia's main Piazza del Duomo with tables outside at which you can dine during warm months. The restaurant also sells local specialties, at its food boutique near the end of Via del Lastrone. At I Sapori della BotteGaia you can buy quality products of the area, including the sausages of a noted producer, *salumi di Marini*, of nearby Agliana. Try the very special *mortadella di Prato*, seasoned with spices from the well-known old Farmacia di Santa Maria Novella in Florence.

Pistoia's entire old center turns into a vast crowded market two mornings each week, on Wednesdays and Saturdays. This is no simple market in a square; rather you'll find street after street and the cathedral square itself crammed with stalls selling every sort of household and personal ware. Food stands include specialties not only of Tuscany, but Naples and Puglia as well.

More interest lies along the streets surrounding the piazzas of the *duomo* and the marketplace. On Via Cavour is the church of San Giovanni with an impressive block-long green-and-white striped marble façade. Inside the dim basilica-like interior, you'll make out a lovely intricately carved Pesani pulpit and a celestial white Visitation by della Robbia. Just down from the main piazza is the not-to-be-missed series of brilliantly colored della Robbia panels fronting the old hospital which is still Pistoia's main one. A set of binoculars can help you to see the intricate detail of the panels. They depict the many acts of mercy ministered by Jesus. Another church, a few blocks away from the main square, is Sant'Andrea, with yet another wonderful pulpit, this one by Nicola Pisano and his sons. Another intimate little church—San Bartolomeo—houses an even earlier example of Romanesque sculpture, stiff figures, but with a lot of expression.

The Duomo itself is filled with splendid art, beginning with the richly decorated Andrea della Robbia lunette under which you enter. Inside, the richly endowed Chapel of St. James boasts an outstanding silver altar of the thirteenth century, with almost 650 solid silver figures. Andrea Pisano designed the octagonal striped bapistry opposite the cathedral; the outside sculptures are splendid examples of the early Romanesque. The inside is imposingly austere, with a remarkable high conical ceiling of simple brick.

Pistoia has an impressive collection of modern sculpture too. Marino Marini was born here; one of his well-known horses occupies the main entrance of the town hall next to the cathedral. A gallery of Marini's works, with sculptures and drawings, is in the old Convento del Tau, a few streets away (Corso Silvano Fedi 30, Tel. 0573-30285; open Monday–Saturday 10am–6pm; holidays from 9:30am–12:30pm, closed Sunday).

A short ride from Pistoia is one of Italy's most impressive modern sculpture parks. Villa Fattoria di Celle is about four kilometers from Pistoia on the road to Montale. Giovanni Gori bought the eighteenth-century villa with its great wooded park in 1969, and made it into an outdoor museum for monumental works by well-known modern artists: Beverly Pepper, Magdalena Abakanowica, Alice Aycoch, Dani Karavan, Sol LeWitt, Pistoletto, Richard Serra, Robert Morris, and many others. At last count there were more than sixty great pieces in the woods. The forest itself is worth the walk, with its small lake, old large firs and oaks, odd nineteenth-century pavilions, and grand avenues to wander through. You'll need a reservation to visit the park. (Villa Fattoria di Celle, Santomato. Reserve by fax 39-0573-479-486 or by email: goricoll@tin.it)

The Apennine road from Pistoia up to the Abetone mountain leads to a cool respite on a hot summer's day, when Florence and the cities around it have become horribly crowded and one longs for a cool day in the hills. Local Pistoians, Luccans, and Florentines traditionally take their summer's refreshment in these verdant hills of vast pine and chestnut forests. Autumn and winter offer a different landscape and other pleasures as well. The changing colors along the forest roads are wondrous in October and November. During the winter months, Abetone, the highest mountain pass in Tuscany, becomes the largest ski resort of the region. (To travel up here during the snowy season, you'll need tire chains.)

From Pistoia, a single road leads up toward Abetone. San Marcello Pistoiese, the principal town of the mountain, lies about twenty-five kilometers from Pistoia. Just before reaching San Marcello (you can come back to it on the return trip to Pistoia) a sign on the right points to Gavinana. This cozy ancient mountain village offers your first real view of the mountains above. Gavinana has an appealing square, complete with fountain and equestrian statue of a local sixteenth-century hero and an impressive lavishly decorated little church—Santa Maria Assunta—that has a number of notable works of art as well: an appealing ancient lion chiseled out of a block of local stone, two lively terracotta bas-reliefs, and two carved wooden figures of an angel and the Virgin Mary. As you leave you'll notice an ancient stone door in the wall that leads up to the church tower.

Continue through Gavinana on the road marked to Lizzano. It offers more splendid views. By now, you are well up into the cool mountains, and reach a kind of primordial dark forest, where the bright sunshine suddenly becomes an almost eerie dark shadow. Continue along the narrow road and emerge into the sunlight to Lizzano, a tiny village whose houses along the road have been frescoed with lively modern naïve paintings of mountain life. Pass through down to the river Lima. Cross the river and you are on the main road that leads up to the pine forests of Abetone.

The first stop along the river on the road to Abetone is Cutigliano, an old bustling resort town, surrounded by woods and a cool summer breeze. It's worth visiting at any time of the year. Ambling through its warren of small streets, you come upon a lovely little old municipality building, fronted by an equally attractive fourteenth-century *loggia*. The façade of the city hall is entirely embellished with coats of arms of every family that has ruled this little town. At the top of Cutigliano is Doganaccia and a funicular that travels farther up the mountain to its peak. Up here, at 2000 meters above sea level, there are lovely walks over grassy meadows as far as the little lake of Scaffaiola, a favorite place for overnight hikers to watch the sun rise.

Cutigliano has several produce shops offering local mountain products, including fruit liquors and grappa, freshly dried wonderfully aromatic mushrooms, and a fine choice of honeys flavored with the wild fruit of the mountains. Also in Cutigliano is da Fagiolino (see page 123), a popular local restaurant. Beyond Cutigliano, on the road to Abetone, at Pianosinatico, there is another fine, unusually interesting, restaurant Silvio La Storia a Tavola (see page 127).

Abetone is the main winter resort of the area, with lots of ski lifts and well-developed slopes and trails. The town itself was mostly built after the Second World War. During its short season of real snow Abetone is quite mobbed on weekends. During the week it's pleasantly empty. Good coffee and pastry shops line the main street, with specialty shops for local products and ski equipment alongside. A favorite after-ski or hiking treat is any number of fresh wild berry tarts and cream snacks.

The chairlifts in Abetone operate during the summer as well, making it a favorite outing for hikers and berry hunters (who, by local legislation to protect professionals, are limited to only as much as they can eat or stuff into their pockets). During August, especially, it can get quite crowded, but even then the mountains make a delightful outing.

From Abetone the road continues down over the mountains to Modena (home of balsamic vinegar, Luciano Pavarotti, and automaker Ferrari) in nearby Emilia-Romagna. To remain in Tuscany, turn around and head back down the mountain past Pianosinatico and Cutigliano to the crossroad at Lima. There you can turn right toward Lucca or left back to Pistoia. Near Lima you'll see a sign to a suspension bridge at Mammiano. Take the little detour here. Before the Second World War, Lima was filled with iron works, many producing the small arms from which Pistoia takes its name. The suspension bridge was built to connect two plants on either side of the river Lima. It's quite an engineering marvel; at forty meters long, it just hangs there like a lacy netting. It's been reinforced in recent years, but I can remember a frightening trip across on my first visit. It's still scary. From lower Mammiano, off the main road to Pistoia, you get the best view of it. Any number of roads from there take you down the mountain, either toward Lucca or back through San Marcello to Pistoia.

SPECIALTIES OF PISTOIA AND ITS MOUNTAINS

Some of the best *porcini* mushrooms in all of Tuscany come from these mountains as do the tastiest wild berries, including the small field blueberries (*mirtilli*), wild strawberries (*fragolini*), blackberries (*more*), and raspberries (*lamponi*). The berries are found in the woods in abundance during the summer months, although, as with *funghi* and chestnuts, permits are needed to pick more than a bagful. The forests are public but professional collectors from nearby villages earn a livelihood from picking and selling the fruits. The berries flavor liqueurs and *grappa*, as well as honeys and marmalades. All can be bought in the specialty shops of Cutigliano and Abetone.

Wild mushrooms—one of the glories of Tuscan cooking—arrive in two seasons here: from late June through July, a limited supply of delicate *castagne porcini* doesn't get much farther than mountain restaurants. During the fall, before the first frost, the main season begins—and ends all too quickly—when fresh *funghi* are the dish of the day everywhere, and the main local sport as well. By 7am—when the first light begins—cars are already climbing the narrow roads to the forests. An hour later it's hard to find a place to park. Seasonal and day permits to pick mushrooms in limited amounts are issued inexpensively in most of the hill towns. In the markets for their short season, *funghi* are costly. A little goes a long way with these heavily perfumed firm mushrooms. They must be wiped clean on top with a moist cloth, and the earth scraped from the stems before they're ready to prepare. The most elegant way of serving *porcini* is to brush the larger caps with good oil, garlic, and salt and grill them over a wood fire. Perfectly firm and fresh *porcini* and the more delicate *ovoli* are also eaten raw in salads, sliced thinly with equally thin slices of Parmesan, all on a bed of arugula. The smaller, less perfect *funghi* are chopped and sautéed in olive oil with parsley and garlic; *funghi trifolati* are served with meats, as pasta sauces, and in *risotto*.

When mushrooms are at their most abundant, a good bit of the crop is laid aside to dry. You can see large slices lying in the open autumn air all over the mountains. Sometimes they are for sale. Stop to buy before they go off to market in their little cellophane sacks; this is the moment when they are at their most pungent, still limp and ready for winter storage in a paper bag or airy tin. Pick the ones that seem most healthy, with firm white interiors, brown on the edges. Fresh *funghi* are also quickly frozen these days. They are nowhere near as tasty as the fresh, but do work as a substitute in cooked dishes.

I've learned a lot from Sauro Signori whose shop in the Pistoia marketplace sells fresh *funghi* when they're available—even in late spring—and large slices of dried as soon as the season ends. He taught me about the rare dried white figs from nearby Carmignano that are sprinkled with fennel seeds and dried in laurel leaves, the best chestnut flour and *polenta*, and the meatiest walnuts from Lari in Pisa's province.

As in other mountain areas of Tuscany, chestnuts are turned into sweet flour, *farina dolce.* The best chestnut flour in these parts, says Sauro, comes from Momigno in the Pistoian hills. The town lies "below 800 meters and has the best soil and climate" for chestnuts. Chestnuts are picked in October, laid to dry for at least two months on a netted screen in a drying room (called *metato*), heated by a fire in the corner that keeps a constant low heat, and then cleaned of their shells, and stone-ground in a traditional mill. The flour begins to arrive in Pistoia in December; the supply continues for several months. By late spring it's all gone.

The most popular chestnut flour dish of the Pistoian hills is *castagnaccia*, the classic semi-sweet baked cake that combines chestnut flour, pine nuts, raisins, olive oil, and rosemary. It is invariably a part of the festive winter meals, especially the traditional one that celebrates the first pressing of olive oil.

The most traditional age-old way of using the sweet, albeit heavy, chestnut flour is for *necci*, a generation ago the daily nourishment in every Pistoian farm home. Flour for normal bread was then still a luxury. There is a splendid way of preparing *necci*, an art little known among the young today. But one of our young friends, Miranda Vitelli, who comes from a village in Pistoia province, still makes them in the traditional manner. I asked her how. It was impossible to explain and she invited us for a *necci* evening. It's a daunting procedure—and all for a simple mix of chestnut flour and water. It was late January. When we arrived, Miranda's husband Paolo was already heating four-centimeter-thick stone discs—each the diameter of a *crepe*—in the open kitchen fireplace. About twenty of them sat on the large iron grill, heating for several hours before the procedure would begin. From her storeroom Miranda brought out several batches of dried large chestnut leaves—still green but brittle—that she had picked in September for the *necci* she would make in January. These she gently boiled to make them pliable. For the twenty *necci*, she made a thick batter from about two pounds of stone-ground chestnut flour and water. Only a pinch of salt was added, nothing more.

The stones were hot. Paolo brought out a kind of umbrella stand bracket, held together by three long wooden columns but otherwise open and just large enough to hold the stack of discs. One by one, with an iron tong, Paolo removed the discs from the fire and placed them in the stand. Miranda covered each disk with three or four wet chestnut leaves (shiny side up), and poured over a ladleful of chestnut batter. More leaves, this time shiny side down, covered the batter, and on top went another stone. Layer by layer, one stone atop another went chestnut leaves, batter, chestnut leaves, until all twenty were stacked into what she called a *castello*. Steam escaped from all sides as the leaves dried instantly in the heat.

Not a minute passed before the *necci* were cooked. One by one Paolo lifted out the stones with his tongs, and we all began to peel off leaves and place the little *crepes* on a serving platter. As the stack went to the table the crisp heap of dried chestnut leaves went into the fire and we sat down to eat the little leaf embossed *crepes* rolled with a choice of two fillings, salted *rigatino*, a fat bacon, or sweet fresh *ricotta* cheese. It was a substantial meal for six. Paolo reminisced about the old days. When his mother was a girl, he said, *necci* were prepared in this way every day, for the children's snack when they went off to school, and as daily bread in those wheat-scarce days.

Cutigliano holds an annual Festa delle Castagne each November that features both *castagnaccia* and *necci*, which are more quickly baked or fried rather than prepared in this elaborate old way.

A prized little waxy potato is harvested in a single mountain town just under Abetone. Melo potatoes are still treasured, but potato farming in the mountains declined and today the Melo doesn't get much farther than the surrounding towns. Area restaurants feature them, especially roasted and served with *funghi*. There's talk of a revival, and Italy's Slow Food movement is encouraging a DOP protection label for the Melo that could encourage local farmers to return to it.

Like other mountain areas in Tuscany, the Pistoia mountains are full of game. The most popular to reach the table are boar and hare. On fall and winter menus everywhere here, *pappardelle alla lepre*, fresh wide noodles with hare sauce, is a favorite. The same light pasta also comes *al cinghiale*, a pungent boar *ragù*.

Another historic winter dish that traditionally marks major winter events in the Apennine foothills is *fegatello di maiale*. The liver of a large pig is cooked in its belly fat and thus preserved to be eaten during the winter. In the Pistoian hills the liver is first mixed with some chopped pork meat, flavored with fennel, laurel, and garlic, and then stuffed into the caul, a thin net-like membrane that surrounds the spleen. The entire package is cooled and preserved in the fat. It solidifies and remains fresh in cold storage the entire winter. I've occasionally seen preserved *fegatello* on restaurant menus in the Pistoia area. In the mountain area of Mount Amiata, the liver is cooked and served fresh in the same way, tender and pink. In the Pistoia area, preserved as it is, it tends to be tougher, to be sliced like a sausage.

Small sheep farmers have fared better than potato farmers in the Pistoian hills. These mountains are fertile ground for the hundreds of small farmers raising small flocks of sheep. They make a special *pecorino*, usually at home, from *latte crudo*, unpasteurized milk, that still eludes the restrictive eye of the European market. Much of the sheep-herding and cheese-making is still done by these small farmers in the traditional way: milk is taken twice a day from grazing pastured sheep and turned immediately into one of the various cheeses. *Ricotta* and *raviggiolo* are eaten fresh, *pecorino* is aged and can be bought at various stages of the aging process—*fresco* or almost fresh, and *stagionato*, aged for a longer period, harder, and more piquant. A dry storeroom serves for ripening and preserving the cheeses. They are very much a local specialty.

TYPICAL RESTAURANTS
& THEIR RECIPES

PISTOIA

LA BOTTEGAIA
Via del Lastrone 4, Pistoia • Tel. 0573-365-602
*Best to reserve, both for lunch and dinner. Closed Sunday lunch and all day
Monday. Prices are moderate.*

This little restaurant just off the marketplace in Pistoia's center has two
entrances. The front door leads on to the busy market. The back door takes
you out to the splendid Piazza del Duomo that is Pistoia's grand center.
On summer evenings ask for a table out back. During the warmer months,
it is possible to dine here in the shadow of the green and white striped
marble baptistry facing the grand old city hall and the cathedral tower, an
unforgettable experience. In the evening the square is gently lit, and, if you
are lucky, you might also dine to the accompaniment of an opera being
rehearsed on the piazza. We were especially fortunate one evening to hear
and sporadically watch a dress rehearsal for *Rigoletto*. Between courses we
wandered over closer to the stage to listen to arias. (There are also noisier
jazz evenings; check before you reserve.)

Carlo Malentacchi and Alessandro Ormi, two friends who love good
food, opened the restaurant in 1996. They chose a good spot. At lunchtime
the restaurant begins to fill just after noon, with students, business people,
groups of women out for lunch, market vendors. They continue to pour in
until after 2pm; often a table serves three seatings. The two owners also run
a little *bottega* at the upper end of the same street that offers specialties of
the area, cheeses, *salumi*, wines, marmalades, and other sundries. At the restaurant, Carlo and Alessandro at times try to gentrify their fare by adding
French (buttery) touches that nevertheless still taste blissfully Italian. They
also like to dress up some dishes in their own manner. "It's an age of spe-
cialization," says Carlo. "I decided to specialize in good things to eat." The
menu changes weekly although some favorites are always available.

A warm summer evening meal can begin with a light salad of thinly sliced peaches and local goat cheese, soft and mild, flavored with raspberry vinegar and olive oil. The light *pappa di zucchini*, a mash of zucchini, bread, and basil, is another summer dish. A *crema di zucchini*, another zucchini soup with a touch of cream, is more sophisticated and quite delicious.

In the winter they do a lot with chickpeas, a Pistoian favorite. Little pancakes of chickpea flour are topped with fresh tomatoes; *gateau di ceci*, a small cake made from the same flour, comes on a salad of baby greens. At times there's a rolled egg *frittata* with the lightest zucchini filling, bathed in a gentle tomato sauce. Or a creamy *risotto* with smoked *scamorza*, a hardened mozzarella-type cheese. For *secondi*, the choices here can be a lightly grilled slice of tuna on fresh vegetables, or, another winter favorite of Pistoians, *fegatello di maiale nella rete*, pork liver preserved in fat. It's served with baked beans. Baby lamb chops are a spring favorite; La BotteGaia serves them on a bed of *polenta*.

An artichoke flan is served on a *pecorino* cheese-based sauce; a peeled cooked potato is stuffed with *ricotta* and egg yolk with a shaving of white truffles. Not to be missed is the *taglierini* smothered in butter and truffles. On market days there is *trippa alla fiorentina* that comes from "the best *tripaio* around," a vendor who sells tripe and other innards from a stall in the open air market out front.

RECIPES FROM LA BOTTEGAIA

Creamed Zucchini Soup
CREMA DI ZUCCHINI

❀

Serves 4-6

½ rib celery, finely chopped
2 shallots, finely chopped
½ carrot, finely chopped
1½ tablespoons butter
1 pound (6 small or 4 medium) dark-green-skinned zucchini, thinly
    sliced into rounds
4 cups vegetable broth
¼ cup cream

Salt and freshly ground pepper
1 slice toasted rustic bread per diner
Extra virgin olive oil

Put the celery, shallots, and carrot into a heavy soup pot with the butter and, over a medium fire, sauté until soft. Add the zucchini slices and cook slowly for another 15 minutes, allowing the zucchini to release its water. Add the broth, cook for another 15 minutes, and add the cream. Mix well, remove from heat, and purée. Add salt and freshly ground pepper to taste.

To serve, place a slice of toast on each plate, drip a bit of olive oil onto each bread slice, and pour the soup over it.

Zucchini and Smoked Scamorza Cheese Risotto
RISOTTO DI SCAMORZA E ZUCCHINE

Serves 4

½ yellow onion, thinly sliced
2½ tablespoons butter
1½ cups Carnaroli or other *risotto* rice
½ cup dry white wine
3 small zucchini, in small cubes
About 4 cups chicken broth
5 ounces smoked mozzarella or *scamorza*, coarsely grated
1 cup grated Parmesan
Freshly ground pepper

Melt the onion in the butter. Add the rice and cook for 3 or 4 minutes. Splash in the wine and let it evaporate. Mix in the zucchini. Add the boiling broth slowly, just covering the *risotto* with each ladleful. When the rice is *al dente* add the smoked cheese and mix well. Remove from heat and add half the Parmesan. Mix and serve immediately, sprinkled with the remaining Parmesan and a grinding of pepper.

Lamb Cutlets in Tomato Sauce
COSTELETTE IN UMIDO

Serves 6

2 pounds baby lamb chops
Flour
3 tablespoons olive oil
1 large shallot, chopped
2 cloves garlic, chopped
2 ribs celery, chopped
½ cup dry white wine
1 14½ ounce can Italian peeled tomatoes
Salt and freshly ground pepper
½ cup white wine

Salt, pepper, and flour the cutlets and brown them quickly in 2 tablespoons hot olive oil. Remove and keep warm.

Add the remaining tablespoon of oil and add the chopped shallot, garlic, and celery. Throw in the white wine, allow to evaporate a bit, and add the drained tomatoes, which you have squashed through your hands. Add more salt and pepper to taste. Replace the lamb chops to cook in the sauce for about 15 minutes, until done.

La BotteGaia serves the chops on a bed of *polenta*.

CUTIGLIANO

DA FAGIOLINO
Piazza Catilina 9, Cutigliano • Tel. 0573-68014
Open for lunch and dinner. Closed Tuesdays and the month of November.
Moderately priced. Reservations recommended during summer and fall.

Trattoria da Fagiolino sits on the relaxed main square in Cutigliano. Diners converge on this popular little eating place from as far as Lucca and Pistoia for a lunch or evening meal, even though the twisting mountain road back down the mountain can challenge the hardiest stomach. (A few inexpensive rooms are available at da Fagiolino for overnight visitors.)

Luigi Innocenti is the third generation of his family to maintain this formidable little inn that specializes in the produce of the area.

Funghi porcini, available from June through mid-July and from September to late November, are prepared in every sort of way. A feast of *funghi* can begin here with *insalata di funghi* or *crostini ai funghi*, or with pasta with *funghi* sauce. Delicious little homemade *gnocchi* (also called *topini*, or little mice, in these parts) are seasoned with marjoram and thinly sliced mushrooms. There is a *gran fritto di funghi*, sliced mushrooms dipped in a light batter and deep fried. The *tagliata di funghi di Fagiolino* (a dish that at first glance resembles a sliced fillet of beef, but it's all mushroom!) can be eaten as a main course.

There are other interesting local dishes to consider here as well. Luigi Innocenti's *zuppa di Fagiolino con cipolline fresche*, a *minestrone* topped with freshly sliced onion, is given a special taste with a bit of prosciutto rind chopped in. His *ravioli al pepolino*, with the traditional *ricotta* and spinach filling, are covered in sauce flavored by local wild thyme called *pepolino*.

Portafoglio alla Fagiolino, a pork roast stuffed with melting cheese and prosciutto and cooked in a *funghi*/wine sauce, is a memorable main course. When in season, game is offered too. Chestnut flour *polenta* — called *manifatoli* — is served with roasted meats during the winter. In springtime, the notable Pescia asparagus is served with a sprinkling of Parmesan.

The best finish to all this is a plate of mixed wild berries accompanied by another house specialty, light, crisp *biscotti* comprised mostly of air and cornflakes. A glass of *vin santo* arrives with the biscuits.

RECIPES FROM DA FAGIOLINO

Vegetable Bread Soup
ZUPPA DI FAGIOLINO CON CIPOLLINE FRESCHE

Serves 6

This is another version of the soup so beloved by Tuscans. Similar ingredients as most, but Fagiolino adds fennel instead of the usual rosemary, and a rind (not fat) of ham, which makes it different.

2 cups *borlotti* or cranberry beans
2 plum tomatoes
1 small yellow onion, thinly sliced
½ leek, thinly sliced
1 small proscuitto rind
3 tablespoons olive oil
2 carrots, thinly sliced in rounds
2 zucchini, thinly sliced in rounds
1 large potato, peeled and cubed
2 ribs celery, cubed
¼ Savoy cabbage, sliced into thin strips
4 kale leaves, tough ribs removed, sliced into thin strips
1 small bunch dried wild fennel sprigs (if not available, use 1 teaspoon
    fennel seeds)
1 small bunch basil leaves
6 small slices day-old rustic bread
1 red onion, thinly sliced
Salt and freshly ground pepper
Extra virgin olive oil at table

Soak the beans overnight and cook them slowly in a large amount of water. Add salt at the end of the cooking. Purée half the beans with some of the water and the tomatoes. Reserve in a bowl, adding the remaining beans to the purée. Reserve the remaining cooking water.

While the beans are cooking, melt the sliced onion and leek in the olive oil with the rind of prosciutto. When soft, add the remaining vegetables (except for the red onion). Salt well and cook over a low flame until the vegetables are all soft, about half an hour. Add the bean mixture. Add the fennel and chopped basil and cook over a slow fire, adding as much of the bean water as is necessary to maintain a fairly thick soup. Add more salt as necessary. Don't allow the soup to become too thin; it should be dense.

When the vegetables are cooked, place the bread in a large oval dish and pour the soup over. Allow to rest for 5 minutes. Slice the red onion over the top and serve with a drizzle of olive oil and a grinding of pepper.

Stuffed Pork Roast

PORTAFOGLIO ALLA FAGIOLINO

❋

Serves 4

1 pound boned pork roast

2 slices mild melting cheese such as Emmenthal or Gruyere

2 slices prosciutto

4-5 sage leaves

Flour

1 tablespoon butter

1 tablespoon olive oil

1 small wineglass white wine

1 cup chicken or meat broth

4 *porcini* mushrooms, chopped (can be frozen; if frozen, add a handful of
dried *porcini* mushrooms)

1 clove garlic, smashed

1 small bunch parsley leaves, chopped

Salt and freshly ground pepper

Slice open the roast without cutting it through. Lay the cheese in the middle, not touching the ends. Over it put the prosciutto and sage leaves. Close and tie firmly. Dust with flour and salt lightly.

In a heavy pot with a cover, brown the roast in the butter and olive oil. Throw over the wine and allow to evaporate somewhat. Add the broth and mushrooms, lower the flame, and cook until soft through, about 1½ hours. Add water if necessary. Toward the end of the cooking add the pressed garlic clove and chopped parsley.

To serve, remove the string, slice, and cover each slice with sauce.

Biscotti

About 2 dozen little cakes

Fagiolino offers these light little cornflake and pine nut biscuits with *vin santo* at the end of every meal.

11 tablespoons unsalted butter, at room temperature
1 cup sugar
3 large eggs
2½ cups flour
2 teaspoons baking powder
1 cup pine nuts, toasted
4 cups cornflakes, crushed
Powdered sugar, optional

Preheat oven to 350 degrees.

Line two baking sheets with baking paper. In a mixer, beat the butter and sugar well until totally blended. Add the eggs, one by one, beating well after each addition. Sift the flour and baking powder in another bowl, and add to the butter mixture, beating until blended. Fold in the pine nuts.

Put the crushed corn flakes into a shallow bowl. Take one heaping tablespoon of the dough mixture, and roll into a ball in the crushed cornflakes. Place on the baking sheets about 1 inch apart. Bake until golden, about 20-25 minutes, and cool. They can be dusted with powdered sugar, but it's not necessary.

PIANOSINATICO

SILVIO LA STORIA A TAVOLA

Via Brennero 181, Pianosinatico • Tel. 0573-629-274
Open for lunch and dinner, except Tuesdays, and, for vacation, 15 days following Easter and in October. Priced inexpensive to moderate. Best to reserve.
Pianosinatico is a little curve in the road between Cutigliano and Abetone,

about ten kilometers before Abetone. Silvio Zanni is a former history professor. His "History at the Table" is a remarkably unpretentious little place well worth the journey. When you've finished a meal at this inexpensive *trattoria* high in the mountains above Pistoia, you'll wonder why it doesn't exist in a more accessible major city, or at least around the corner from where you live. There's a good reason. Chef Silvio Zanni grew up in nearby Cutigliano, and after years of teaching in Prato and then Paris, came back home to do his favorite thing: creating splendid things to eat. He takes his role seriously. The jauntily perched chef's toque sits well on his friendly gray head. He claims to have five hundred *primi* at the ready, many of them invented by him, using only — or mostly — local ingredients.

Silvio graduated with a degree in philosophy at Bologna and taught medieval history for years before seriously turning to the kitchen. He can regale you with talk that mixes food and history, holding forth on Tuscan medieval cooking citing Brunelleschi's shopping lists or Pontormo's diaries. He claims an atavistic right to his culinary skills; his grandfather was a famous Cutigliano hotelier/chef, at a time when the little resort played host to Italy's aristocracy each summer.

Silvio's partner, Andrea Vannucci, serves, and knows as much about local specialties and the dishes served here. He will tell you about the local wheat that is ground into the special flour used to make pasta and bread. He lists the various local goat cheeses made from *latte crudo*, or raw milk, that have been rewarded with a special certificate from the prestigious Slow Food Presidio.

It's the *antipasti* and first courses that Silvio is most proud of. The restaurant usually offers three *antipasti* and five different *primi* as a tasting menu each day. I recommend the tasting menu. If you can save space, the *secondi* of various grilled and roasted meats are also very good. The *antipasto* can be an incomparable combination of the esteemed Melo potatoes in a truffle sauce, or *crostini* of liver and tuna fish combined into a tasty spread. *Crostini di funghi* are a special treat during the fall and late spring as well. The pasta dishes have mostly been invented in Silvio's kitchen. There's one with a colorful beet sauce, another one with red or white onions, a third with carrots and smoked bacon. *Ravioli* are covered in a fresh oil steeped in the local wild mint called *nipotella*. The creamed soups include a light chickpea *velluta* as well as one of fresh peas combined with *funghi*.

Liver and Tuna Crostini
CROSTINI DI FEGATO E TONNO

❀

Makes about 30 crostini

1 clove garlic
2 tablespoons olive oil
5 chicken livers
1 (6 ounce) can tuna fish packed in oil, drained well
1 small shot glass *vin santo* or port
2 tablespoons tomato paste
Chopped parsley
Salt and freshly ground pepper
1 long baguette

Heat the garlic with the oil. When the oil begins to bubble, add the chicken livers and tuna. When the livers have lost their red color, add the *vin santo* and allow to evaporate. Add the tomato concentrate and enough water to cover the livers and tuna fish. Cook for about 15 minutes. Add some fresh parsley, taste for salt and pepper, and blend. Serve on sliced baguette.

Silvio dips the bread quickly in broth before smearing on the paste. It's good but not necessary. You can also serve the mixture on crackers.

Summer Tomato Pasta
PASTA POMODORO ESTIVA

❀

Serves 4-5

1 pound cherry tomatoes
¾ pound *spaghetti*
½ cup extra virgin olive oil
1 large handful of fresh herbs that can include marjoram, rosemary, sage, thyme, oregano, savory, and basil
1 small hot chili pepper, seeds removed and chopped
Salt and freshly ground pepper
½ cup shaved Parmesan, with additional at table

Chop the tomatoes into small cubes and put them in a colander with a sprinkling of salt to drain while the pasta cooks. Prepare a serving bowl with a cover.

Put the pasta to cook in lots of boiling salted water. In a small pan, heat the oil and add the chopped herbs and chili pepper. Just as the oil begins to sizzle, turn off the heat. When the pasta is cooked, place the tomatoes in the bottom of the serving dish. Drain the pasta, add it to the tomatoes. Add a good sprinkling of salt and freshly ground pepper, pour over the herbed oil, mix, and cover for several minutes. Serve with slices of Parmesan shaved over the top.

Fusilli with a Carrot and Bacon Sauce
FUSILLI CON CAROTE E PANCETTA

Serves 4

This invention of Sylvio can't really be called traditional, but he certainly is and the pasta is good enough to include.

1½ tablespoons olive oil
3½ ounces *pancetta* or bacon, in small cubes
5 carrots, grated through the largest holes of the grater
¼ cup cognac or brandy
2 tablespoons cream
1 pound *fusilli*
1 small handful chopped parsley leaves
Salt and freshly ground pepper

In a saucepan large enough to hold the pasta as well as the sauce, heat the oil and add the bacon. After two minutes add the carrots. Cook over a slow heat until the carrots are cooked. Add the cognac and allow to evaporate. Add the cream and heat to mix well. Remove from heat.

Cook the pasta in lots of boiling salted water. Drain the pasta but don't shake the colander—a bit of water should cling to the pasta. Over a low heat, add to the sauce. Add the parsley and cook together for a few minutes. Taste for seasoning and pour into a heated serving bowl.

Tagliatelle with Creamy Onion Sauce
TAGLIATELLE CON CIPOLLE CREMOSE

Serves 4-5

2 large red onions, very thinly sliced
1 tablespoon fresh olive oil
1 cup red wine
1 tablespoon cream
1 pound egg *tagliatelle*

Sauté the onions in the oil until just soft. Add the wine, bring to a boil, lower the heat, and cook gently until the onions are completely soft. Cook the *tagliatelle* just for a minute, drain, and add to the sauce. Add the cream and mix well. Cook until the pasta is soft (adding water if necessary) and serve immediately.

Farfalle with Red Beet Sauce
FARFALLE CON BARBABIETOLE

Serves 4-5

Another Silvio invention.

4 medium beets
Salt
3 cloves garlic, crushed and chopped
4 tablespoons olive oil
½ cup vegetable broth
2 tablespoons fresh cream
1 pound *farfalle*
Small bunch basil, chopped

Cook the beets in a good amount of salted water until they are cooked but still firm. Peel the beets, cut them in half, and slice fairly thinly. Heat the oil with the crushed and chopped garlic, and when it begins to bubble, add the beets. Cook for a minute, mixing well, and stir in the cream. Set aside.

Bring a big pan of salted water to a boil and throw in the pasta. While it is still very *al dente*, drain, and add to the beets. Throw in the basil and cook another minute or so until the pasta is cooked and the sauce absorbed.

Cream of Chickpea Soup

VELLUTA DI CECI

❁

Serves 6-8

2 cups chickpeas, soaked overnight with a pinch of bicarbonate of soda
½ onion, sliced thinly
2 tablespoons olive oil
1 sprig rosemary
Leaves of 1 sprig sage
2 cups vegetable broth (or more), divided
1 tablespoon tomato paste
1 teaspoon butter
Freshly ground pepper
Fresh extra virgin olive oil at table

Drain the soaked chickpeas, and in fresh water, cook the chickpeas until soft. Melt the onion in the olive oil, and add the drained, cooked chickpeas, along with the rosemary, sage and half a cup of broth. Cook for several minutes, and blend. Put the mixture back in the pan, add the tomato paste and enough broth to make a light creamy soup. At the end, add the butter and serve hot with pepper and some olive oil at table.

CHAPTER 5

The Mugello

THE MUGELLO WAS ONCE THE SUMMER PLAY-
GROUND OF THE MEDICI FAMILY, WHO BOUGHT
most of its southern hills from various noble families in the fifteenth and
sixteenth centuries. It lies conveniently just to the north of Florence, in the
cool foothills of the Apennine Mountains, an inviting retreat in the steamy
summer months in the valley. You can still see the fortifications, castles,
villas, hunting lodges, and bishops' palaces that went up during Medici
control. The family even founded experimental farms to bring better nourishment to their Florentine subjects. A flourishing milk industry is the
single visible trace of that initiative, but telltale fortress towers and remaining castles become evident soon after you leave Florence.

The Medici remnants are in verdant valleys of the lower Mugello.
In the upper hills are Alpine-like landscapes of vast beauty that stretch
into Emilia-Romagna. It's one of those places to return time and again, yet
remains one of the lesser-known and little visited parts of Tuscany.

Reaching this awesome beauty can be trying. The valley roads north of
Florence are busy with industry, especially around Borgo San Lorenzo and
Rufina. But once you get beyond the cement factories and carelessly tossed
together housing estates, you'll find yourself almost alone in one of the
more spectacularly beautiful mountain landscapes of Tuscany. It is a land
of well-preserved natural parks perfect for trekking and horseback riding.
Imposing churches, interesting towns, and some tasty traditional dishes
add to its attractions. The narrow inside roads are blessedly unspoiled; you
drive for long stretches through lovely pastured pine and chestnut-covered
mountains without meeting another car. The most you'll come upon is a
warning sign for an unseen cow. (You can also go by rail, on the newly
renovated Faentina railroad line that meanders from Florence up into the
hills to Marradi.)

Make a point to visit or at least pass by one of the stately Medici villas and buildings that include Villa Demidoff, Castello di Cafaggiolo, the Palazzo de Vicari in Scarperia, and Castello del Trebbio.

I've tried different ways to get to the Mugello from Florence. There is the most obvious, from the Barberino exit on the *autostrada* to Bologna. My favorite, however, is to head east from Florence to Pontessieve and there turn north through Rufina to Vicchio. Rufina is about a forty-five minute drive from Florence, and from there it's a short trip to Dicomano. (A detour at Dicomano takes you up to a lovely church at San Godenzo.) From Vicchio, head toward Borgo San Lorenzo where a right turn leads up to the mountains, where vistas open and you'll reach the remote mountain towns of Marradi and Palazzuolo sul Senio. After that it's back down the mountain to Scarperia and other towns below.

Rufina is not yet really the Mugello; it's the northernmost area where the wines of Chianti are produced. A good bit of commercial Chianti, Chianti Ruffina, is bottled here, and you can almost smell the wine as you near town. The town is mostly interesting for its wine production; there are tastings along the way. Further up the road at Dicomano, turn off for a small detour to San Godenzo, with its noble eleventh-century church of the same name (or San Gaudenzo, as he was originally called). The body of the saint lies in state, glowing beautifully embalmed in an open case. More captivating is the lovely painting by Bernando Daddi of the Virgin and several saints. San Godenzo had its big moment in the first years of the fourteenth century, when Ghibelline forces gathered here in an attempt to return to Guelph Florence; Dante Alighieri was among them.

The translucently shadowed valley around Vicchio is Giotto land. He was born in nearby Vespignano where his house is now a small museum, La Casa Natale di Giotto (Summer, open Tuesday on request; Thursday, Saturday, and Sunday from 10am–noon and 3:30–6:30pm; winter, Saturday and Sunday 10am–noon and 3:30pm–6:30pm). Some claim that the Renaissance itself burst onto the scene from these low hills. Franco Utili, a lightly bearded gentle Vicchio native who dwells on local lore (and traditional food) described it all to me one day. "Walk out from Giotto's house," he suggested, "into the pastured woodland, and you'll find Ponte di Cimabue—Cimabue's bridge, where Cimabue happened upon the young shepherd Giotto sketching his sheep in the field." Impressed by his skill,

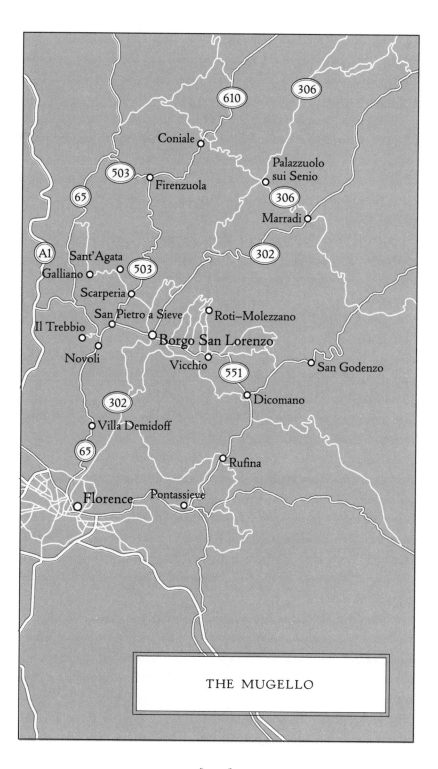

THE MUGELLO

Cimabue invited the boy to his workshop. "*Ecco*, the Renaissance blossomed!" Franco exclaimed. Cimabue was the link, and Giotto began the chain. If you walk through those woods and fields today, he says, you'll see and understand why. I did and came away convinced.

Fra Angelico also came from Vicchio and in the old town hall the Museo Fra Angelico is dedicated to sacred art. It's open the same hours as that of Giotto. Another museum to visit is Il Museo della Civilta Contadino, a historical exposition of rural life in this area. (For visiting hours and other information about these three museums, call the Vicchio commune, 055-843-921.)

Casa di Caccia (see page 145), a small restored lodge about twelve kilometers north of Vicchio, houses a restaurant worth the detour; from its pleasant terrace dining room you have a view of the entire valley of the lower Mugello.

From Vicchio and Vespignano, the main road leads west toward Borgo San Lorenzo. Skirting the city, you can turn right to the provincial road through Panicaglia that brings you through pleasant landscapes to the upper Mugello, to Marradi and Palazzuolo along the Senio river, the area I love best. From the wide valleys in the lower Mugello you rise into the high mountains over narrow passes through meadowed pine and chestnut forests and dazzling views on all sides. This is the Toscana Romagnola, green mountains with rounded peaks that roll off into distant Emilia-Romagna. Head first for Marradi, then across the mountain landscape to Palazzuolo sul Senio. Both towns are perfect little alpine Italian villages preserved almost in the state they were hundreds of years ago. And both boast admirable restaurants. In Marradi is Il Camino (see page 148) with its reputation as the best restaurant in the area. Palazzuolo has Locanda Senio (see page 151), a cozy inn just off the main old square, a little fourteenth-century town center.

From Palazzuolo another beautiful almost deserted road with singular mountain and valley views runs up to Coniale and back down to Firenzuola, a bleak little old town with a big history that was almost bombed out of existence during the Second World War. Garibaldi, fleeing his enemies, made his way across these passes in the freezing winter of 1848, traversing the Apennines in an arduous trek from Livorno to Ravenna. The inscription on the facade of one city hall assures visitors that, fleeing from the French army, Giuseppe Garibaldi slept here one night *"assieme con la moglie"* (together with his wife).

Firenzuola still retains the old Porto Fiorentina, arcaded streets, and has reconstructed old *palazzi* to give you an idea of what it once was. There is also an evocative little museum dedicated to *pietra serena*, the velvety grey travertine stone that was once quarried and worked here and that faces and fronts so many lovely Romanesque churches. (Museo della Pietra Serena, Rocca di Firenzuola, Tel. 055-8199434-5; June 15–September 15, Monday, Friday, and Saturday 4pm–7pm; Sunday 11am–1pm and 4pm–7pm; September 16–June 14, Saturday 3pm–5pm and Sunday 11am–1pm and 2pm–5pm)

The drive back down toward the valley through another mountain pass brings you to Scarperia, once the main trading town of the Mugello. In the eighteenth century a modern road was built over the parallel Futa pass, today part of the main *autostrada* link between Florence and Bologna, and Scarperia was left by the wayside. The town thus has become something of a minor attraction, but its remnants of greatness remain. Walking up the narrow old main street you come upon an oversized and commanding castle—the Palazzo dei Vicari—looking as though it was simply parachuted into this street of an otherwise low-built medieval little town. Awesome, even overbearing, it is a perfect display of the architecture of power. ("Stalin as an architect," my husband mused upon first laying eyes on the *palazzo*, "had nothing on the old Medici. Only their taste was better.") The Palazzo dei Vicari was built by the Medici to house their appointed bishops. It wears their coats of arms ornately across its front like a proudly decorated overweight aging general. Each of the many reigning bishops added his own. The castle's overwhelming tower and thick crenellated walls—fronting an inordinately small piazza and the dwarfed Romanesque church of Saints Jacopo and Filippo—seem to possess the entire town even today. Off to the side on the piazza, the little Gothic chapel of Santa Maria has a fifteenth-century vaulted ceiling and a lovely old Madonna.

The Palazzo houses a museum for another of Scarperia's historic traditions, the hand production of knives. Somewhat euphemistically it's called a Sharp Tools museum. (Palazzo dei Vicari e Museo dei Ferri Taglienti, Tel. 055-846-8165; June 1–September 15, Wednesday–Friday, 3:30pm–7:30pm, Saturday, Sunday, and holidays, 10am–1pm and 3pm–6:30pm;

September 16–May 31, Saturday, Sunday, and holidays, 10am–1pm and 3pm–6:30pm.)

Fine hunting knives have been crafted in Scarperia for hundreds of years, developing into a first-rate artisan cutlery industry that is still a mainstay of its economy. On both sides of the road leading up to the Palazzo dei Vicari, fine handmade cutlery shops offer their wares, selling a wide range of kitchen knives, handsome carving sets, and well-honed table knives, an irresistible temptation to buy. Just around the corner from the Palazzo, you can watch knives being crafted in the factory shop of Saladini (Via Solferino 19). Owner Pierre Baldini will be happy to show you around and sell you anything you want from his ready supply on the second floor. From there you can wander the back streets of Scarperia.

Scarperia celebrates a major festival, the Diotto on every September 8th, to honor its bishops and commemorate the founding of the town in 1306. The festival is replete with medieval costumes, tournaments, and a procession of banner-waving young men marching through the streets. Banner-waving is something of a Tuscan art. It's featured in town festivals all over the region (Tel. 055-843-161).

Just outside Scarperia to the north, an authentically restored grand old building of the Borghese family houses the Fattoria il Palagio (see page 154), once a farm building and now an impressive restaurant and inn.

From Scarperia, head for nearby Sant'Agata, possessing one of the more notable little churches of the region, the ninth-century Romanesque Pieve di Sant'Agata. Continue on the road to Galliano, but soon turn to the left for the road that brings you to San Piero a Sieve. Follow the signs for Castello del Trebbio, perhaps the most historic Medici house in the area. Designed and built in the fifteenth century by the noted Renaissance architect Michelozzo Michelozzi for Cosimo de'Medici, this imposing castle was described memorably by historian Hugh Thomas as a place where a person with a sense of history will be forgiven if he persuades himself that even though remote, here is the heart of civilization.

There's a fine view of the valley below, where so many great travellers passed and many continued on to Il Trebbio. "Imagine Lorenzo de Medici walking under the pergola with Poliziano or Luigi Pulci, his country neighbor, or Dante nearby plotting with the Ubaldini, Giotto walking with his sheep, Becket, Goethe, Montaigne and Boswell traveling past," writes

Thomas. Here also passed Galileo, Leonardo, Michelangelo, Masaccio, and many others. The castle, now in private hands, can be visited in groups from Monday through Friday (Tel. 055-845-8793).

From Il Trebbio it's a short drive to Novoli where you'll find a main artery to Florence that takes you past another sixteenth-century Medici villa, once the magnificent home of Cosimo's eldest son. The grand house fell into ruin, and was rebuilt completely as Villa Demidoff in the nineteenth century by Prince Paolo Demidoff, son of the Russian ambassador to Florence, thus the name. Its splendid gardens are filled with grottos, water games, grotesque figures by Buontalenti, and the gigantic statue *Apennino* by Giambologna. (Both sculptor/architects are well represented in the Boboli gardens in Florence as well.) The park is open to the public weekends between March and October, and host to cultural events as well (Tel. 055-409-427; or 409-155).

SPECIALTIES OF THE MUGELLO

Along with their many villas and castles, the Medici brought milk farming to the Mugello. Il Trebbio was a vast agricultural holding as well as a hunting estate. They called their nearby milk farm Panna (which means cream in Italian) and imported Alpine cows to bring nourishment to the Florentines. (Panna, still a locality near Barbarino, has rolling meadows, but no Medici cows to be seen.) Milk production, by descendents of the Alpine cows brought from Switzerland by the Medici family, continues to this day. We all drink Mukki milk, eat Mukki bio-yogurt, and other dairy products that have evolved from the Medici incentive in the fourteenth century. It's one of the Mugello's major industries. A particular beef called Limousin cattle is also a Mugello specialty, and here is considered on a par with the better known Chianina beef.

As in other regions of Tuscany, various saints' days and holy periods of the year are observed with traditional foods in the Mugello. During carnival, the pre-Lenten season, *cenci*, or fried pastry strips, appear here and elsewhere, as do *migliacci* (millet cake). The forty days of Lent—the *Quaresima*—are commemorated here as elsewhere with a dry little cocoa mini-biscuit shaped into alphabet letters. On Ash Wednesday, in Borgo San Lorenzo, plates of *polenta* are offered in the main square to begin the fast before Easter. Another traditional Lenten dish, *farinata con gli Zoccoli*, adds beans to the *polenta*, making a hearty soup that turns almost solid. After a day, it can be sliced and fried for a second meal.

In anticipation of spring, on the day of San Giuseppe, March 19th, Tuscans eat a sweet fritter of eggs and rice called *frittelle di San Giuseppe*, to celebrate the moment hens begin laying again after their winter suspension. Every area, including the Mugello, has its own variant of the fritter. On Easter and Ascension Day come spring lamb and baby artichokes, and *ravioli* made with potatoes and *pecorino*. An especially tasty white potato, grown in the area around Firenzuolo, goes into this special *ravioli* of the Mugello, a traditional dish here and in neighboring Casentino all year round.

In the upper reaches of the Mugello, chestnuts, wild mushrooms, and game have always been the necessary sustenance during the difficult seasons. The chestnut is considered the tree of life in mountainous parts of Italy. Without chestnuts and their flour the mountain people could not have survived winters; chestnuts became the mainstay of the kitchen. And so they are today.

DOC and IGP labels on a bag or tin are a great source of pride to the producers who earn these designations for excellence. Only extraordinary foods or wines that are produced in a particular place are awarded a DOC, IGP, or DOP designation. The *marron buono* (or "good chestnuts") of Marradi are that famous. These are designated IGP, meaning a place of Geographical Protection. We all look forward to the first chestnuts of the season, in late September and early October. Fall has arrived; chestnuts are here. If you're lucky enough to have a chestnut forest as we do, you gather them from the ground once the hard little spiked coating has split and the nut falls out. This simple nut is the *castagna*. A larger, shinier nut, one that doesn't grow in our own woods, begins to appear in local markets in and around the Mugello a little later. This is the *marrone* of the Mugello. (The difference is like that between *prosecco* and a fine champagne.) While both species get roasted—in the Mugello roasted chestnuts are called *bruciati* or burned—and boiled, chestnuts are also ground into flour and made into creams. *Marroni* come from trees that have been pruned, nurtured, and coaxed over the centuries into producing larger perfectly shaped beauties. These generally go into elegant glazed desserts. *Marroni* come onto the market later than chestnuts, renewing the excitement of the year's first encounter. The season is a short one; by December all you'll find is dried chestnuts and their flour.

There are famous fall *sagras* and *feste* of *marroni* throughout the Mugello. Marradi's and Palazzuolo's are the best known. It's a good time to get on the old restored Faentina steam-engine railroad in Florence that takes you on a special trip up into *marrone* land and its festivals. Every Sunday during October an early special train leaves from Bologna, Rimini, or Florence to bring you to Marradi, its *marron buono*, and the special dishes that are created from them. A bus from the Marradi station can carry you on over a scenic road to Palazzuolo as well.

Recently, a group of innovative young people in these high mountains have begun a noticeable renewal of old food traditions, introducing organically grown products and marketing them as such. The movement has not only introduced some great new products but a rebirth of much traditional agriculture here. Land in the upper Mugello is meager, it's not easy to grow a great deal. Sheep have their small pastures, grains have their limited plots. Large industrial farming is out of the question. In the past farmers made a bare subsistence living.

Now a number of cooperatives have begun operating, young farmers and producers joining together to offer choice products that find a sophisticated market throughout and beyond Tuscany. They all know one another and work together as friends. One group has begun an artisan production of organic pasta products and *farro*. The micro-climate in these mountains, I'm told, is as ideal for the growing of *farro* as the Garfagnana. The label is Rio Maggio and has become a precious one. Another group of friends has created an organic cheese cooperative using ancient cheese-making methods from the milk of grazing goats. The co-op turns out a limited number of fine organic goat cheeses; they've recently broadened the range of goat life in this region with the importation of an Alpine goat. Their cows and sheep also freely graze on the grassy meadows of the mountain. The fresh *ricotta* and *raviggiolo* cheeses are remarkably good; the aged *pecorino* as well. You can see and buy a fine selection of them at the Agricoop in Palazzuolo.

Marco Minardi calls himself *il porcaro medievale* after his medieval progenitor who allowed his herd of pigs to wander through the woods, calling them home each evening to sleep. With his wife Rosita he produces pork products from pigs that forage the fresh grasses of the woods. He turns out fresh pork cuts as well as smoked and dried *salumi*.

As in other mountain regions of Tuscany, a great number of various wild herbs and greens go into the food of the Mugello as well as flavored *grappas*, brandies, digestives, honeys, and marmalades. Venture into La Dispensa della Locanda Senio in Palazzuolo and you'll find homemade *grappa* flavored with berries, juniper, sage, or various other wild herbs. Chestnut honey and chestnut cream as well as various wild berry marmalades are also on the shelves in this small enticing shop.

In the fall and late spring, *porcini* mushrooms are on every menu. Another popular mushroom here is the *prugnolo*, that sprouts in meadows just after the snows have melted.

And, as in other woodsy regions of Tuscany, a plethora of game dishes appears on the menus of the Mugello.

VICCHIO

CASA DI CACCIA

Roti-Molezzano, a suburb of Vicchio • Tel. 055-840-7629

Lunch and dinner daily in the summer; closed Tuesday during other months.
Closed for fifteen days during February. Prices are moderate.
Reservations recommended.

With patience and perseverance, a twenty-minute drive from the main square at Vicchio will bring you to this old cheese maker's domain, now a restored gathering place for hunters. You'll get the kind of meal that hunters relish. A group of young *cacciatore* bought the old ruin about fifteen years ago; they spiffed it up and turned it over to Mirella Settori, who runs the kitchen along with the entire large restaurant today.

From Vicchio's main square, take the road in the direction of Santa Maria a Vezzano; there are indications to Casa di Caccia all along the way. The view is splendid; after all, this is Giotto country. Continue along the road for about ten kilometers, and signs will bring you to the restaurant. A good stretch of the road is unpaved, but easily passable. You'll come upon the main sign for the restaurant just about at the moment you think you're totally lost. I'd suggest your first time there be for lunch, not only to see where you are going, but for the lovely views as well.

Mirella Settori is a robust, outdoorsy woman who is justly proud of the restaurant she has created. She lives above the remote place. It seems to contain her life and passion for the kitchen. Her menu changes not only with the seasons, but with the game that is available on a daily basis as well. Antipasto features prosciutto of wild boar and roebuck, a pate of wild boar served with a tangy strawberry marmalade, along with the usual *crostini* and local *salumi*. Pastas are all made in the restaurant kitchen; both the *ravioli di scamorza con tartufo* made with a cheese resembling mozzarella, and the *ravioli con pecorino*, her version of the noted potato *ravioli*, are special. The glass-enclosed terrace dining room is bright and cheery, open to the woods and valleys around. Main courses to try are game, such as hare with a truffled stuffing, and wild boar in a wine sauce. A good dessert to try is a *panna cotta* with a memorable sauce of wild berries.

RECIPES FROM CASA DI CACCIA

Scamorza Ravioli with Truffle Oil
RAVIOLI DI SCAMORZA CON OLIO DI TARTUFI

Makes about 50 ravioli

Scamorza cheese is part of the mozzarella family, a bit more flavorful. It dissolves entirely when you cook the *ravioli*, forming a meltingly creamy filling. Rather than square *ravioli*, I find it easier to make a half-moon shaped filled pasta—*tortellini*—by cutting circles with a 2-inch glass, adding a spoonful of filling, and then folding the circle in half and pressing the edges closed.

1¼ cups plain white flour
3 eggs
1 tablespoon extra virgin olive oil
Salt
2 pounds *scamorza* or other firm creamy melting cheese
1 egg yolk, beaten
Truffle oil and/or truffle butter
1 black truffle (if available)

To make the pasta, put the flour, three eggs, and the olive oil in a food processor and process until it forms a ball. Remove and knead until shiny and malleable, about 10 minutes. Allow to rest covered in plastic wrap or under a cloth for at least half an hour.

Grate the *scamorza* through the largest holes of a grater. With two forks, mix well with the egg yolk until the cheese takes on a uniform orange glow.

Divide the pasta into about 4 balls. While working with one, keep the remaining balls covered. Roll out the pasta as thin as possible and, with a large-mouthed glass, cut out circles from the sheet of dough. Put a scant teaspoon of filling in the middle of each, fold over and pinch closed.

Drop the *ravioli* into a large pan of boiling, well-salted water, remove with a slotted spoon as they rise to the top, and serve with a good covering of truffle oil and/or truffle butter and, if available, slivered black truffles.

Piquant Strawberry Marmalade
MARMELLATA DI FRAGOLE

1¼ pounds strawberries
3 tablespoons balsamic vinegar
2 tablespoons sugar

Combine all the ingredients in a saucepan and cook over a low fire until the mix reaches a marmalade consistency. At Casa di Caccia the marmalade is served with a country paté. It also goes well with a hunk of *pecorino* at the end of a meal.

Panna Cotta with Wild Berry Sauce
PANNA COTTA AI FRUTTI DI BOSCO

Serves 10

FOR THE PANNA COTTA:
½ cup cold water
4 teaspoons unflavored gelatin
4 cups cream
1 cup sugar
1 vanilla bean

FOR THE SAUCE:
4 cups mixed wild berries
⅓ cup sugar

To make the *panna cotta*: in a small metal bowl, sprinkle the gelatin into the water and allow to stand for about 10 minutes. Put the bowl into a pan of simmering water to melt the gelatin entirely, about a minute or 2. Split the vanilla bean and scrape out the seeds. In another pan, combine the vanilla seeds, cream, sugar, and bring to a boil. Simmer for 2 minutes, remove from heat, and mix the gelatin into the cream. Whisk until well blended.

Fill 4 individual molds, allow to cool, and refrigerate.

To make the sauce, boil together the berries and sugar for about 5 minutes. Purée half of the mixture, and stir it back into the other berries.

To serve, turn out the *panna cotta* onto small flat plates and divide the sauce over each.

MARRADI

IL CAMINO

Viale Baccarini 38, Marradi (near the railway station) • Tel. 055-804-5069

Open daily for lunch and dinner. Closed Wednesday and one week during June. Prices are moderate. Best to reserve.

An elegant-looking family runs this unpretentious little gem of a restaurant. Golden-haired mama Rita Bassetti is in the kitchen, her long tresses pulled tightly back into a long ponytail. Her pretty daughter Simona, as brunette as her mother is blonde, is *sous-chef*. Son-in-law Mirko — also golden flecked — is *maestro di sala*, welcoming guests and enthusiastically detailing each of the several specialties the restaurant offers each day.

Marradi is on the direct route to the Romagna region above Tuscany, and Il Camino presents a cuisine that reflects both areas. This fusion of two great Italian regions is delectable. Sauces seem to be richer, the bread contains salt unlike Tuscan bread you'll find elsewhere. Most specialties at Il Camino are seasonal, "of the moment," as cook Rita puts it. Peas are picked in the morning, prepared for lunch; *funghi* arrive daily. The pasta served is not only fresh, but rolled and cut as you order.

There is a menu, but Mirko avoids giving it to diners; he would rather tell you about the specialties of the day. Always on hand, and a must, is a trio of warm *crostini* served on soft absorbent bread rather than the usual firmer, crustier sliced baguette-type bread or toast: liver paté, creamed asparagus, and a wild mushroom stew that are fresh in season and frozen at the right moment for the rest of the year. Mediterranean-style baby lamb is usually on the menu, as are *bocconcini ai funghi*, bite-sized chunks of chicken and *funghi* stewed together and served on a bed of *polenta*.

As Marradi is the home of the grand *marron buono*, the treat of Il Camino is the chestnut pudding, best in the fall when chestnuts are freshest.

Chicken Stew with Wild Mushrooms
BOCCONCINI AI FUNGHI

Serves 6

Serve this delectable dish on a bed of *polenta* or mashed potatoes.

3 large chicken legs with thighs
1 onion
1 carrot
2 or 3 cloves garlic
1 bunch chopped parsley
3 tablespoons olive oil
10 ounces fresh or frozen wild *porcini* mushrooms, chopped
1 cup hot chicken broth

Have your butcher bone and skin 3 large chicken legs with thighs. The meat should weigh about 2 pounds. Chop into fairly large bite-sized pieces.

Coarsely chop the onion, carrot, and garlic; chop the parsley more finely. In a pan large enough to hold all the ingredients, sauté the onion, carrot, garlic, and parsley in the olive oil. Add the chicken pieces and sauté for a few minutes until they have lost their color. Add the mushrooms. (If frozen, allow to defrost before adding.)

Cook for 10 minutes over a low flame, and add the chicken broth. Cook more rapidly until the sauce takes on a slightly thickened consistency, about 10 more minutes.

Chestnut Pudding
BUDINO DI MARRONI

❋

Serves 8

1 cup sugar (to caramelize mold)
1 pound shelled chestnuts (about 2 pounds unshelled)
½ teaspoon salt
Peel of 1 lemon
4 eggs, beaten
1¼ cups sugar
2 vanilla beans
1½ ounces chocolate
2 tablespoons brandy
2 tablespoons rum
About ½ cup milk

Preheat the oven to 300 degrees.

First, prepare the mold with caramelized sugar by heating 1 cup of sugar, slowly, in a heavy skillet, stirring constantly with a wooden spoon until sugar melts and is free of lumps. When the sugar turns a caramel color, remove it from the heat and pour it into a 6-cup mold. Set aside.

If the chestnuts are fresh and unshelled, make a cross on the flat side of each with a sharp knife, and place either over a flame in a chestnut pan or in the hot oven until they open enough to peel the outer shell. Cover the peeled chestnuts with water, bring to a boil, add the salt and lemon peel, and cook over a medium flame until soft. Pass through a food processor or potato masher to make a purée of about 1 pound. Mix in the eggs, and add the sugar, the vanilla, the chocolate, and the liquors. Add enough milk (about ½ cup) to make a semi-liquid, mix well, and pour into the mold.

Bake for 3 hours, until the custard is firm. Turn out and serve.

PALAZZUOLO SUL SENIO

———————— ·❈· ————————

LOCANDA SENIO

Via Borgo dell'Ore 1/3, Palazzuolo sul Senio • Tel. 055-804-6019

The restaurant (it is also a small six-room hotel that is open year-round) is open continually from May through October, other months from Thursday through Sunday. It's a small place, with only eight tables and it's always wise to telephone beforehand. Prices are moderate to high, depending on what you eat and drink.

Ercole Liga is the generous, gregarious, and knowledgeable host of this warm and welcoming *locanda* (inn). He and his wife Roberta have turned their place into a perfect nest of lovingly prepared and tasty home produce, which Ercole deliciously describes in his own series of small publications. He designs and prints descriptions of his menus, their history, often their recipes, in four languages. It's fun to talk about food with him. Ercole is a Romagnolo by birth who moved to Roberta's Tuscan mountains after his studies and ten years as a businessman in Milan.

Ercole is one of the young entrepreneurs of the upper Mugello who are bringing back tradition as they fight for the environment. He runs a small *dispensa* across the road where he sells Roberta's jams and his own *grappa* and mountain liqueurs together with the products of his friends. Every morning Roberta bakes a variety of breads for the restaurant, a goodly number that includes—beyond the normal crusty unsalted Tuscan variety—one with chestnut flour, Parmesan rolls, rosemary flatbread, grape-dotted *focaccia*, and plenty of others. There's an amazing little fried puff of dough that has its origins in Ercole's home district of Romagna, crisp and soft little fritters called *crescentine*, served with three little bowls of spreads. One is a soft, locally produced goat cheese, *raviggiolo*, another a homemade chestnut paste, and the third a sauce of sharp tomatoes. You open the hot little puff, smear on some cheese, and over it either the sweet chestnut paste or the sharp tomato. Either combination is very good.

The menu at Locanda Senio is all mountain food. Several kinds of *menu degustazione* at a fixed price are available, an opportunity to taste the specialties of the moment. One is a "medieval pork" meal, the pork arriving from the nearby *porcaro medievale.*

First courses are the best. A light salad of various mountain greens and aromatic wild herbs is dressed with salt and fresh olive oil, and surrounded by tiny cubes of hot freshly deep-fried potatoes. You can also have *tagliatelle di farro* from Rio Maggio in a sauce of local *ricotta* cheese, a rich smooth *pappa al pomodoro,* or a *farro* salad with beans, capers, and thyme. *Secondi,* main courses, varied as they are, also concentrate on local mountain fare. Among them: sausages with chestnuts and oranges, pork from the "medieval" herd of *il porcaro,* and goat in tarragon and mint.

Roberta, a totally self-taught cook, leaves the local mountains behind as she makes a Bavarian cream dessert that would be credible in the most elegant city restaurant. The presentation is perfect; a mint green molded cream on a white plate, covered with fresh cream and decorated with mint leaves and little shaved pale green gratings of mint-flavored chocolate across the plate.

RECIPES FROM LOCANDA SENIO

Tomato Bread Soup
PAPPA AL POMODORO DI LOCANDA SENIO

Serves 6

1 onion, finely chopped
2 tablespoons olive oil
1 tablespoon tomato sauce
2 pounds (about 6 large) tomatoes, with juice and seeds squeezed out, coarsely chopped
3 slices day or two-day old Tuscan bread
2 cloves garlic, peeled and chopped
1 bunch basil leaves, chopped
Salt and freshly ground pepper
Extra virgin olive oil at table

Sauté the onion in the olive oil, add the tomato sauce and the tomatoes, and cook over a low fire until most of the liquid has evaporated. In a deep pot, place the bread, garlic, and basil, barely cover with water, and cook for 5 minutes. Add the tomatoes and continue to cook until the entire mixture becomes pulpy. Add salt and pepper to taste. Blend in a food processor or blender, taste for seasonings and serve with a drizzle of olive oil.

Medieval Farro Salad
INSALATA DI FARRO MEDIEVALE
❀
Serves 10

1¼ cups cooked *borlotti* or cranberry beans, soaked overnight
2 cups *farro*
1 cup capers, preserved in vinegar
1 large bunch thyme (or summer savory)
Extra virgin olive oil
Salt and freshly ground pepper

Cook the beans over a very low heat until they are totally soft but still holding their form. Reserve.

Cook the *farro* in boiling salted water for about half an hour, until it is cooked through but still *al dente*. Drain and rinse with cold water. Drain the beans and mix well with the *farro*.

Wash the capers well, and add to the *farro* along with the cooked beans and chopped herbs. Dress with a good olive oil, add salt and freshly ground pepper to taste, and serve warm or at room temperature. Add more oil at table.

Medieval Pork Roast with Juniper Berries and Pomegranate
ARROSTO DI MAIALE MEDIEVALE
❀
Serves 4

This old recipe offered by Locanda Senio "promises to dispel the bad spirits and bring a healthy air to the home."

1 fillet of pork tenderloin, about 1½ pounds
15 juniper berries, crushed in a mortar
1 tablespoon seasoned lard, chopped

Juice of 1 or 2 pomegranates, plus some whole kernels
Salt and freshly ground pepper

Split the tenderloin. Salt and pepper the meat and sprinkle the crushed juniper berries on the inside. Fold together and secure with a string.

Use a heavy pan with a cover that is large enough to hold the entire roast. Melt the lard in the pan, add the roast, and brown it well. Pour the pomegranate juice over the roast, cover the pan, and continue to cook for about 10 minutes. Uncover and allow to cook another 10 minutes. Remove the meat and reduce the sauce to gravy. To serve, slice the meat, pour the pan juices over it, and sprinkle with pomegranate kernels. Baked leeks and fried artichokes are suggested as accompaniment.

SCARPERIA

FATTORIA IL PALAGIO
Viale Dante 99, Scarperia • Tel. 055-846-376
Open daily for lunch and dinner. Closed Mondays and from August 6 through the end of August. Prices moderate to expensive.

A visit to Fattoria il Palagio transports you back to earlier times, when large estates had their tenant farmers and their *fattoria*, the central farm building of the estate. The restaurant was once an administrative center and a collection point where tenant farmers brought their produce to sell and to tithe a portion to the estate. Fattoria il Pelagio was the largest in the area, belonging to the noble Borghese family. The manor house is still next door. The case *coloniche* or tenant farmhouses have been sold off to be renovated as country retreats. Great old cedar trees that date from the seventeenth century still front the *fattoria*. The large old building has been carefully and precisely restored by energetic Mirella Lorensi, who, with her husband Leonardo Mazzani in the kitchen, and son Mirko as administrator, owns it now. They've converted it into a large restaurant and halls for receptions. Mirko and Mirella will take the interested visitor on a detailed tour, pointing out how the *fattoria* once worked.

The big halls, now restaurants and reception rooms, are beamed and arched in their original state. These were the granaries, with hand-hewed stones covering the openings in the floor through which the grain was poured. A clever device separated the smaller grains from the larger. The smaller grains went straight on to the mill, to be ground into flour for bread and pasta. The larger were set aside as seeds. Names of tenant farmers, the years, and amount of wheat they brought—in *quintale*, or hundreds of kilos—have been left scratched into the old walls; one still visible dates back to 1748. Handmade terracotta floors, worn rich with time and oil, are in place, as is the old step just outside the office where farmers humbly awaited their final accounting from the administrator at his desk in the counting house. The wine cellars have been left with their large chestnut brown barrels, alas now empty, but still commandingly filling the hall. An old glazed terracotta Bacchus decorates a wall in the wine cellar, over the spigots of the wine barrels that have been preserved within. Gently arched windows have been uncovered, brick domed ceilings and walls carefully restored.

The renovations were made tastefully and enthusiastically during the first years of the restaurant. Mirella claims she was simply uncovering the magic of the place. At the same time, Leonardo developed his kitchen skills. They'd more or less inherited their purpose, having helped out in the small restaurant Mirella's parents opened in Scarperia in the 1970s. Mirella is a former elementary school teacher, Leonardo was a metal worker in Florence. When Mirella's parents retired the two of them took over the smaller restaurant, then bought the *fattoria* and started remaking it. Today it has become a landmark institution.

The menu at Fattoria il Palagio is Florentine. A variety of *antipasti* includes various *crostini*, grilled eggplant, tomato/mozzarella combinations, prosciutto and sausages, a *ribollita* and other warm soups in the winter, *panzanella* (bread salad) in the warmer seasons. The Mugello *tortelli di patate* are generously filled, and served in a rich and savory duck sauce. Leonardo makes a good *risotto* in a way that can also save time for the entertaining home cook as well. (See recipe below.) In season, the asparagus *risotto* is especially good.

Main courses include generous helpings of Florentine specialties, *tagliate* (slices of thick steaks), a Florentine beefsteak, or pork cooked in milk. Desserts include the *torta della casa*, always worth trying.

Pappardelle with Duck Ragù
PAPPARDELLE CON SALSA ANATRA

⊛

Serves 6 amply

1 duck, boned and cut up into large pieces
2 tablespoons olive oil
1 sprig sage leaves (about 8 leaves), chopped
2 cloves garlic, chopped
1 carrot, finely chopped
1 celery rib, finely chopped
1 onion, finely chopped
1½ cups tomato sauce
Salt and freshly ground pepper
1 pound *pappardelle*
Grated Parmesan at table

Remove as much fat and skin from the duck as possible. Heat the oil with the sage and garlic, and brown the duck pieces on all sides. Add the chopped carrot, celery, and onion, mix, and continue to simmer for another 10 minutes. Add the tomato sauce, salt and pepper, and simmer gently for 2 hours. If the sauce begins to dry out, add a bit of water. It should remain liquid.

Remove the duck pieces and shred the meat into small pieces. Return the duck to the sauce and keep warm. Boil the *pappardelle* in lots of boiling salted water, drain, mix in the sauce, and serve with grated Parmesan.

Asparagus Risotto
RISOTTO CON GLI ASPARAGI

✦

Serves 6

Some years ago, a fine chef in Chianti taught me how to make *risotto* in a pressure cooker. With his precise instructions, it turned out reasonably well. Leonardo improves on this particular time-saver. He makes his with a pre-cooked *risotto* rice, cooks the rice alone in a low oven for 15 minutes before beginning the actual preparation. For the home cook, when entertaining, it's a way of avoiding lengthy preparation at the last minute.

2 cups pre-cooked *risotto* rice
4-5 cups vegetable or chicken broth
1¼ pounds asparagus
1 onion, chopped
½ cup grated Parmesan, and additional at table

Preheat the oven to 325 degrees.

Put the rice into a flameproof oven casserole and barely cover with broth. Leave for 15 minutes; when you take it out, the rice should still be somewhat hard. Set aside until you begin to prepare the *risotto*. When you begin to prepare the *risotto*, have a pan of boiling broth on a low flame.

Chop the asparagus into ½-inch pieces. Sauté the onion in the oil and add the asparagus. Cook for 5 minutes. Put the pan with the rice on a low flame, and add about half the asparagus mixture, along with enough broth to just cover the rice again, stirring all the while. When the broth is absorbed, add the remaining asparagus, and continue to cook gently, adding broth as needed. When the rice has absorbed the broth, continue to add more, little by little, until the *risotto* is cooked and the rice still firm. Add the cheese, allow to rest a minute, and serve with more Parmesan at table.

2

(3)

(1)

1

(4)

(5)

CHAPTER 6

The Casentino and Tiber Valley

THE CASENTINO AND TIBER VALLEY COMBINE A WORLD OF LOVELY LANDSCAPES AND RETREATS, art, and good food between the headwaters of two great rivers: from here the Arno flows down to Florence and Pisa before reaching the Mediterranean and the Tiber begins its journey to Rome and the sea at nearby Ostia. The Passo della Consuma—the easiest mountain pass through the Apennine range—brings you there. It is a half-hour's drive from Florence through Pontessieve to reach the pass.

On the other side of the pass you'll find the towns of Stia, Poppi, and Bibbiena, and the monasteries of Camaldoli and La Verna, the birthplaces of Michelangelo and Piero della Francesca, and the finest examples of Piero's art.

As you climb the pass, the woods open to views of the valleys and towns below. The austere Romanesque abbey of Vallombrosa lies just off the way with its botanical gardens containing an impressive collection of pines and other Mediterranean plants. In less global times, Vallombrosa was the preferred summer retreat for Florentines escaping the city's torrid heat; the legendary art historian Bernard Berenson had his vacation villa here in an old hunting lodge overlooking the mountain range.

The vast national park of Monte Falterona begins as you descend the pass. It's divided into various forests and parks that extend from the Casentino into the mountains of the Mugello, the Upper Tiber Valley, and neighboring Emilia-Romagna. Long before it was a national park, Dante wrote of "the cool rustic waters of the Casentino that trickle down into the Arno."

Two castles come into view as soon as you head down the mountain to the Casentino. The first, along the road that leads to Stia, is a majestic ruin; upon inspection you can see that it once had fourteen towers surrounded by three walls. The second is the imposing town hall of Poppi that still looms high over the entire valley.

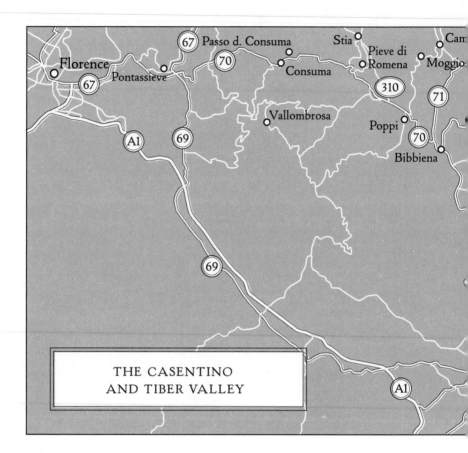

THE CASENTINO
AND TIBER VALLEY

Both were once part of the vast domain of the Guidi counts, rulers over a good part of northern Tuscany from the eleventh to the thirteenth centuries. They had originally come down from Lombardy and built themselves fortified citadels here. One still sees Guidi traces everywhere in Tuscany, from Cerreto Guidi and Vinci in the Montalbano area to the one in Poppi. Some of these castles were remodeled during the Renaissance by the Medici when Florence—through battle or purchase—moved in to dominate the area and alter the political and cultural landscape.

Two battles that turned Florence into a major regional power took place in the narrow valleys of the Casentino and Tiberina. The Battle of Campaldino, in 1289, was ferociously fought just below the town of Poppi. Warriors from Florence, Lucca, Pistoia, Prato, Siena, Volterra, and even Bologna massed against Arezzo. Dante Alighieri served in the cavalry (and writes about it in the *Purgatory*). It was an interesting moment. Politi-

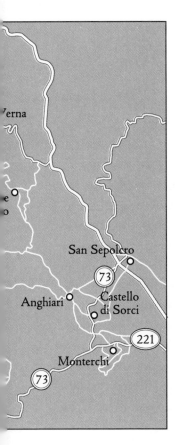

cally, at times it matches our own. The Bishop of Arezzo, it seems, was caught out trying to sell his entire See to the Florentines to ensure a lifetime's annuity for himself and his nephew; he was executed and the Aretinos — i.e., the people of Arezzo — battled Florence to regain their lost pride. They lost even more, both in men and in territory.

A small arrow to the left as you descend the Passo della Consuma indicates the road to Stia. Follow it, and you arrive at the grand Guidi castle ruin. One of the loveliest Romanesque churches in Tuscany lies just a few kilometers beyond. A small sign at the ruin indicates the way to Pieve di Romena. This narrow little road is definitely the best way to approach the noble simple church from the rear. You suddenly come upon the soft gray round apse colonnaded with the most delicate Romanesque columns and blind arches. Ask Signora Cipriani at the house opposite (Tel. 0575-542-027) for the key to see the bare grace and finely decorated column capitals of the church within.

Stia is nowadays best known for its potato *ravioli* and for the *casentino*, a brilliantly colored warm wool cloak produced here. Traditionally worn by monks, mountaineers, and shepherds, during the last century, with the addition of a little fur collar and brass buttons, it became the fashionable winter wrap of the Florentine bourgeoisie. Hand woven in the most flattering bright green or orange (the color of a Sicilian blood orange), the *casentino* is still produced in Stia by a single mill. There are two shops on the fine old square — Piazza Tanucci — that sell them. No longer rough-loomed and hand sewn, the warm cloth is still in great demand, and comes in many bright colors and forms: coats, jackets, hats, and even scuff slippers. There's a comfortable little *trattoria*, Filetto (see page 170), on the same square.

The other imposing castle of the Guidi sits atop the old town of Poppi, jutting out against the skyline like a virtual copy of Florence's Palazzo Signoria. The twelfth-century castle is said to have been the model for the larger Florentine palace. After the Battle of Anghiari in 1440, the Guidi made their formal surrender to the Florentines here. Ponte a Poppi, the commercial center below the old town, has an inviting bar on its main square, Osteria del Tempo Perso (Inn of A Lost Time), where you can learn all about the specialties of the area while you drink your coffee and sample some of them. Cheeses, marmalades, honeys, and pork products are all there for the eating, and for sale as well (Osteria del Tempo Perso, Via Roma 79, Ponte a Poppi, Tel. 0575-529-996. Open daily except Sunday).

From Poppi it's a lovely ride up into the Foreste delle Casentinesi to the monastery and hermitage of Camaldoli. Take the road up through the beech-filled forest through Moggiona where you'll find a well-established little *trattoria*, Il Cedro (see page 172). The monastery and its hermitage, which date back to the eleventh century, are peaceful places, at home in sylvan surroundings. The monastery, a cluster of small hut-like houses around a larger building, was founded as a pilgrimage; the monks were charged since time immemorial with the responsibility to maintain the environment. This they still do well; they may be the most ecologically minded group within the Church. The monks at Camaldoli are strictly vegetarian and grow their own food. They welcome guests and are hosts to inter-faith meetings and other spiritual events throughout the year.

Don't miss the impressive old chestnut-paneled *farmacia/bottega* at Camaldoli. Balsamic bath oils and other therapeutic lotions and creams, honey, and its by-products are on sale. Unlike many other monasteries nowadays, the monks at Camaldoli don't import their potions, but still produce them here according to their own ancient formulas. Ingredients come from botanical gardens on the grounds dating back to the fifteenth century; a small museum room adjacent to the pharmacy details the medicinal and curative offerings over the years. The Camaldoli monks also run—as they always have—a traditional olive mill, the Pieve di Micciano, where oil is pressed today as it was in the thirteenth century. They decant particularly pleasing oil from the *mosto*, the pulp that is left over from the crushed olives. The nearby hermitage, Eremo, has an enticing old library to visit. (Tel. 0575-556-163 for a schedule of events. In addition, the ancient pharmacy selling elixirs and beauty products is open from 9am–12:30pm and from

2:30pm–6pm except Wednesday during the winter. Tel. 0575-556-143)

Bibbiena, another major town in the Casentino valley, has an impressive historic center. From the piazza of the old town there are great views of the entire valley. Even better views can be had from the road leading from Bibbiena to Chiusi del Verna and the monastery of La Verna. From La Verna, the road through the Tiber valley leads to Caprese Michelangelo, San Sepolcro, and Anghiari.

Try to reach the magnificent monastery of La Verna before the tour buses arrive. If you arrive at a quiet moment, it can be a wondrous experience. Dante called it the "rough crag" between the Tiber and Arno rivers. Tradition tells us that Saint Francis received the stigmata here. You'll find a collection of graceful old buildings and chapels housing dozens of the loveliest glazed Andrea della Robbia reliefs. A wide piazza looks out over the valleys and mountains. Walk down to the stream below where there's a shrine to Saint Francis. It's a magical place (Tel. 0575-5341).

I asked one of the younger monks at La Verna, Brother Filippo, how they produced all the many magic curative potions, herbal elixirs, and exotic liqueurs I found on sale there. He couldn't really tell me; with a wry smile, he suggested I look more closely at the labels. While the herbal liqueurs were still produced according to original ancient recipes they were bottled somewhere else and the soaps and bath oils were not really different from the sort of thing one finds in health stores everywhere. "We young priests here," he said somewhat plaintively, "no longer even have the ancient recipes." The monks at Camaldoli, however, do produce the products sold there.

The Tiber valley under La Verna gave birth to two of Italy's most revered Renaissance artists, Michelangelo and Piero della Francesca. Caprese Michelangelo is the birthplace of the former. Michelangelo never spent much time here, but did claim that he had sucked in his love of the traditional chiseling tools with his wet nurse's milk. Caprese was proud enough of its native son to rename the town after him and open a little museum in the house where he was born (Museo Michelangelo, open daily; call 0575-793-776 for hours).

Piero della Francesca was born, and died, not far away, in the small valley town of San Sepolcro. Several of his most exciting works hang in the Civic Museum here. His splendid *Resurrection* and another polyptych of the Madonna and saints make the museum a mandatory stop. Through a large window cut into the museum wall it's now possible to view the *Resurrection* (Aldous Huxley called it simply "the best picture in the world") from the square outside. At night it's lit up (Museo Civico, Via Aggiunti 65, open daily). Just down the street from the Civic Museum, at number 30 via Aggiunti, is the little *trattoria*, Da Ventura (see page 175).

Across the valley from San Sepolcro is the old town of Anghiari. The Battle of Anghiari—which finally and firmly established Florentine rule in the area—was fought in the Tiber valley between the two towns in 1440. It could not have been such an enormous battle as has been claimed; we know that only one life was lost when a warrior fell off his horse. It did gain a firm place in the history of art on a wall in Florence's Palazzo Signoria where Leonardo da Vinci began a noted fresco of the battle. It remained unfinished perhaps because Leonardo had not mastered the art of fresco as he had mastered almost everything else. The unfinished, badly-peeling fresco was later painted over by Giorgio Vasari. Only a few preliminary drawings and a copy by Rubens are left to assure us of its original wonder.

Everywhere in this area, you sense the local reverence for tradition. Stop at the *antico frantoio* (old olive mill), Ravagni, located just outside Anghiari (Antico Frantoio Ravagni, Ravagni 4, Tel. 0575-789-244). The mill still operates as it has since the fifteenth century. The most heavenly aromatic scent from hundreds of years of oil pressing hits you as soon as you walk in. Their oil-pressing method has changed little. The olives are still hauled by hand up an ancient winding wrought-iron staircase to the top level and poured down into a basin with the widest grinding stones I've ever seen. The mash then goes through old mat-lined presses. It drips out as oil into large vats. The steel vats for storing the pressed oil are the single modern addition. (In the past, huge terracotta jars served this purpose.) Francesco Bartolomei, the young son of the family that has owned the mill since the eighteenth century, shows the visitor around. You can buy their lightly piquant oil at the entrance. There is also an inviting tasting room inside, and an outdoor terrace fitted with tables to enjoy the oil with appropriate accompaniment.

Anghiari is an imposing medieval town high on a hill overlooking the Tiber valley and a good place to explore old artisan customs still strong in these parts. The town is well known for its wood and iron workshops, its fine carpenters, famed furniture restorers, stonemasons, handmade textiles, and antique shops. The main street is lined with little *botteghe* for olive oil products and wrought iron.

The annual Mostra Mercato dell'artigianato, from April 25 through May 1 each year, is an artisans' fair that attracts visitors from all over the region. (For further information, call Botteghe Artigiane, 0575-749-279, or the tourist office, 0575-789-522) On August 15th — Ferragosto — an open air dinner and theatrical performance take place in a little square here. Visitors are welcome.

The old local tradition of furniture restoration has led to the establishment of an international school here attended by students from all over the world. The renowned Busatti linen and cotton textiles are made in Anghiari. The shop in the old Morgalanti Palace still has shuttle looms working in its basement and the showrooms upstairs have an impressive display of traditionally designed hand-loomed fabrics and tablecloths.

Immediately coming upon the square under the old town you'll find an interesting little bread shop, Al Cantuccio (Tel. 0575-788-547; open daily except all day Monday and Sunday mornings.). Its *forno a legna* (wood-burning oven) turns out all sorts of bread-based dishes. A few tables at which to enjoy them are scattered about. It is the perfect spot for a light luncheon. Cicalino Gennaioli owns the little *forno* with his wife Domitella; he bakes the bread; she cooks lunch. A thin bread fried in boiling oil, the *ciacia fritta*, is served to crowds on Wednesday market days and Sunday afternoons. Pizzas can be had at lunchtime every day; especially good is the one made with only onion and tomato. There's also a *piatto del giorno*, which changes from day to day, *gnocchi* one day, a pasta or soup on another, and sometimes a lovely stewed *trippa* or *ribollita*. Al Cantuccio also serves a winter *bruschetta* of the popular Tuscan winter kale leaves, *cavolo nero*. The chopped leaves are first cooked gently in a bit of simmering water, then squeezed, salted, and sautéed in fresh olive oil and garlic. Fresh bread is toasted over the open fire, rubbed with half a clove of garlic and dipped quickly in and out of the cooking water. The kale is layered on top. An array of freshly-baked raisin-dotted, anise-flavored biscuits is another temptation. One of the more original restaurants in the area — La Nena (see page 177) — is just up the street.

You'll pass another very popular eating place in the former granary on the estate of Castello di Sorci (see page 180) along the road from Anghiari to Arezzo. The same road takes you to old Monterchi, well worth a visit just to view Piero della Francesca's famous painting, *Madonna del Parto*. In years past it could be viewed in its original home, a remote little chapel in the middle of a field just outside town. Alas, no more. It could not be restored and properly protected where it was; it has been removed to Monterchi to a museum of its own, with explanations and pictorial details of its full restoration. Follow the signs. (Museo della Madonna del Parto, summer, open 9am–1pm and 2pm–7pm; winter 9am–1pm and 2pm–5pm) From Monterchi the road leads directly to Arezzo.

SPECIALTIES OF THE CASENTINO
AND TIBERINA

Like so many traditional dishes elsewhere in difficult mountain regions, specialties of the Casentino and Tiber valley began as smart and tasty ways to make the most of available produce. Even eking out a living was difficult. Vegetables that grew in summer and could be stored in winter provided most sustenance, along with grazing animals and their milk products, mostly cheeses. Many Casentino dishes originated with shepherds who took their flocks each winter down to the more hospitable areas of the Maremma. Food from the Maremma came back with them to the Casentino. They had to pay duties and taxes along the way, often in the form of small cheeses. The tradition of Tuscany's most special cheese, *pecorino*, wandered with them from place to place. Grazing land is perfect here in the warmer months. Casentino shepherds made notable cheeses, and still do so today.

Potatoes and onions, poor man's staples in most places, make appetizing dishes in the Casentino, full of imagination and substance. A local light potato called *patata di cetica* goes into the *ravioli*; *acquacotta* (cooked water), imported from the mountains of Maremma, originally consisted of little more than onions sautéed in oil and covered with boiling water. With today's additions of seasonal vegetables and herbs, it can be as delicious as celebrated French soups. It's an admirable first or main course.

Stone-ground wheat still goes into local bread and the pasta *bringoli*. *Bringoli* are made with only flour and water—no eggs—hand-rolled and pulled into stringy noodles and sauced with *sugo finto* or "fake sauce," a local specialty. It's made to taste like the traditional *ragù*, but austerely without meat.

Lessons learned at our mother's table die hard. At home as children we never ate two starches at a single meal, so pasta stuffed with potatoes seemed a dubious proposition until I tried it. In this traditionally poor country *tortelli di patate* have long been a staple dish. Beef *ragù* goes over it today; before WWII, meat sauce was added only on holidays. I first discovered potato *ravioli* in the Casentino at Stia, but it's popular just across the mountains in the Mugello too.

Another dish of the Casentino and Tiber valleys is the *scottiglia*, an ancient stew of less desirable meat cuts simmered in a red wine and tomato sauce until deliciously edible. Tiny snails — found on bushes everywhere — make another well-considered meal here. The little creatures are cooked for several hours in a rich tomato sauce and then plucked from their shells with a toothpick. The remaining sauce is sopped up with crusty bread.

Wild fennel grows in these valleys in profusion, and is used abundantly to flavor dishes. The *porchetta*, a highly flavored pork roast you'll find at roadside stands throughout Tuscany, usually stuffed with rosemary or sage, is here flavored with wild fennel. One favorite local salami is the *finocchiona*, a pork sausage flavored with wild fennel seeds. The Casentino prosciutto is exceptionally tasty, salty, and lean. A slice resembles a small brown plate.

Casentino is also the land of the spicy *peperoncino*, often used instead of black pepper. A typical *bruschetta* is little more than fresh olive oil on a thick slice of Tuscan bread sprinkled with a mixture of oregano, salt, and piquant *peperoncino* flakes.

Like in other once difficult mountain areas of Tuscany, beans, chestnut flour, and maize find their way into many substantial dishes. Chestnut flour and cornmeal are still ground as they always were, between two (often ancient) stone wheels. In the fall and early winter, wild mushrooms also make their way into almost every dish.

If you've never tasted truly fresh beans at the end of summer, Tuscany is the place to try them. Beans are available — but not the same — everywhere. Tuscans speak about the simple bean, *il fagiolo*, with an endearing ardor elsewhere reserved for more elegant food. The pursuit of that perfect specimen — the delicious fresh local bean — is fervent. Fresh from the plant at the end of summer it has a velvet texture and a skin that's almost imperceptible. Dried beans are a big winter staple and cooked into so many dishes that few beans that are freshly dried at the end of summer last beyond late spring. In Tuscany there is little time for them to really harden or shrivel — the harvest is eaten quickly. The Casentino boasts a small delicately flavored yellow bean, Zolfino, grown in a small area around Poppi and Bibbieno. It is as meltingly smooth as a bean can be. My husband calls this and its Valdinievole cousin, the Sorano bean, "Tuscan caviar." Sorano and Zolfino beans are almost unknown outside their regions; the harvest is tiny. The Zolfino can be bought dearly here, and for bean lovers, the expense is worth it. No soaking is necessary. It is cooked slowly, at a simmer, in a bath of water, sage, garlic, oil, and just a touch of tomato.

Hard biscuits served with *vin santo* are a tradition in these parts much as in the rest of Tuscany. The biscuits are slightly different here; raisins and anise are the favorite flavorings. The local *panino*—elsewhere a sandwich—is an odd form of bread flavored with herbs and raisins; *berlingozzi* are more like hard doughnuts, flavored heavily and deliciously with anise.

STIA

FILETTO

Piazza Tanucci 9, Stia • Tel. 0575-583-631

Filetto is difficult to see from the piazza. Look under the sign saying Folterra, a previous restaurant on the spot. Open for lunch and dinner during the summer months; lunch only in winter. Closed Thursday and Saturday, and the months of June and November. Reservations are recommended for Sunday lunch. Priced moderately.

The Piazza Tanucci in Stia is an elegant old square, ascending gently up to a grand fountain and lovely Romanesque church. Tuscan piazzas that ascend or descend a hill to form a dramatic natural amphitheater (Siena's Campo is the most famous but there are many others) are especially moving. No town-planning board today would approve such an odd plan. Stia's gracious little old square would have undoubtedly been leveled by a modern engineer, so gaze upon it gratefully. It's lovely.

Filetto is a comfortably old *trattoria*. It sits about halfway up on the left of the square. In summers there's outdoor eating space as well. It's a perfect place to watch life on the square and eat a typical meal. The restaurant has been in the Francalanci family for four generations. Even on Thursday, when the restaurant is closed the owner—and cook—can be found next door serving up local cold cuts and cheese at the bar/*tabacchi* the family owns there.

After the *antipasti*, a most typical *secondo* is *tortelli di patate*, the traditional pasta of Stia. The customary sauce is the *ragù*, but one can also eat them in a simple fresh tomato sauce, or just dressed with butter and sage. Other pastas are dressed with *capra* (goat) or *cinghiale* (wild boar) sauce. Filetto's *acquacotta* is a spicy bread soup, made with the addition of chopped pork. A wood-burning kitchen fire provides any number of grilled meats, from ham to lamb.

Potato Tortelli (or Ravioli)
TORTELLI DI PATATE

Serves 8 (about 60 ravioli)

FOR THE DOUGH:
2 cups flour
Good pinch of salt
4 eggs
2 tablespoons olive oil

FOR THE FILLING:
1 pound (about 2) mature fluffy potatoes
2 garlic cloves, chopped
1 bunch parsley leaves, chopped
4 tablespoons extra virgin olive oil
1 tablespoon tomato paste
2 tablespoons grated Parmesan
Nutmeg
Salt and pepper

To make the dough: mix together the flour, salt, eggs and olive oil, knead until flexible and shiny, and roll out into long thin strips to fill for *ravioli*.

To prepare the filling: boil the potatoes, peel them, and mash through potato mill. Mix with all the other ingredients to form a light paste. Lay a scant teaspoon about every 3 inches along the pasta leaves, cover with another leaf of pasta, and slice into rectangular *ravioli* shapes. Make sure each is sealed.

Bring to boil a large pan of salted water and drop in the *tortelli*, several at a time. As soon as they float to the top, remove with a slotted spoon to a warm bowl. Serve with a meat *ragù* or *sugo finto* (see page 174).

MOGGIONA

———— ≫≋:⊚:≋≪ ————

IL CEDRO

Moggiona di Poppi • Tel. 0575-556-080

Open for lunch and dinner. Closed Mondays; reservations recommended.
Prices inexpensive to moderate.

Not far from lower Poppi, on the road to the forest monasteries of Camaldoli and Eremo, is the little town of Moggiona. There you'll find a most typical small restaurant, Il Cedro, snuggled in against the landscape.

Mariangela Tassini is the third generation of her family to run Il Cedro. Her mother still does the cooking and strictly follows the basic culinary rules of her own grandmother. Italians often lament the loss of their traditional cuisine but in almost every out-of-the-way Tuscan town, it's possible to find an *osteria* or *trattoria* that still clings to the old ways. In the Poppi area, Il Cedro does it well.

Peperoncino — that ubiquitous little hot red pepper — flavors almost everything, but judiciously. Curiously, nothing you eat seems overly sharp. Black pepper is used sparingly.

The restaurant reflects the simple peasant kitchen that's always existed in this 700-meter high mountain valley. Main ingredients are the basics: potatoes, onions, and seasonal, locally grown vegetables. In the winter that means cabbage, fennel, artichokes, and *cardo* (cardoons, celery like clusters of bitter stalks of wild artichokes). In other seasons, lighter zucchini are eaten, along with zucchini flowers, dipped in batter, fried, and served. Pasta is mostly with *sugo finto*, the meatless sauce of the Casentino. A meat *ragù*, however, goes over *tortelli di patata*, the simple potato stuffed *ravioli*. As is typical in the area, Mariangela tells you that even today the *tortelli* are a dish for celebration.

In restaurants like this, you discover how different dishes with the same name can be. *Acquacotta* ("boiled water") is a good example. Born in the Maremma by the woodsmen boiling sliced onions to pour over bread for their lunch in the forest, it's taken on more sophisticated dressings everywhere. Different restaurants add a variety of seasonal vegetables and *funghi* when they are available. It is a clever use of the most prevalent vegetables.

At Il Cedro it is still basically an onion and tomato *pappa*, topped with a crusty layer of grated aged *pecorino* cheese.

Il Cedro has its meat dishes, mostly rabbit, local lamb, and game in their seasons. In early spring, when wild fennel begins to pop in the fields, rabbits are stuffed and roasted with it atop slices of garden fennel bulbs. Fennel seeds are also added, and it imparts a heady anise flavor to the already tasty meat.

RECIPES FROM IL CEDRO

"Boiled Water"
ACQUACOTTA

Serves 4-5

Use canned peeled tomatoes in this dish, especially in the winter. One large tin should do. The bread should be Tuscan, i.e. not salted, of stone ground flour, which holds its shape when soaked.

1 pound (about 4 cups) yellow onions, cut in half and thinly sliced
½ cup good olive oil
1¼ pounds (about 6 large) tomatoes, skinned
Salt
1 small hot pepper, or to taste, chopped
1 cup vegetable or meat broth
1 1-pound loaf stale Tuscan bread
1 cup aged grated *pecorino*

Preheat the oven to 400 degrees.

Put the onions into a large pan, add the oil, and sauté quickly over fairly high heat, mixing often, until they are soft and golden. Squash the tomatoes into the onions and add as much hot pepper. Add the broth, and remove from fire. Layer the bread in a terrine or oval dish and pour the soup over it. Sprinkle half the pecorino over the top and put into a hot oven for 10 minutes. Serve with the remaining cheese at table.

"Fake Sauce"

SUGO FINTO

Makes enough sauce for 4 servings of pasta

2-3 yellow onions, finely chopped
1 whole *peperoncino*, finely chopped
3 tablespoons extra virgin olive oil
1 glassful red wine
1¼ pounds tomatoes, peeled, or 1 large (1 pound 12 ounce) can of
    Italian plum tomatoes
Salt
Grated Parmesan at table

Melt the onions, together with some salt and the *peperoncino*, over a slow fire in a pan deep enough to hold the finished sauce. After about 20 minutes, when the onions are soft and just golden, throw in the wine. Raise the heat and allow the liquid to evaporate. Cut up the skinned tomatoes and add to the sauce. Cook over a moderate flame until the sauce is reduced to a fairly thick consistency, about 10 minutes. Taste for seasoning and add salt. Serve over thin pasta with Parmesan.

Fennel-flavored Rabbit

CONIGLIO IN PORCHETTA

Serves 6

1 medium-sized rabbit, cleaned and splayed open
Salt and freshly ground black pepper
Olive oil
2 fennel bulbs, sliced
1 tablespoon fennel seeds
Wild fennel branches, if available
4 cloves garlic, smashed

Preheat the oven to 350 degrees.

Wash the rabbit well, rub inside and out with salt, pepper, and olive oil. Mix the smashed garlic with the fennel seeds. Put the sliced fennel in a bowl with a tablespoon of olive oil and some salt, and mix well. Lay the slices in a layer in a roasting pan, and put the rabbit on top of them. Fill the cavity of the rabbit with fennel seeds and garlic and, if available, a few branches of dried wild fennel. Bake for about 50 minutes. During the last 5 minutes of baking, cover the dish with aluminum foil. The rabbit makes its own juices to spoon over.

SAN SEPOLCRO

DA VENTURA
Via Aggiunti 30, San Sepolcro • Tel. 0575-742-560
Open for lunch and dinner. Closed Sunday evening and Monday.
Prices moderate; reservations recommended for Sunday lunch.

Marco Tofanelli is another of the young third-generation family members to run a typical restaurant in these parts. His grandfather first opened Da Ventura, and over the years Marco has introduced some innovations, even a special menu for vegetarians. The restaurant is a favorite with families of the area out for Sunday lunch.

Da Ventura offers familiar local dishes with variations designed in its own kitchen. Names might be the same, but either the ingredients or way of cooking them are a bit different. One good example is the familiar Florentine *ribollita*, made with a rich vegetable *minestrone* rather than the fairly simple bean soup you find in Florence. It's still served in much the same way, over stale bread and heated in the oven.

In wild mushroom season, Da Ventura offers a salad of *funghi ovoli*. You can see baskets of *ovoli* in most Tuscan markets in early fall. They are pure white *funghi* that emerge from a bright orange coat. At first sight, they are firm orange ovals. Later they develop into delicate white mushrooms. The sooner they are picked and eaten, the firmer the mushroom. Marco Tofanelli makes a salad of them with slices of Parmesan and a dressing of lemon and fresh olive oil. If truffles are in season, he'll add a slice or two of those as well; here the truffle is black.

Hand-rolled *bringoli* pasta is light, of plain white flour and water that absorbs sauce particularly well. Da Ventura serves *bringoli* with a sauce of *pancetta*, sausages, and sliced mushrooms called *sugo alla ghiotta*. (*Ghiotto*, the noun, has a double meaning in Italian; it can mean both a glutton and a delicacy. At Da Ventura I think it means both.)

Antipasti, vegetables, and sweets are offered from open trolleys brought to the table. *Antipasti* include sausages of the area, salads, stuffed vegetables, *sformati*, baked fennel in Béchamel, and a mix of little onions with orange.

RECIPES FROM DA VENTURA

Sausage and Mushroom Sauce
SUGO ALLA GHIOTTA

Makes enough sauce for 6 servings of pasta

1 medium carrot
1 sprig celery
1 small onion
3 tablespoons extra virgin olive oil
2 ounces *pancetta*
½ pound sausage meat (about 2 fresh sausages)
8 ounces fresh white button mushrooms
1¼ pounds skinned and seeded tomatoes (can be tinned)
1 small hot *peperoncino*, chopped (optional)

Chop the carrot, celery, and onion together, and sauté in 2 tablespoons oil in a small pan. Put the remaining tablespoon oil, the chopped *pancetta*, and sausage meat into another pan large enough to hold the finished sauce, and cook until the meat has become browned and crisp, about 10 minutes. Add the chopped vegetables, lower the flame, and sauté until they are just soft, about 10 more minutes.

Add the mushrooms and cook for another few minutes, until they are well coated and just beginning to release their juices. Squeeze in the tomatoes with your hands, add the chopped hot pepper if desired, and cook for 20 minutes over a low flame. Serve with a simple *spaghetti*, or, if available, fresh *bringoli*.

Mushroom Salad

INSALATA DI OVOLI

⚜

Serves 4

Ovoli are one of the rare wild mushrooms, delicate in taste, firm, egg-shaped and covered with an orange skin before they open. The limited supply can be found in the fall months. I've substituted fresh large *champignon* mushrooms, which work wonderfully. The salad should be made at the last minute. Slice both the mushrooms and the cheese with a cheese slicer.

8 ounces fresh large *champignon* mushrooms, cleaned and thinly sliced
3½ ounces Parmesan, sliced as thinly as possible in wide sheets
1 small bunch arugula
Juice of 1 small lemon
¼ cup fresh virgin olive oil
Salt and lots of freshly ground pepper

Place the mushrooms in a wide serving dish. Sprinkle over some salt and lay the Parmesan on top, and leaves of arugula on top of that. Add a good grinding of black pepper, sprinkle the lemon juice, then the oil, over the top. Mix gently and serve.

ANGHIARI

⸺⟫⟪⊚⟫⟪⸺

LA NENA

Corso Matteotti 10-14, Anghiari • Tel. 0575-789-491
Open for lunch and dinner, closed Mondays and first two weeks of July.
Prices are moderate.

The Corso Matteotti is Anghiari's main street. It runs steeply straight up from the main square. La Nena is at the top. Three food-loving partners — cook Palmira Alberti, along with managers Paolo Severi and Sergio Cappetti — do everything here, and know their food well. They took over the long-time *trattoria* some years ago from the previous owner-cook, *nonna* (grandmother) Elvira. Her *sugo finto* still covers the *bringoli*.

Today the partners feel the challenge to find new ways to keep the traditions and be innovative at the same time. So they've added wild berries to the *porcini* mushrooms that make up *risotto Galeotto*. It's fun and delicious. The *sformato selvaggino* is a custard of game purée, served with a sauce that contains local truffles and wild mushrooms. More traditional is the *passato di fagioli*, a thick bean soup with the addition of the thinnest homemade noodles. All the *salumi*—the antipasto cold cuts—are made in the restaurant as well.

RECIPES FROM LA NENA

Risotto with Mushrooms and Wild Berries
RISOTTO GALEOTTO

Serves 6

10 ounces *porcini* mushrooms (can be frozen)

2 cloves garlic, crushed

3 tablespoons extra virgin olive oil

1 small onion, finely chopped

2 tablespoons butter

2 cups *risotto* rice

1 large wine glass white wine

About 4 cups chicken broth

4 tablespoons frozen wild berries (blackberries, wild strawberries,
blueberries) with their syrup

Sliced truffle, if available

2 tablespoons cream

Chop the mushrooms well, and sauté with the garlic in the olive oil, and set aside.

Bring the broth to a boil and keep it simmering on the stove until ready to use. In another pan large enough to hold the finished *risotto*, sauté the onion in the butter, and add the rice. Stir for a minute over a medium flame, and throw in a glass of white wine. Allow the wine to completely evaporate, then add enough chicken broth to cover the rice. Cook, stirring every now and again, adding broth as it is needed. After about 15 minutes of cooking, add the sautéed mushrooms and the wild berries with some of their syrup. Continue to cook until the rice is *al dente*. At the last minute, add the truffle and cream. Mix well and serve.

Bean Soup with Tagliolini
PASSATO DI FAGIOLI CANNELLINI

Serves 4

1 cup *cannellini* beans, soaked overnight
3 cloves garlic
2 sprigs fresh sage
1 medium carrot
1 onion
1 rib celery
4 tablespoons extra virgin olive oil, and additional at table
1 small (6 ounce) can tomato paste
Vegetable stock (or water)
½ pound fresh egg *tagliolini*
Salt and freshly ground pepper

Together with 1 clove of garlic and the sage, cook the soaked beans at a bare simmer in enough water to cover them by about 2 inches. Add a good amount of salt at the last minute.

While the beans are cooking, finely chop the remaining garlic, carrot, onion, and celery and sauté for 10 minutes in 4 tablespoons of olive oil. Add the tomato paste and ½ cup water or vegetable stock. Add the beans and their water, and cook for another 15 minutes until all the vegetables are completely soft. Purée. The soup should be of light creamy consistency to allow the *tagliolini* to cook easily. If need be, add more water or stock.

Add the *tagliolini* and cook for another minute, until the pasta is *al dente*. Serve warm with a good drizzle of fresh oil.

ON THE ROAD TO MONTERCHI

——— ⚜ ———

LA LOCANDA AL CASTELLO DI SORCI

On the road from Anghiari to Monterchi • Tel. 0575-788-022

Open lunch and dinner, closed Mondays. Reservations recommended on weekends. Prices inexpensive.

Not far from Anghiari is an impressive old castle, on whose grounds you'll find one of the simplest traditional restaurants in the area inside the old granary of Castello di Sorci.

La Locanda is a big family affair. This historic seat of the Sorci family was in bad shape when Primetto Barelli bought it in 1970, and began to turn it into the festive place it is today. Now his children have grown up, and are working there. La Locanda is a stone's throw from the castle, which is available for larger celebrations.

The menu is fixed, and it's the kind of meal you'll get at an Italian peasant wedding or baptism. It's a grand *festa* for a pittance: self-service platters put in the middle of the table, piled high, from which to eat as much as you want. Ask for seconds and you'll have them within minutes. Everything served is the typical food of the region: an *antipasto* of local prosciutto, various cold cuts and tomato *bruschetta*, thick slabs of toast smeared with a purée of peeled plum tomatoes gently spiced with hot pepper, garlic, and olive oil. Two *primi* come next, one always homemade *tagliolini*, the other a choice among sauced *polenta*, *risotto*, and, a favorite of mine, thick chickpea soup laden with *quadrucci*, or pasta squares. The main course is a variety of *arostiti* (roasted rabbit, chicken, duck, pork, goose, and turkey) served up on one big platter for the table. The exception is Friday, when traditional *baccala* (salt cod) in a tomato, wine, and fresh olive oil sauce, is the main course. There are roasted potatoes and salads to accompany, and a bottle of wine to boot. To finish, as much *vin santo* as you can drink, accompanied by some homemade dry pound cake, the local *torcole*.

The atmosphere is festive, the sound level overwhelming, especially at Sunday lunch, the day large families celebrate the noonday meal together. Ask for a table on the second-floor enclosed terrace; while a bit narrow, it's the room with the greatest character.

Tomato Bruschetta
BRUSCHETTA DI POMODORO

Serves 4

2 cloves garlic
2 tablespoons olive oil
6 Italian plum tomatoes, peeled and seeded, or 1 (1 pound 12 ounce)
  can peeled tomatoes, chopped into small pieces
Good pinch *peperoncino* (hot red pepper)
1 small bunch basil, chopped
Salt
4 thick slices rustic bread, toasted

Press 1 clove garlic into the oil over a medium fire. As soon as the oil begins to bubble, add the tomatoes (mashing them in the pan) and pepper. Cook until thick. Add the basil and salt, and set aside. Halve the remaining garlic clove, and rub onto the toasted bread. Cover the toast with a spoonful of sauce and serve warm.

Thick Chickpea Soup
PASSATO DI CECI

Serves 4

½ pound dried chickpeas, soaked overnight
2 sprigs rosemary
3 cloves garlic
3 tablespoons extra virgin olive oil, plus additional at table
2 large tomatoes, skinned and chopped
½ cup chicken broth
¾ cup *quadrucci* or small soup pasta, such as *tubettini* or *orzo*
Salt and freshly ground pepper

Cook the chickpeas slowly, in water to cover by about 2 inches, together with 1 sprig of rosemary and 1 garlic clove. When cooked, drain, reserving the water. Purée about ¾ of the chickpeas with enough of the reserved water to make a thick purée. Return the purée and the chickpeas to their pot.

Squash the remaining garlic cloves in the oil over a medium heat. When the oil begins to bubble around the garlic, add the tomatoes and remaining rosemary leaves. Add the chicken broth, and cook for 10 minutes. Purée, and add to the chickpea soup along with the pasta. Cook until it is *al dente*, about 10 minutes. If the soup is too thick, add more of the reserved water or chicken stock. Taste for salt, add a good grinding of pepper, and serve with fresh oil at table.

CHAPTER 7

Valdichiana and Crete Senese

THE VALDICHIANA AND NEIGHBORING CRETE
SENESE ARE TUSCANY AT ITS MOST PHOTOGENIC.
Lying to the east and south of Siena are landscapes of almost unsullied
beauty. The hilly pastures meld into the voluptuous, rounded, crater-etched
hills of the Crete Senese. Few factories and modern housing schemes disturb
the rolling pastures and intermittent woods, the contrast of cypress and red
earth. Ancient towns dot the olive and vineyard laden hills.

I have an odd tendency to divide Tuscany down its middle, not by
mountains, woods, or valleys, but into east and west of the major Flor-
ence/Rome *autostrada*. For whatever reason, trips are confined to one side
or the other of the motorway. This one is to the west, leaving the *autostrada*
at Monte San Savino to a road that passes through Lucignano in Valdichiana, Trequanda, and Montefollonico, then into the hills of the Crete
Senese. There's another town called Lucignano along that way, and other
towns such as Buonconvento, San Giovanni d'Asso, and Asciano. Almost
the entire way has surprises and little traffic. It is filled with unspoiled
hill towns settled in the Middle Ages on Etruscan and Roman ruins still
evident today. Wander through their narrow streets, admire their frescoed
churches, attend a local festival if you're lucky enough to find one. It is the
simple enjoyment of an ancient culture that lingers.

About 10 kilometers south of the *autostrada* exit at Monte San
Savino lies the fortified little village Lucignano, a thick-walled medieval
enclosure with a perfect concentric urban structure like few others in Italy.
Enter one of the four great portals. You'll find a series of ring roads that once
housed the various strata of society. The first ring is the imposing Corso Matteotti with its stately townhouses and a major castle—Le Logge—backing
onto and forming the outer wall. (The weekly market, on Thursdays, runs
completely around this ring road.) Narrow old passageways lead to the
second ring, and a third. At the top is the tranquil Piazza del Tribunale. You

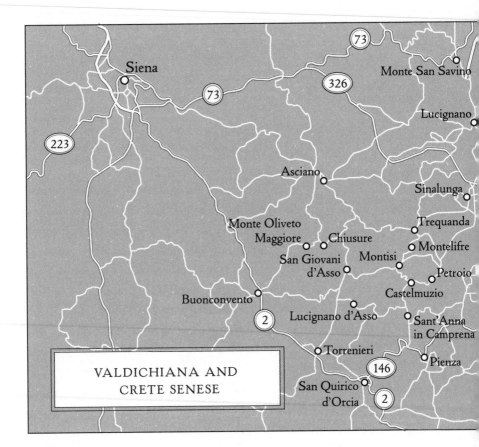

VALDICHIANA AND
CRETE SENESE

can also climb the graceful rounded staircase opposite the castle that brings you to the top. You'll meet several lovely Romanesque churches along the way. The Civic Museum on the Piazza del Tribunale is well worth a visit. It holds one of the more noted shrines of the region, a more than six-foot-high "Golden Tree of Life" (or *Albero di Lucignano*), a Gothic relic of gilded branches, enamels, and flowers of crystal and coral. A few fine Luca Signorelli paintings and an impressive early Crucifixion are a welcome addition to the visit (Museo Communale di Lucignano, Tel. 0575-838-001; summer open Tuesday, Thursday, Friday, Saturday, and Sunday 10am–1pm, and 2:30pm–6 pm; winter, 5:30pm closing on weekdays and 6pm closing on Saturday and Sunday; closed Monday and open Wednesday only to groups).

From Lucignano south, you'll hit a bit of urban sprawl around Sinelunga. Continue on to Trequanda, another fortified town. The castle of the Cacciaconti, a feudal family who once ran the entire area, still dominates the little

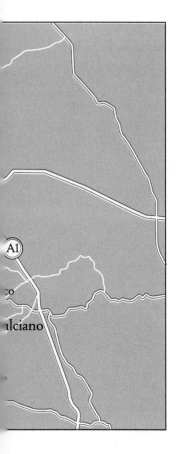

village, its entrance at one end of the main square. A fine *trattoria* just off the main square carries the nickname given to one of the Cacciacontis, Il Conte Matto ("The Crazy Count") (see page 196).

The wonder of the town is a little checkerboard-façaded church that sits off to the side of the main (and only) square. Sts. Pietro e Andrea is filled with rare treasures, paintings by Sodoma, Giovanni di Paolo, and sculpture by Sansovino, and a splendid walnut urn holding the remains of Bonizzella Cacciaconti, a saintly thirteenth-century member of the ruling family. After her death the good Bonizzella was forgotten for a few centuries and but for a miraculous occurrence might still be so. A swarm of bees is said to have formed a hive in a wall niche of the church. When, years after Bonizzella's death, the villagers went to collect honey from the hive they discovered her remains just in back of it giving off a lovely odor of incense. The remains were removed to her present resting place in the walnut urn. The veneration of Bonizzella continues. The church isn't opened very often, but during the second week of May, when swarms of bees are said to reappear at the spot, it is Bonizzella's moment and the time to easily see the lovely single-naved church. At other times, ask at the wine/tourist shop at the corner opposite the church; someone there should know how to find the key.

Near Trequanda are other small hill towns — Montisi, Petroio, and Castelmuzio. They seem like they've been there forever, untouched by earthquake, blight, or man-made wars. Not quite true, but in each of them a number of charming authentic urban centers remain to wander through and admire: Montisi with its thirteenth-century granary, Castelmuzio, reached by a curving two-kilometer drive through lovely woods, and Petroio, noted for its small workshops producing hand-crafted earthenware pots. You'll hit the first workshop as soon as you arrive on the outskirts. A high slim furnace tower tells you you're there; go in through the open doors and discover how the famous large terracotta pots of Tuscany are crafted. Further on into town, a small museum documents and displays the old terracotta produced here. (Museo della Terracotta di Petroio, Via Valgelata 10, Tel. 0577-665-188, summer open Saturday and Sunday 10am–12:30pm and Thursday and Friday 4pm–7pm; winter Saturday and Sunday only, or by appointment).

Midway between Trequanda and Montisi, you'll be struck by a dramatic view of the remains of the old Castello di Montelifre, one of the many strongholds of the Cacciaconti family. It was reduced to a ruin in the fifteenth century, when the Sienese discovered a nest of conspirators there during battle with the Florentines. An able mercenary chieftain managed to reduce it to the remnant it is today. Then, as the story goes, the elders of Siena deliberated how to reward the fine warrior who had saved Siena from great peril. One notable suggested he receive a gold medal, embedded with precious stones; another urged that he be given high office. After much discussion, they solved the problem by making him a saint. They had to kill him to do so, but thought the solution politically and morally fitting. Such are politics and morality. Within the ruined walls, there is a little *borgo* today of reconstructed vacation homes.

Further south, off the road to Pienza, you can visit the ancient monastery of Sant'Anna in Camprena, where "The English Patient" was filmed a few years ago, partly in the beautifully frescoed refectory, painted in the sixteenth century by Giovanni Antonio Brazzi. Better known as Sodoma, he was mentioned contemptuously by Vasari who described his licentious ways with young boys, not an unusual practice among some of the best-known Renaissance artists. The name stuck even after Brazzi married and raised a respectable family.

From the terrace at Sant'Anna, there is a lovely view west to the Crete Senese hills. The former monastery today is an *agriturismo* (subsidized farm-hotel) that offers language and culture classes at a nearby school. It's possible to stay on the premises and study Italian culture for as long as you like. A small shop of home-grown wine and produce forms part of the complex. (For more information, email camprena@diocesimontepuliciano. it or scuolacamprena@bccmp.com. Telephone and fax at the monastery: 0578-748-037. Telephone at Scuola Camprena: 0578-749-404)

Before continuing on to the road that takes you up through the Crete Senese, the little twelfth-century village of Montefollonico lies off the way to the left. Still remarkably intact, the town traces its lineage to Etruscan times, with stone vestiges dating from the sixth century. It is a miniature medieval city. The main alleyways are perfectly preserved. The large old *porta*, almost an antechamber between two arched gates, brings you into town. The Romans pretty well destroyed most of Montefollonico; what you see today are homes and churches built during and after the twelfth century. Montefollonico is also the home of one of the better known inn/ restaurants of Tuscany, La Chiusa (see page 199).

Once you reach the Crete Senese, the change of landscape is remarkable. The bare open pasture is broken only by dramatic craters and evenly spaced tall, graceful dark cypresses. *Crete* refers to the clay soil that has hardened over the years. It is from these voluptuous hills that the ubiquitous "Siena red" building bricks come. The rounded hills are a velvet green covered by rich pasture grass that feeds some of Italy's finest cattle and sheep. Only just after it's been plowed do you see the rich brick-red upturned soil.

As you travel through the Crete Senese, it becomes clear why sheep cheese and lamb are so special here. The hills never lose their rich cushion of green except where they drop off into odd crinkly craters. This is fine cheese country. Pasturing sheep can be seen from March through late fall.

From Montefollonico follow the signs to Pienza, past San Quirico d'Orcia to Torrenieri. Turn right at Torrenieri on the smaller road that leads to San Giovanni d'Asso. It's along this road that a small sign to the right takes you to the tiny town of Lucignano d'Asso where you'll find one of the best offerings of local cheeses at the little *alimentari*, a perfect place to sample them along with the cold cuts of the Crete.

Lucignano d'Asso is little more than a cluster of ancient houses. Upon arriving, you immediately encounter a modest door with an *Alimentari* sign above. At first sight it is totally unassuming, a little shop of staples and vegetables with a second small room offering a few worn wooden tables and chairs. Then you see the vast display of cheeses and sausages. Eraldo Gianneti not only sells the best cheeses of the area but serves lunch here seven days a week. He and his wife are old-timers in these parts, known to everyone. Their son is a sculptor, a few of his pieces lie around at the back. At lunchtime Eraldo's is crowded with lunch arrivals and take-out customers, entire families, workers, members of the local *carabinieri*. Lunch at Eraldo's means a platter of sheep cheeses and cold meats served with good country bread and a simple table wine. The cheeses vary: oval and slightly aged *marzolino di Pienza* is the first cheese of spring, sold either plain or lustily flavored with some local white truffles or sharp *peperoncino*; *roscozino* is a fresh white delicate cheese; Pienza *pecorino delle fosse* is sharper, having been aged in a hole in the ground; another even sharper and longer aged cheese is *morchiata reserva*. It has the aura and taste of an old wine. If you want to be sure about a table, call Eraldo beforehand (Tel. 0577-803-109). Lunch won't be more than a few euros, the temptation to take away favorites will cost more. The prosciutto and sausages come from farmers nearby.

From Eraldo's and Lucignano d'Asso, head back to the crossroad at Torrenieri and continue along the old Roman highway, Via Cassia, to Buonconvento. The old town of Buonconvento lies flat alongside the Via Cassia. It's a village of enormous charm, a few narrow streets of medieval splendidly ornamented red brick palaces that give the town a fine aristo-cratic air. You immediately sense that the old *borgo* well reflects its name, which means a happy, fortunate community of good souls.

At Buonconvento the old Roman highway coincides with the medieval Francigena, the pilgrim route to Rome from northern Europe. Buoncon-vento was a stopover along the way. Behind the main Via Socino are medi-eval alleyways; Via Oscura ends in a delicious little square where summer dinners are held and other festivities take place. A traditional festival of grain threshing is held here in July, and on the third and fourth Sundays of September, the *Sagra della Valdarbia* takes place when local specialties are offered for tasting and costumed folklore events engulf the town.

Henri VII of Luxemburg—known here as Arrigo VII—is some-thing of a mythical figure in Buonconvento. On his way to his corona-tion as Holy Roman Emperor in Rome in the early fourteenth century, after causing quite a bit of trouble in the area, he died here. Had he lived, a plaque on Buonconvento's city hall assures us, he might have realized Dante's "magnanimous illusion," to achieve the "*aggrandizemento*" and "peace" of all Italy. *Sic transit.* There is a rabbit dish named after him today at Da Mario, a most original local restaurant along Via Soncino.

Several interesting shops line the main street. The most tempting is the Dolcezza di Nanni, a bread and pastry shop that grew out of Nanni's old bread *forno* to become an international business that today supplies homemade biscuits and cakes to Queen Elizabeth, Harrods of London, and other illustrious clients. Floriana Giuliana, Nanni's wife, and her help are all sunshine, brightly dressed in Floriana-designed smocks with caps to match. Among the wares — in addition to breads leavened with their own yeast — are various fruit and citrus-flavored cakes, homemade *cantucci*, and other biscuits with the most Tuscan names such as *ossi di morto* ("bones of the dead") and *brutti ma buoni* ("ugly but tasty"). It's a cheery little shop where local gossip and friendly exchange go on all morning.

Across the street from Nanni is the Cantiniere Ghiotto, where owner Barbara Isolani is happy to tell you where all her local specialties come from and what is special about the different sausages, honeys, cheeses, jams, and other wares for sale here. And up the street you'll find the *trattoria* Da Mario (see page 202).

The road from Buonconvento takes you to the noble abbey of Monte Oliveto Maggiore, the major attraction of the area. Travel back through the soothing landscape of the Crete Senese into the tranquil woods surrounding the famous monastery. Monte Oliveto Maggiore is likely to be crowded at times but is surely worth the visit even in high season. The grand fourteenth-century Benedictine monastery is a model of Renaissance architecture with a lovely cloister extravagantly frescoed by Luca Signorelli and Giovanni Antonio Bazzi (Sodoma). The frescoes have an almost modern feel. The long walk down from the great gated entrance to the abbey through the cypress-lined road is lovely; the climb back up is not nearly as challenging as it looks. The monks are still hard at work producing most of the things you'll find in the small shop: honeys, wines, liqueurs, and various elixirs. (I highly recommend the orange honey.) Skin and beauty products sold here are made elsewhere (Monte Oliveto Maggiore; summer, open daily and Sunday 9am–noon and 3pm–6pm, winter hours are the same, but closing at 5pm; Tel. 0577-706-611 or fax 0577-707-670 for schedule of Mass).

From Monte Oliveto it's a short drive to Chiusure, a pretty old terracotta village, where the little Locanda Paradiso (Tel. 0577-707-016) an inviting light-lunch stop. The front room includes the regulars at tables in front of the bar, looking like a nineteenth-century Tuscan Macchiaioli painting, *chiaroscuro* with touches of color. Walk through to another little kitchen room, fire burning, where you can sit and eat a *ribollita*, or a plate of *pici*, the local pasta, or some of the fine *pecorino* and sausages of the area.

At San Giovanni d'Asso, you'll find an enticing park, Bosco della Ragnaia, that has been cut out of the woody landscape by Sheppard Craig, an American artist living here. With the help of local youngsters Craig has developed an array of alluring walks and small tranquil spaces through an eight-hectare forest. The walks are lined with local building blocks of tufa, the volcanic rock from which so many Etruscan tombs are built. You don't immediately notice the enormous work that has gone into sculpting a garden in a wood. It's only when you become aware of an umbrella pine that spreads majestically from a lonely, soaring, bare curved trunk that you realize it's all been planned and worked out. The small sculpted spaces are marked by enigmatic engraved thoughts: "Everywhere you can see a part... nowhere can you see all...." Four engraved stones on the "Hill of Painted Posts", tell us, as Craig suggests, how "things happen:" "Always, Sometimes, Never, Often." Another terracotta tile reads *aporia*, the Greek word for doubt. The garden isn't gated; entrance is free. The only admonition on the welcoming sign asks the visitor not to smoke.

San Giovanni d'Asso is also a commercial center for the delectable white truffle of the area. A truffle festival is held every mid-November and the town has recently opened the first museum in Italy dedicated to the light-colored little tuber (The Museo del Tartufo, Piazza Gramsci 1, Tel. 0577-803-101; open weekends 10am–1pm and 2pm–6pm. During season you can also arrange a truffle excursion: Assotartufi, Tel. 0577-803-076).

Another stop — or at least pass-by — in San Giovanni d'Asso is the *pieve* of San Pietro in Villore, a little eleventh-century church at the end of the old town. It is permanently closed but worth passing to see the façade, a fine example of the many local *pieve*, simple rural churches with exteriors decorated with the earliest kind of Romanesque symbols.

The road from San Giovanni d'Asso to Asciano is another scenic drive through the Crete Senese. As you arrive in Asciano, directly in front of you is the basilica of Sant'Agata. Atop an imposing staircase, the church is set well above the town. Here is the main town of the Crete Senese, though no longer the great commercial center it once was. In the past, artisans and farmers sold their wares and shared their skills at the weekly market. You could hire a *segatino* here, a man who would cut your overgrown grass with his small moon-shaped *falcia*, or sickle. Here too the potter sold his terracotta pots, the hat and shoe makers sold their goods, and tanners their sheep hides. Remnants of what once was can still be found on the second Sunday of every month at a handicraft market.

A walk down the main street, Corso Matteotti, brings you past the old civic tower and its imposing clock, to Palazzo Corboli, an old noble home that now houses the Civic Museum. Within you'll find a handsome collection of sacred art, including a work by Duccio, a little crucifix by Giovanni Pisano, and two beautiful wooden angels of the thirteenth century. It is an impressive collection. (Museo Civico Archeologico e d'Arte Sacra, Corso Matteotti, open all year, but call to make sure. Tel. 0577-719-524.) Next door, in the same *palazzo*, is Locanda del Ponte del Garbo (see page 206), serving local specialties and Neapolitan pizzas.

From Asciano, the old Laurentana road passes through the last of the Crete Senese and leads you to Siena.

SPECIALTIES OF VALDICHIANA
AND CRETE SENESE

Some of the world's finest beef comes out of the Valdichiana. The hefty white Chianina steer—named after the local Chiana valley—has become one of the more prolific beefs everywhere, but nowadays is bred less in Tuscany itself. The breed, known for its succulent, less fibrous meat, spread throughout Tuscany and later to the world from its origins near Trequanda. The Chianina provides the beef lover's dream, the famed Florentine beefsteak. A restaurant that serves real Chianina will note the fact on its menu.

Once upon a time Chianina steers pulled Etruscan plows, were praised by Roman poets, and sculpted by Roman artists. Only a few years ago, one still saw yoked pairs of Chianina steers slowly pulling the same wooden plows you find on ancient Roman urns. Nowadays, the white steers mostly just loll on the pastures.

The province is home to another unique animal, the Cinta Senese, a wispy black wild pig sporting an odd wide white band around its middle (hence the appellation *cinta*, or belt). Nowadays, it is cultivated but remains free-roaming. Cinta pigs have become a protected species and are farmed throughout the Siena area. This particular pig has been around for hundreds of years. Ambrogio Lorenzetti included one in his famous fresco *Buon Governo* (Good Government) that covers a large wall in Siena's Palazzo Communale. The Cinta Senese feeds in open woodland on acorns and tubers. Slaughtered young, it provides pungent meat that is seasoned with local herbs to make the many preserved pork products of the area. A blood sausage, *buristo*, and a spicy boiled mélange of pork parts called *soppressata*, are especially tasty. The fennel-flavored *finocchiata*, a sausage seasoned with fennel seeds, is firm and rosy, slimmer than in other parts of Tuscany. *Pan'unto* is also something to try, especially in winter; it is little more than a slice of good thick farm bread smeared with the lard of the Cinta Senese and roasted in a wood fire oven, a traditional farm dish.

Lamb and cheese figure strongly in the local cuisine. The sheep of the Crete Senese provide a tasty rack of lamb along with some of the finest *pecorino* and *ricotta* in all of Italy. The *pecorino* is especially known for its aromatic flavor that results from open grazing on the grassy knolls of the Crete. Added tastes, such as hot little red peppers and local white truffles, are recent innovations. The latest "designer cheeses" aren't just a fashion; they have added variety and quality to ubiquitous Tuscan cheeses. Sardinian shepherds can claim the credit for making Siena *pecorino* so good. They arrived as migrants in the mid-twentieth century from their impoverished island. After some were allegedly involved in a spell of lucrative but hazardous kidnappings of rich residents for high ransoms, the Sardinian shepherds, on abandoned farmlands, revived the ancient art of unadulterated cheese-making that dates from the Etruscans. The late-arrival Sardinians have now become well-to-do land owners and sheep farmers throughout the area. A large variety of delicious new cheeses is now produced here, from fresh white *ricotta* and *raviggiolo* and mild *pecorino* to the sharper aged variety that can be both eaten at the table or grated onto pasta. They come with red or black rinds. The red means *semistagionato*, i.e., aged for about three months; the black designates the more mature cheese of Pienza, aged for at least six months. There's one great cheese aged in a cave called "*del grotto.*" Cheeses of all ages are served with a variety of piquant marmalades and honeys as a nice sweet course to finish dinner.

The Crete Senese is also one of Tuscany's prime areas for the white truffle. *Bianco di Crete Senese* affords a lucrative livelihood today to farmers around San Giovanni d'Asso. The season begins in September and goes on through December. The major moment is in mid-November at the truffle festival. Tuscan truffles, especially those of San Giovanni and San Miniato, now rival those of Piemonte. You'll find wild mushrooms here, too, especially *porcini*, on fall and winter menus.

The pasta specialty of the area is the *pici*, a slim pasta hand-rolled and elongated in alternating movements by practiced hands. The skill has been inherited from centuries of forebears. It resembles the *bringoli* of Casentino and the Tiber Valley, just a touch more delicate. The width of *pici* differs from cook to cook, and community to community even within the province. I've eaten it rolled to the size of half a little finger in Pienza, and in matchstick widths nearby. *Pici* is usually served with a pungent garlic/tomato sauce called *aglione* or a less savory *ragù*, but it goes well with every kind of sauce.

TREQUANDA
———— ᵕᵕ⁝⊛⁝ᵕᵕ ————

IL CONTE MATTO

Via Maresca 1, Trequanda • Tel. 0577-662-079

Lunch and dinner daily; closed Tuesdays and month of January.

Prices moderate. Reservations recommended.

Il Conte Matto, or "The Crazy Count" (the people of Trequanda always considered the ruling Cacciaconti family mad, hence the name) is just off the main Garibaldi square in Trequanda. It has belonged to the Arrigucci family since 1983, when Chiara and Davide's grandmother closed her bar to open the first (and still only) restaurant in this small town. It is just down the street from the Cacciaconti castle on the main square. The restaurant specializes in the favorites of the area during the seasons they appear. Uncle Libio Graziani runs the kitchen, applying the basics and improvising the recipes of Grandmother Tosca's original *cucina*. Chiara, who runs the dining room, calls her grandmother's dishes still the best of the menu.

An antipasto of local *salumi* made from the wild Cinta Senese pig begins a meal; the local prosciutto, *pancetta*, and *salumi* laced with seasoned fat seem more savory in these parts. There are also *crostini di cacciotta*, toasted bread with a slice of melted soft cheese sprinkled with local truffles.

I found the summer version of *pappa al pomodoro* the lightest I've eaten anywhere. The simple vegetable and tomato broth is full of delicious vegetable tastes and crusts of bread. The hand rolled *pici* come with whatever sauce you choose; one is just some simple fried garlic, super fresh olive oil, breadcrumbs, and salt.

Eggplant Custard with Tomato and Basil Sauce
SFORMATINO DI MELANZANE CON
POMODORO E BASILICO

Serves 4

You can prepare this textured custard in a baking dish or 4 large individual molds. If you use a baking dish, slice the custard onto a serving platter and pour the sauce over it. The individual molds can be turned out onto the sauce.

FOR THE CUSTARD:

1 pound eggplant, peeled and coarsely chopped
Extra virgin olive oil
¾ cup heavy cream
1 egg, plus one yolk
3 heaping tablespoons grated Parmesan, plus additional at table

FOR THE SAUCE:

1½ pounds (about 4 large) ripe tomatoes, peeled and seeded
3 sprigs basil, chopped, and some additional whole leaves for garnish
1 tablespoon red wine vinegar
Salt and freshly ground pepper

Preheat the oven to 300 degrees.

Put the eggplant into a colander, mix some salt through it, and leave to rest for at least half an hour in order to rid it of any bitter juices. Squeeze it dry in a towel, then sauté gently in 2 tablespoons olive oil until soft. If need be, add a bit of boiling water and allow to cook out. Place the eggplant, the cream, the egg, egg yolk, and Parmesan into a food processor and blend until amalgamated.

Put the mixture into individual molds or a baking dish, and place in a *bain marie* of boiling water. Bake for half an hour, if individual molds, or 45 minutes if using a baking dish. Test for doneness by sticking a sharp knife into the custard. If it comes out clean, it's done. Cool well.

Meanwhile, blend the tomatoes and basil together, and pour into a bowl. Mix in the vinegar, and add salt and pepper to taste. Serve the custard with the sauce, garnished with fresh basil leaves. Serve with more sauce and Parmesan at table.

Summer Tomato Soup
PAPPA AL POMODORO

Serves 4

1 large onion, chopped or coarsely sliced
1 rib celery, sliced
2 cloves garlic, sliced
1 carrot, sliced
2 tablespoons extra virgin olive oil, plus additional at table
1 bay leaf
1 bunch parsley leaves, chopped finely
1 small hot *peperoncino* (red pepper), seeds removed, chopped
½ cup white wine
4 cups vegetable broth
5 sprigs basil leaves, chopped
¾ pound tomatoes, peeled and sliced (about 2 medium)
Salt and freshly ground pepper
3 small slices rustic bread, cubed and toasted
Grated Parmesan

Sauté the onion, celery, garlic, and carrot in 2 tablespoons olive oil for about 5 minutes. When they begin to soften add the bay leaf, parsley, and *peperoncino*. Add the white wine and continue to cook until it evaporates. Add the vegetable broth, bring to a boil, and add the chopped basil leaves and the sliced tomatoes. Lower the flame and cook for half an hour. Remove the bay leaf. Place the toasted bread in the bottom of a soup tureen, pour the soup over it, add Parmesan and a dripping of olive oil and serve warm or at room temperature.

MONTEFOLLONICO

———— ⚜ ————

LA CHIUSA

Via della Madonnina 88, Montefollonico • Tel. 0577-669-668

Fax 0577-669-593; Email info@ristorantelachiusa.it

Lunch and dinner daily; closed Tuesday. Expensive.

Reservations recommended.

La Chiusa would be my choice for the pricey stop along the way. The restaurant/inn — in a beautifully restored old olive mill — sits under the small village of Montefollonico, with a view from its windows of nearby Pienza and Montepulciano. There are fifteen rooms to let, some of them with a jacuzzi and open fireplace in the bath.

Owner/chef is Dania Mansotti, a chic and lively Florentine. She manages her kitchen dressed straight out of a fashion magazine. The food is stylish too. Dania turns traditional local fare into highly refined dishes. Lamb is coated with rosemary, garlic, and *pancetta* before going into the oven in a bath of red wine. Beef is large and thick, cut from the fine Chianina of the area. Dania spent a good part of her youth by the sea. While a good distance from the sea, La Chiusa is notable for its seafood. *Zuppa di teste*, an incredibly rich broth made with heads of scampi, is served over toasted whole-wheat bread slices topped with a sliver of Parmesan and two large crayfish. The soup is a meal in itself.

Dania's thick puréed chickpea and pasta soup is topped with crayfish for an added taste. The freshly-made *pici*, half a little finger round, are coated with a special *ragù*. A local woman rolling *pici* in front of your table is a featured presentation in the dining room. Artichokes, a major winter and early spring product of the area, are stuffed with puréed artichokes and capers, served on a large platter generously dripped with a syrupy reduced balsamic vinegar sauce. Sweet balsamic vinegar, not too long ago known only in the Emilia-Romagna region of Italy, is nowadays a mainstay of kitchens throughout Tuscany.

Dania showed me how to reduce balsamic vinegar to syrup. A jam thermometer is a necessary tool in order to save the sauce from turning into hard and brittle sugar. Begin by pouring 1½ quarts of vinegar into a small saucepan. Bring it to a boil and keep a watchful eye on it as it cooks down. After fifteen or twenty minutes, it will begin to coat a spoon. Keep an eye on the temperature. When it reaches a soft ball consistency (about 230 degrees), remove it from the heat and cool it. It keeps forever.

Artichoke Hearts Stuffed with Artichoke Purée
CARCIOFI RIPIENI

Serves 6

If you have leftover stuffing, add some mayonnaise and serve as a pate on crackers with drinks before dinner.

3 tablespoons capers, packed in salt if available; otherwise, in vinegar
10 large globe artichokes, with their stems
2 large lemons
6 tablespoons extra virgin olive oil, plus additional for drizzling
2 cloves garlic, smashed
2 tablespoons breadcrumbs
Dry white wine
½ cup reduced Balsamic vinegar syrup (see above)
Salt and freshly ground pepper

Drain and soak the capers in water, whether they are in vinegar or salt. Fill two large bowls with cold water and add the juice of a lemon to each, saving the juiced halves to rub the artichokes. Slice the stem from each artichoke and rub all the cut sides with a lemon half. Peel each stem to the light inner core, slice, and toss into one of the bowls of acidulated water.

Pluck off the outer leaves from each artichoke until you reach the pale green tender leaves inside. Trim around the bottom. Slice 6 of the 10 artichokes from the top to about 2 inches in height, scoop out the center with a sharp knife, and toss them into the second bowl of water. Cut the four remaining artichokes into quarters, and remove the fuzzy core. If they are very large, cut in half again. Add to the stem pieces in the first bowl of water.

In a large sauté pan, heat 3 tablespoons of the olive oil and add the smashed garlic cloves. When the oil around them begins to bubble, add the drained stem and artichoke pieces from the first bowl, and cook for about 10 minutes, adding about half a glass of water and allowing it to cook out. The artichokes should then be fairly soft. Purée the entire contents of the pan and set aside.

Mix the breadcrumbs into the purée. Drain the capers from their soaking water and purée. Add to the puréed artichokes, taste, and add salt and freshly ground pepper.

Remove the remaining 6 artichokes from the water and dry well, gently pressing the leaves outward to form a good cavity. Fill each with a round of the stuffing and place in a pan just large enough to hold all six. Pour half a glass of water around the artichokes, and then add enough wine to bring the liquid up to a touch beneath the filling. (Don't get the filling wet.) Drip the remaining oil over the top, cover and seal with some aluminum foil, and cook gently for about 15 minutes, until the hearts are cooked. Keep warm.

With a small spoon, drip some rounds of the balsamic syrup on each serving plate and place the artichoke in the middle. Serve warm.

Roast Leg of Lamb

AGNELLO AL FORNO

Serves 6

1 leg of lamb (about 5 pounds)
2 ounces *pancetta*, chopped
3 sprigs rosemary
2 garlic cloves
Salt
2-3 glasses dry red wine

Heat the oven to 450 degrees.

Bring the lamb to room temperature. Blend the *pancetta*, rosemary, garlic, and salt together into a paste, and rub all over the leg.

Put the lamb in a deep roasting pan and bake for about half an hour. Remove from oven and pour over the red wine. Replace, lower the heat to 350 degrees, and bake for another half an hour.

Remove the lamb to a serving platter, and, over a high flame, reduce the liquid remaining in the pan to a sauce consistency. Serve in a separate sauceboat to pour over the sliced lamb.

BUONCONVENTO

DA MARIO
Via Soncino 60, Buonconvento • Tel. 0577-806-157
Lunch and dinner daily; closed Saturdays. Inexpensive.
Reservations recommended.

Da Mario is a family restaurant par excellence. Mario Pallassini died some years ago, but his wife Alfa—now nearing 90—still runs the kitchen. Grandson Christian invents new dishes, such as *ragù* of rooster crests (I did not ask how many roosters lost their crests for one *ragù*) and a rabbit stewed in red wine, in homage to Henri VII, who died in Buonconvento in the fourteenth century. Christian's mother Anna and her sister Nara alternate between the kitchen and the dining room, mixing with the regulars. Two other grandsons run the upstairs and downstairs dining rooms, and in the summer, are out back serving in the large courtyard.

You are never quite sure here who is family and who's paying. A few single men come for lunch and dinner every day; others—usually workers on a local building site—arrive in groups for the evening meal. Beyond that there are local and foreign guests who've discovered the good simple food of this very basic but imaginative *trattoria*. The room downstairs fills early; late-comers are accommodated upstairs. Everyone hugs hello and goodbye. All in all, it promises a fun evening.

There is a single menu atop the refrigerated showcase just outside the kitchen. Few look at it. Most eat what Nara or Anna suggests. Try one of Christian's new concoctions that usually turns out to be a perfect combination of ingredients (such as a thick bean and mussel soup, the mussels floating in their little boat shells amid the beans). First courses include a soothing lentil and rice soup, or *tagliatelle* with hare sauce. The *pici* are topped with *aglione*, a savory sauce of concentrated tomato laced with garlic. You can also have the *pici* with a simple *ragù*. Another of Christian's deliciously innovative dishes is a guinea hen in citrus sauce. There's also a pork fillet richly sauced in balsamic vinegar. Just listen to what's offered and dine on the dish of the moment.

Pici with Thick, Garlicky Tomato Sauce
PICI AGLIONE

Serves 6

2 cups canned, peeled Italian plum tomatoes
4 cloves garlic
½ cup extra virgin olive oil
Salt and freshly ground pepper
1 pound *pici* or *spaghetti*
Toasted breadcrumbs

Drain the tomatoes. Cut them open to release inner juices. Chop and drain again. Smash 2 of the garlic cloves, cut them into slivers, and put them into a heavy pan with the oil. When the oil begins to bubble around the garlic, add the tomatoes and a good amount of salt and pepper.

Coarsely chop the remaining 2 cloves of garlic, and add to the sauce. Cook for about 15 minutes, until the garlic is softened and the sauce nice and thick. Add more salt and pepper to taste.

Cook the *pici* or other pasta in well-salted boiling water until just *al dente*, drain, and mix with the sauce. Top with toasted breadcrumbs and serve.

Loin of Pork in Balsamic Vinegar

MAIALE AL ACETO BALSAMICO

❋

Serves 6

1 onion, sliced
3 tablespoons extra virgin olive oil
½ cup balsamic vinegar
Pinch of sugar
1 small sprig of fresh sage leaves, chopped
1 loin of pork, about 2 pounds
Salt and freshly ground pepper

Sauté the onion in 1 tablespoon of the olive oil, add the vinegar and a pinch of sugar. Cook until the onion is completely soft and purée. Set aside.

Heat the sage in the remaining 2 tablespoons of oil. Brown the loin on all sides and cook for 5 or 6 minutes. Remove the fillet and slice into ¾-inch slices. Put back into the pan, pour the balsamic dressing over the meat, and cook until the pork is done, another 5 minutes.

Rabbit in Wine Vinegar

CONIGLIO DI ARRIGO VII

❋

Serves 6

1 rabbit, cut into 8 serving pieces
Extra virgin olive oil
3 cloves garlic
4 sprig rosemary
1 cup red wine vinegar
½ cup chicken stock
1 bunch parsley leaves
6 thin slices toasted rustic bread
Salt

Prepare this dish in a heavy pot wide enough to hold the rabbit pieces in one layer. Salt the rabbit and put into the pot. Pour 2 tablespoons of olive oil and 2 chopped garlic cloves over the rabbit, mixing to coat the rabbit pieces entirely. Add 3 sprigs of rosemary. Heat, turning the pieces over to brown a bit.

Pour the vinegar into the pot and cook over a high flame until the vinegar is reduced by half. Add the chicken stock, lower the heat, and cook gently, partially covered, mixing often. Add water if necessary as the dish cooks. Toward the end, add the fourth sprig of rosemary. Chop the remaining garlic clove finely with the parsley leaves and add when the rabbit is almost cooked, in about an hour.

To serve, place a slice of toast on each plate, and top with a piece or two of rabbit and a good dousing of sauce. The rabbit can also be served with rice or mashed potatoes instead of toast.

Guinea Hen in Citrus Sauce
FARAONA IN AGRUMI

Serves 6

1 large guinea hen, in 8 pieces
2 navel oranges
2 unwaxed lemons
3 tablespoons olive oil
1 small onion, chopped
2 sprigs sage leaves, chopped
2 cloves garlic, smashed and chopped
½ cup cognac
Salt and freshly ground pepper

Remove the fat from the guinea hen, then wash and pat it dry. Season the pieces with salt and pepper and set aside.

Remove the zest from the oranges and lemons, slice it into thin strips, and drop into boiling water for about 30 seconds. Drain. Juice the oranges and lemons.

In a large pan with cover, heat the oil with the chopped onion, and all but a little of the sage and garlic. Allow to bubble for a minute and add the guinea hen. Brown the pieces well on all sides. Add the cognac and continue to cook until the cognac evaporates. Add the orange and lemon juice, the zest, and cook over a medium heat, covered, for about half an hour, until the guinea hen is almost done.

With a slotted spoon remove the guinea hen and reduce the liquid over high heat until it is a thick sauce. Replace the poultry and cook slowly until the meat is completely tender. Taste for salt and pepper, place the pieces on a serving dish, and pour the sauce over them.

ASCIANO

LOCANDA DEL PONTE DEL GARBO
Corso Matteotti 126-128, Asciano • Tel. 0577-718-011
It's a pensione too, thus is never closed. Inexpensive.

Gianni Veglio and his wife Giovanna opened their restaurant here after years of owning Italian restaurants in Latin America and Germany. They wanted a small friendly town in Tuscany, found Asciano, and opened Locanda del Ponte del Garbo. The restaurant adjoins the eighteenth-century Palazzo Corboli, the museum of sacred art in Asciano. Gianni Veglio is a displaced Sicilian from Salerno, and you find flavors of his origins tapping into the food here. He brings his incomparable mozzarella and *ricotta* cheeses from the south each week; his pizzas are thick and hearty as in Naples, and come in tastes that are just a bit different, like a whiff of pineapples added to prosciutto, mozzarella, and tomatoes—Tuscan food with a southern touch.

Gianni is the cook, Giovanna runs the large dining room. The *fegatini* for the *bruschetta* are made with chicken livers and white wine, a tasty variation on the usual red. There are interesting soups on the menu, including both broccoli and potato. Mostly the menu features local specialties, *pici* (with an anchovy sauce) and different wild game of the area. You'll find fish on the menu as well.

Chicken Liver Bruschetta
FEGATINI BRUSCHETTA

Serves 6

This particular version of a very Tuscan *crostini* or *bruschetta* has a special tang. If it seems too acerbic, add a bit more cream.

½ pound chicken livers
White wine vinegar
2 tablespoons extra virgin olive oil
1 shallot, chopped
½ cup dry white wine
1 tablespoon cream
18 capers under salt, soaked and drained
6 slices toasted Tuscan bread
Salt and freshly ground pepper

Marinate the livers in vinegar for half an hour. Drain, pat dry, and chop up a bit. Heat the olive oil with the shallot. When the oil begins to bubble around the shallot, add the chicken livers, and sauté. Add a good bit of salt and pepper. After a minute or two, add the wine and cook for about 15 minutes, until the wine has evaporated and the livers are cooked through. Remove from the pan and chop well, either by hand or in a food processor. Add the cream and mix. Spread the liver on the toast and top each toast with 3 capers.

Broccoli Soup

ZUPPA DI BROCCOLI

Serves 4

1¼ pounds broccoli (about 1 head)
2 tablespoons cream
1½ ounces slivered almonds
Salt and freshly ground pepper

Peel the broccoli stems and chop them coarsely. Break up the flowerets. Boil a pot of salted water, just enough water to cover the broccoli, and add the broccoli. Cook until soft, around 10 minutes. Drain, reserving the water. Blend the broccoli with a bit of its water and put back into the pot. Add the cream, and as much water to make a dense soup. Put the almonds in a mortar or pulverizer and pound into a paste. Add the paste to the soup, along with salt and freshly ground pepper. Heat and serve.

e

b

c

CHAPTER 8

Montelupo Fiorentina and San Miniato on to Val d'Era

T HE VALLEYS TO THE WEST OF FLORENCE TEEM WITH SMALL INDUSTRY, NOT A PARTICULARLY enticing lure for the tourist. But go beyond the crowded valley to find pleasant hills and old hill towns. Montelupo, where this trip begins, is the center of Tuscany's artisan ceramic industry. San Miniato, the next stop, has come to rival Piemonte in its rich truffle production. Montopoli's aristocratic past under Florentine rule endows its narrow streets with elegance. Palaia and Peccioli in Pisa's Val d'Era hold some nice surprises as well. The trip is almost entirely through little traveled countryside.

Montelupo Fiorentina is a short drive down the Arno along the Florence-Pisa-Livorno (Fi-Pi-Li) *superstrada*. It is my favorite place to buy wedding gifts. The town and its immediate surroundings are filled with small artisan workshops making highly decorative, old-fashioned platters, jars, and bowls with traditional patterns in much the same way as was done during the Renaissance. The high art of tin-oxide glazed ceramics — *maiolica* — arrived in Pisa from Spain with Moorish traders during the thirteenth century. As Montelupo and its river clay — necessary to the production of *maiolica* — lie along the old Roman road linking Florence and Pisa, you can surmise some connection. It was only later, during the Renaissance, that ceramic decoration became the high art form one sees in museums today. The new tableware had a civilizing influence too. During the Renaissance the rich tossed away the old boards from which they ate and replaced them with the elegant new tableware.

The original designs, colorful and intricate, are meticulously hand copied all over town. My favorite workshop is Tuscia, along the road from the Florence highway to town, at Via Chiantigiana 264 in Lastra a Signa. It is fascinating to watch the skilled artisans painstakingly dabbing and painting throughout the day. The old patterns are rendered more or less faithfully. Check the originals in Montelupo's Museo Archaeologico e della Ceramica in the center of town (Via Sinibaldi, Tel. 0571-51352, open Tuesday through Sunday, 10am–6pm) and pick up something similar at a reasonable price at Tuscia and elsewhere. At the end of June there's a big international ceramics fair (Usually the third week in June, open along the streets every evening from 6pm to midnight and on Sunday from 10am to midnight. Check with the tourist office, Tel. 0571-518-993, Fax 0571-911-421). In addition, many Sundays throughout the year — from March through October — are given over to an open air ceramics market.

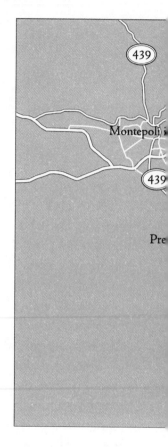

Montelupo is the beginning of a pleasant tour to the west through olive- and vine-laden hills brightened in summer by radiant sunflowers. It's a bit tricky to maneuver the minor roads away from the industry- and traffic-infested Arno valley, but with a bit of attentive map reading, it should be no problem. It took me several tries, but I finally worked out a route that is indeed lovely and takes you first to the ancient town of San Miniato and its truffles.

From Montelupo take the road to Sammontana. Continue on through Villanuova, and when you reach the traffic light at Pozzale, take a left turn. You cannot go straight across the road, which is what you'd like to do, but it doesn't really matter. Go left and follow the road through Monterappoli to Granaiola, where you'll begin to see signs to San Miniato. Follow the signs over the hills. While struggling to find an asphalted route over the hills, I stopped a friendly looking man in Monterappoli and gathered a nice historical footnote. "How might I find the loveliest and most quiet road to San Miniato?" I asked. An odd request, he obviously thought. It would be longer through too many curves, he protested. I assured him I wanted an unfettered landscape that would not take me through the roads surrounding Empoli. This prompted him to tell me the story of Empoli's tiny military force attacking San Miniato in the thirteenth century. (The various towns

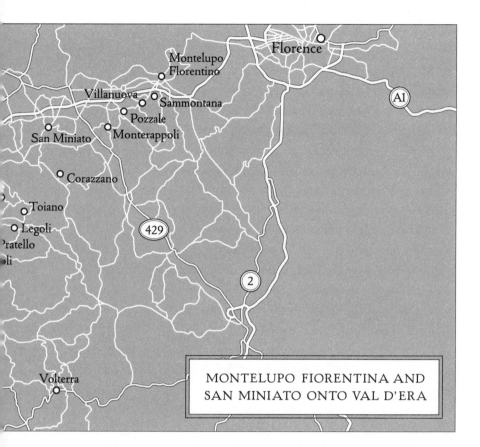

MONTELUPO FIORENTINA AND
SAN MINIATO ONTO VAL D'ERA

were continually fighting one another.) In order to look menacing and grand, the little band collected all the goats it could find, tied candles to their horns, lit them, and with the well-lit animals marched on in grand style taking on the appearance of a huge military force. Needless to say, they won handily.

Following their footsteps, you reach San Miniato from the rear. You'll first catch sight of the town by its tall thin tower topped by three oddly ragged round brick columns. Travel around on the circumferential road to the old center where there's limited parking on the main Piazza del Popolo. (If you arrive on a festive occasion, or during truffle season in November, it's best to use the ample parking lot under the old wall and walk up to town.)

San Miniato has a big history, albeit a tragic recent past—another footnote. I first visited San Miniato some years ago, still under the shock of a film I'd just seen. "La Notte di San Lorenzo" (in English, "The Night of Shooting Stars"), made in the 1970s by the brothers Paolo and Vittorio

Taviano, natives of San Miniato. Much of it was locally filmed. The film retells the disaster that befell San Miniato during the German occupation in 1944. During that fatal summer, the town was under siege, with sharp battles between the advancing American army and the retreating Germans. Local partisans were fighting alongside the Americans. Most townspeople had fled and the Germans locked the entire remaining population inside the *duomo*. During the battle, an American shell hit the cathedral, bringing down a major column and causing the deaths of 50 people. In the immediate post-war years after the American liberation, it was easier to blame the Germans whose fault it actually had been. When the film was made, photos of the actual battle as well as from the film were posted prominently all over town. The people of San Miniato were reliving their shock. The film takes its Italian name from the battle between partisans and Germans on August 10th, the feast day of San Lorenzo. It follows the correct sequence of events but to spare local feelings the brothers recreated the *duomo* scene inside the cathedral of nearby Empoli.

The many grand rulers who passed through these hills left an impressive number of beautiful buildings in San Miniato. Ottone the First passed in the tenth century, Frederick Redbeard in the twelfth, and later in the same century, his son, Henry IV. Local lore tells us that Countess Matilde of Canossa, one of the legendary figures of the time, was born in San Miniato in the eleventh century. Her father Bonificio, the Marquis of Tuscany, not a pleasant man, is said to have lived here at the time. Upon his death by assassination — her two older siblings had already died — the nine-year-old Matilde became heiress to vast lands that spread from Emilia-Romagna through much of northern Tuscany. She was one of the more powerful women of the Middle Ages, a veritable warrior who consolidated Bonificio's widespread holdings. She negotiated a famous peace between Henry IV and Pope Gregory VII, who was said to have been her lover as well. The Medici later founded the city of Livorno on top of one of her fortresses. Her great citadels and castles can be seen all the way from the Garfagnana and Mugello down to the Val d'Era southwest of San Miniato. Her main residence was in Canossa in Emilia-Romagna, the castle where she hosted Henry IV and the Pope. She's better known there than in Tuscany.

As each ruler passed through San Miniato, and occasionally stayed a while, castles, towers, and churches were built in the city. What's left of them still gives the town an important and impressive look. The last emperor to drop in officially was Napoleon III, when he came to see a relative who was running it. San Miniato is a small place, but with a lovely elegant feel and some very grandly decorated churches. Today the town is most famous for its truffles, little brown marvels that rival the better known Piemonte variety.

From San Miniato it's a short drive to Montopoli in Val d'Arno. Stay along the inner road, don't follow the road down to the heavily trafficked road to Pisa. Leave San Miniato on the road to Serra, and from there to Montopoli. Along the way is a detour to Corazzano and a little restaurant, Taverna dell'Ozio (see page 220), where you'll find the best of local food.

Montopoli lives its history. Written records carry the town's existence to long before Florentine rule, as far back as 746. The Florentine grandee Gino di Neri Capponi—his namesake still lives in Florence—captured the town from the Pisans in the fourteenth century, and erected an impressive tower that still overlooks the surrounding countryside. He also built one of the most elegant villas of the entire Tuscan countryside just outside Montopoli, Varramista, designed by the noted Florentine sculptor Bartolommeo Ammannati, architect of the Pitti Palace. In recent years Varramista has been owned by the Agnelli automobile family, and has become an important wine producer.

Around Montopoli's main Piazza Michele are still standing some fine old buildings, the Bishop's Palace, the Podesta's Palace, and the Antique Chancellery Palace with its newly restored portico. On the same square the inn/restaurant Quattro Gigli (see page 224) is well worth a visit. It prides itself on an historical menu of recreated old Montopoli specialties.

The remains of the earlier tenth-century castle are a short walk off the square. The castle is today only a simple tower; the rest was destroyed in 1944. Down the road is the fine church of Saints Stefano and Giovanni Battista. And there is a new little archaeological museum along the main street, based on collections of another ancient Florentine family, the Baldinovinetti, whose country house in the nearby village of Marti is still lived in by the family. It's housed in the Palazzo Guicciardini, another well-known name of Renaissance Florence (Museo Civico; summer, open Tuesday, Thursday, and Friday 10am–1pm and 4pm–7pm, and Saturday and Sunday, 10am–1pm and 4pm–7pm; winter, Wednesday and Friday 10am–1pm and

Saturday and Sunday 10am–1pm and 3pm–6pm).

The road from Montopoli to Palaia brings you to the Val d'Era, a tranquil valley marked by dramatic *chalanti* (sandstone cliffs), eroded through the millennia as an inland sea that once covered the valley gradually receded. It is after Palaia, on the road to the deserted little medieval town of Toiano, that you get the best view of the cliffs.

Walled Palaia, with its two impressive portals at either end of a rather drab main street, has its most interesting features above the second large gate: the Church of Sant'Andrea, built over the ruins of a Roman temple with a lovely brick façade and impressive group of saints by Andrea della Robbia, and a spectacular view from what was once the *rocca*, or castle, at the top of the town. It's worth the somewhat precarious climb along a dirt path up to the little grassy plot just to have the full view of the valley around, all the way to Volterra in the south and the peaks of the Apennine mountains to the north.

The loveliest visit in Palaia is just below the old town: the large Pieve di San Martino, built and signed — on the capitol of a simple column — by the early Renaissance sculptor Andrea Pisano. The high-vaulted awesomely pure interior is entirely of brick, including its well-designed columns and Gothic shaped apse. The church is usually closed, but across the road lives young Giacomo, who knows it well and will open the severely barred side door to show you around and graciously explain all the intricacies of the church. An ancient hand-hewn baptismal font sits in a corner.

On the way to San Martino, just outside the old walls, is a favorite restaurant of the area, Il Pettirosso (see page 227), with a terrace that takes in the lovely views around. Inside the walls is also a small welcoming wine bar/restaurant, Antica Farmacia, open only evenings (Via del Popolo 51, Telephone for reservations 0587-622-149; closed Wednesdays).

From Palaia, the road continues to Peccioli. A few kilometers along this road you'll see a sign on the left to Borgo Medievale di Toiano. The six kilometer narrow road is a worthwhile detour along a ridge that, to the left, is marked by the dramatic spires and etched sandstone cliffs of the once inland sea. Follow the asphalted road; it becomes a navigable dirt track at the very end, and runs directly into the bridge that leads to the deserted little walled village, now, almost unnoticeably, being gently restored. A few houses seem to be occupied; the only sign of life we encountered on a visit was the mailman, motor-biking into the village in his bright yellow and blue uniform, obviously to deliver the post. The other single bit of color was the tiny cemetery at the entrance, eerily kept in a flush of color with flowers on every tomb. It is apparently maintained by former villagers still attached to the place.

Return to the main road and follow it past the village of Montefoscoli to Peccioli, a further excursion into the graceful valleys and surrounding hills of the Val d'Era. A small turnoff to the left at Montefoscoli will take you to Legoli, where the small Chapel of Santa Caterina, set in a grove of cypress trees, was frescoed by Benozzo Gozzoli in the fourteenth century when he escaped from the Pisa plague to these woods. You can go on from here through Pratello to Peccioli, or return along the same road through Montefoscoli. Peccioli is a small old town, with a few surprising attractions in addition to the graceful, perfectly proportioned twelfth-century church of San Verano overlooking the valley. First there's the parking garage, underneath the town, with an elevator that delivers you right to the main square. Second is a museum of rare Russian icons, the collection of Francesco Bigazzi, an Italian journalist who spent years in Russia and donated his collection to Peccioli. The museum is housed in the medieval Palazzo Pretorio on the square (Segni della Santa Russia; for museum hours, telephone 0587-672-877). And then there's the prehistoric park, a walk among life-sized dinosaurs in a private garden that's open to the public as well (Parco Preistorico, Via dei Cappuccini, open all day; Tel. 0587-636-030). On the Piazza del Carmine, the square at the top of town as you drive in, is the most sophisticated restaurant of the area, La Greppia (see page 230).

You can continue from Peccioli to Volterra, about twelve miles to the south, or return to Florence on the road that joins the *superstrada* just beyond the estate of Varramista. Drive up through the landscaped grounds to the architectural beauty that was once the residence of Gino di Neri Capponi and most recently of the Agnelli family (Call to reserve; Tel. 0571-44711).

SPECIALTIES OF MONTELUPO FIORENTINA AND SAN MINIATO

The heavenly, intensely aromatic little tuber known as the white truffle is the major product of the area. Less well-known than those of Alba in Piemonte, they are just as good and rather less expensive. White truffles—brown outside, flecked inside—have been coveted for ages. The Romans thought them an aphrodisiac, precious enough to demand payment in gold coin. They are different both in quality and in texture from the black truffle—where one grows, the other does not. Neither ideally lasts for more than a few days, no matter how you try to preserve it. The highest quality truffle is round and smooth, easily cleaned of the bits of earth that cling to it. It is usually stored in a jar of rice that absorbs a good bit of the aroma and makes a wonderful *risotto*. The truffle itself is never cooked. It is probably at its best simply shaved over fresh buttered *tagliatelle*.

San Miniato's white truffle is treasured in these parts, considered by locals the best in the world. (The "biggest truffle in the world," weighing over 25 kilos, was shipped from San Miniato to President Dwight Eisenhower in 1954; it could not have been all that aromatic. In 2004 a London restaurateur paid $52,000 for a San Miniato truffle at auction.) Nowadays, farmers are successfully seeking out truffles all over Tuscany, in the Crete Senese, the Pistoian Hills, the Garfagnana, even the Casentino and Tiberina. San Miniato still holds first place. Its international truffle fair the last three weekends of November has become a major annual event. You can buy a truffle, or just smell and eat. (For more information, call 0571-418-739 or 0571-42745.) Truffles can actually be found here a good part of the year. The most aromatic noble white truffle has a limited season, from late September through December; others, like the more delicate *marzuolo* (or *bianchetta*), go on and on through April. There's also a lesser variety called *scorzone* that can be found even later. The height of the season is November.

Throughout the year *tartufi* are the talk of the town, in San Miniato and in the surrounding hills as well, where more than 700 professional truffle-hunters are either training their dogs, or out scavenging in the woods. Truffling is a local sport. I went off on a training exercise with Bruno

Castaldi, a grizzly bear of a man, whose humor and affection for the pup he was training to hunt truffles immediately dispelled any suspicion I might have had that animal exploitation for man's pleasure was at work here. I met this *tartufaio* almost accidentally, struck as I was by a bunch of wild asparagus he was grasping like a bridal bouquet. He arrived from the woods at a restaurant in Corazzano, not far from San Miniato, where I was having my fill of spring truffles. His asparagus were not the trim slim "wild" variety one finds in early spring markets, but the ones we go out looking for in the nearby forests. I could see from the awkward angles of the asparagus that they were the real thing, as precious in early spring as the *porcini* mushrooms we forage in the autumn. With great exuberance, Bruno described the *risotto* and pasta sauces that bring out the best of these little delicacies. Our conversation inevitably turned to truffles, and Bruno invited me out to the woods with his ten-month-old puppy for a lesson in hunting truffles. The truffle woods were directly across from the restaurant.

Bruno has five truffle hounds, and normally takes out two at a time to hunt. The one I met, Tita, is the youngest, a dog of indeterminate heritage who looks like a mini-Labrador. Tita adored the hunt. In his deep-pocketed overcoat, Bruno kept a sack of puppy snacks; each time Tita hungrily and happily nosed out a truffle, she was rewarded. Bruno snatched the truffle; Tita munched the snacks. We walked the edge of the forest. The hunt was in fact virtual since Bruno had earlier planted the little tubers for training purposes about half a foot down. Tita, a gentle and affectionate young dog, found them all.

CORAZZANO

TAVERNA DELL'OZIO

Via Zara 85, Corazzano • Tel. 0571-462-862

Corazzano is a little known crossroads about twelve miles from San Miniato.
Reservations are necessary for both lunch and dinner, especially during truffle
seasons. The taverna sits on the main road through Corazzano.
It is closed Mondays, and at lunchtime during August.
Prices are inexpensive to moderate.

This unobtrusive little restaurant is a splendid place to enjoy a meal of truffles. Corazzano is best reached from San Miniato, a pleasant drive of some ten kilometers through undulating wine country. Simone Fiaschi is the owner/chef, a portly man with a grand resemblance to Pavarotti; he claims a lovely tenor voice as well. Simone comes from a family of *norcini*, once a highly valued (now almost extinct) profession throughout Tuscany: itinerant pork butchers who roamed the countryside, from one farmer to another, slaughtering and seasoning mature pigs in a way that assured preservation and use of every single part of the animal. *Norcini* salted the hind legs (prosciutto) and the front legs (*spalla*), cooked, seasoned, and stuffed the sausages, boiled down the blood for the *mallegata* or blood sausage, and carved the roasts and the ribs. By the time the *norcino* was finished, meat for the entire year had been prepared to hang and dry in a cool cellar.

Simone, who runs the restaurant together with his wife Silvia, carries on the tradition, preserving his own meats. A glance at the prosciuttos and sausages hanging in his cellar, aging alongside the cheeses and preserved mushrooms and olives on the shelves, is a tempting invitation to try them all as *antipasto*. A favorite sausage is his *briciolona*, soft and pepper-spiced, looking like the better-known *finocchiona* sausage, but without the traditional fennel seeds. Pasta courses include, in truffle and *funghi* season, *tagliatelle con tartufi* or *funghi*, and delicate thistle/*ricotta*-filled *ravioli*, with butter and shaved truffle sauce. The wide variety of interesting main courses is unusual, attesting to Simone's delight in creating savory meats. He prepares different game dishes: *colombina* (wild pigeon) in a rich wine/tomato sauce, *lepre* (wild hare) in a combination of a dozen spices, steak of *capriolo* (wild goat) topped with a shaving of truffles, and pheasant in truffle sauce. An entire milk-fed three-month-old pork can be ordered beforehand, stuffed with sage and juniper berries, and roasted in a sweet-sour sauce.

RECIPES FROM TAVERNA DELL'OZIO

Mushrooms Preserved in Oil
FUNGHI SOTT'OLIO

❀

Makes a 1-quart jar

2 cups white wine
2 cups white wine vinegar
1 tablespoon salt
2 pounds small, perfectly white and firm white button mushrooms
20 whole peppercorns
2 cups corn oil or extra virgin olive oil

Boil together for 5 minutes the wine, vinegar, and a good tablespoon of salt. Slice off the bottom of the mushroom stems, and either peel or wipe the mushroom caps with a wet cloth. Drop them in the boiling liquid for 3 minutes, then drain, and spread on a clean cloth or kitchen toweling to dry a bit.

Place the mushrooms in a clean glass jar, add the peppercorns, and cover with oil. (Simone uses corn oil; I prefer olive oil.) Store in a cool place. The mushrooms are ready for eating in a day or two, and last well for up to a month. They do not have to be refrigerated.

Mixed Vegetables

CAPONATA

❂

Serves 4

Simone Tuscanizes this southern dish, and serves it on a *bruschetta*, or as accompaniment to his roasts.

1 large eggplant (not peeled)
1 large red onion
1 large red bell pepper
3 medium zucchini
2 ribs celery
2 ripe tomatoes
2 cloves garlic
1 sprig fresh oregano
1 bunch basil
½ cup fresh virgin olive oil
Salt and freshly ground pepper

Cut the eggplant into bite-sized pieces of about 1½ inches square, place in a colander with a good sprinkling of salt, and allow to sit while you prepare the other vegetables. Wash and cut all the vegetables into bite-sized pieces, about 1 inch square. Rinse and drain the eggplant. Heat the oil in a large pan and gently sauté the onion with the garlic, oregano, and basil. After 5 minutes add the vegetables, along with the drained and rinsed eggplant, and cook gently for 30 minutes. Add salt and pepper to taste. Serve warm or at room temperature.

Hare in Sweet-Sour Sauce
LEPRE IN SALSA DOLCE/FORTE

❀

Serves 6-8

This rich sauce does not divulge its ingredients easily but the combination of spices is enormously satisfying. Originally from the East, such spices are used quite often in Tuscan cooking, from flavoring preserved olives to enhancing game dishes. If a hare is not available, a rabbit will substitute well; it's less gamey but very good. Hare is larger than rabbit; a rabbit will serve 4-6.

1 hare or rabbit, divided into small pieces, and marinated overnight in a
   mixture of ⅓ white wine vinegar, ⅓ water, and ⅓ white wine, enough
   in all to cover
2 carrots
2 ribs celery
1 large onion
1 bunch parsley leaves
3 tablespoons extra virgin olive oil
2 sprigs rosemary
1 clove garlic
2 tablespoons tomato paste dissolved in ½ cup water
A pinch each of the following powdered spices, or as many as you can
   find: coriander seeds, nutmeg, cinnamon, anisette, cloves, and allspice.
   (The spices should add up to about 1 tablespoon.)
1 handful pine nuts

Finely chop the carrots, celery, onion, and parsley, and sauté in olive oil in a pan large enough to hold the entire dish. Remove the pieces of hare from the marinade and dry well. Add to the pan and brown gently for about 5 minutes on all sides and remove to a plate.

Chop the rosemary and garlic together and add to the pan along with the tomato concentrate, the spices, and the pine nuts. Put the hare back into this pan, along with any juices that have accumulated. Lower the heat and cook slowly, covered, until the hare is tender. Hare will need about 45 minutes, rabbit less.

MONTOPOLI

QUATTRO GIGLI AND TRATTORIA

DELL'ORCIO INTERRATO

On the main square, Montopoli · Tel. 0571-466-878

Open for lunch and dinner, closed Mondays. Prices are moderate in the trattoria, more expensive in Quattro Gigli.

Quattro Gigli is a welcoming little *pensione*. Two different restaurants occupy a number of rooms in what were once the storage cellars: the elegant Quattro Gigli and the simpler Trattoria dell'Orcio Interrato, both serving traditional foods of the area. The inn sits on terraced land, and the cellars look out onto the garden and surrounding hills. In warm weather ask for a table on the terrace with a view of the surrounding countryside.

The historic menus at both Quattro Gigli and Trattoria dell'Orcio Interrato are the happy result of owner Luigi Puccioni's passion for old Florentine manuscripts and local lore. Wife and chief chef Fulvia develops and modernizes the historic recipes dating from the fifteenth century. Meals derived from ancient recipes are more likely to be interesting than mouth watering, but here they work. The two restaurants sit cozily in a warren of cellars and terraces under a fourteenth-century palace all done up in local pottery and old church artifacts. Don't be put off by the touch of fancy artifact and pretentious service; the tableware may resemble that of a new Milanese restaurant, but the food is traditional and good.

Luigi's old hand-printed books tell of fruit-flavored game and spices that arrived in Tuscany from the East and North Africa. The nobility, he notes, ate from the sky, mostly the birds they hunted; the middle classes could afford meat, and the poor — progenitors of today's fashionable *cucina povera* — ate only what they could grow. Butter was for the privileged, olive oil for the farmer. The food at Quattro Gigli is more that of the upper classes, but the Trattoria dell' Orcio Interrato offers simpler fare.

The dining terrace of the *trattoria* is a delight, overlooking a garden of persimmon and cherry trees and all the fresh herbs that go into the food. The menu changes with the seasons, to include only fresh and available ingredients. A fall chicken breast, for instance, is poached in pomegranate juice with almonds. *Antipasti* include a terrine of wild boar, accompanied by marmalade of onions and apples; there's a pasta of fresh cheese *gnocchi* with a fifteenth-century sauce of ground hazelnuts and rosemary, another is *ricotta*-filled *ravioli* covered with pear sauce. Homemade fresh pasta, *torcionetti*, come with a rabbit, olive, and eggplant sauce. In November the menu takes on the truffle, and for a special treat, there's lots of it here to try: *trippa di tartufo* is not innards smothered in truffles (as the name may suggest), but rolled and thinly sliced *crepes* in a truffle sauce. *Crostini di tartufo* are covered with a simple light cheese topped with a good grating of truffles. *Pici con tartufi* are thin hand-rolled pasta in a sauce of fresh *pecorino* and a generous grating of truffles.

Chianina beef and *Cinta Senese* pork come from the Lorenzetti farm in nearby Montaione. The *lonzino di cinta* is a seventeenth-century main course; in September it is served over a peach purée not at all sweet, rather quite delicious. Desserts include a white almond cream, served with a lovely spread of fruit sauces.

RECIPES FROM QUATTRO GIGLI AND TRATTORIA
DELL'ORCIO INTERRATO

Fresh Cheese Gnocchi in a Hazelnut Sauce
GNOCCHI CON SALSA DI NOCCIOLI

❋

Serves 6-8

FOR THE GNOCCHI:
3 cups goat cheese *ricotta*
1 ¾ cups flour
6 egg yolks
Salt
1 teaspoon freshly ground nutmeg, plus additional for finishing

FOR THE SAUCE:
⅓ cup butter, plus additional for finishing
1 sprig rosemary
1 cup ground hazelnuts, lightly toasted and ground
½ cup cream

Pinch of salt

½ cup grated Parmesan cheese, for finishing, and additional at table

To make the *gnocchi*, whip the *ricotta* until creamy in a mixer or food processor. Add the flour slowly, working it well into the cheese. Add the egg yolks one by one and continue to process until well blended. Remove to a bowl, add a good amount of salt and a teaspoon of freshly ground nutmeg. The consistency should be a paste that can be scooped by a spoon and dropped into boiling water, neither too solid nor too liquid. Set aside while you make the sauce.

To make the sauce, melt ⅓ cup butter with the leaves of rosemary over a medium flame. Don't allow the butter to burn, but let the rosemary steep a bit. Remove the rosemary and whisk in the toasted hazelnuts. Add the cream to make a thick liquid sauce. Add a pinch of salt, mix well, and heat just to the boiling point.

Bring a large pan of salted water to boil, and, working with a teaspoon, drop small balls of dough into the water. Allow to cook for a few minutes, until the *gnocchi* rise to the top. Remove to a warm buttered dish, adding bits of butter to each layer. Pour over the sauce, mix gently, add the nutmeg and Parmesan, and over it, the hazelnut sauce. Serve with more grated Parmesan at the table.

Sage Frittata

LA SALVIATA

❁

Serves 6 as antipasto

Leaves of 5 sage sprigs (about 20 leaves)

6 eggs

½ cup *ricotta*

½ cup Parmesan, grated

Salt

1½ tablespoons extra virgin olive oil

Pound the sage into a paste, either in a mortar or food processor. Beat the eggs with the *ricotta* and add the Parmesan. Add the sage and a good amount of salt, and mix well.

Heat the olive oil in a large frying pan, and throw in the egg mixture. Either turn the *frittata* over so that the other side cooks, or cover it with a lid so it cooks through without turning. When the *frittata* is just cooked through, turn out onto a serving plate and serve warm or at room temperature.

PALAIA

IL PETTIROSSO

Via San Martino 15, Palaia • Tel. 0587-622-111

Reservations aren't absolutely necessary, but to have a table ready it's advisable to call ahead. In warm weather ask for the terrace from where there's a nice view. Prices are moderate, depending on what you choose. Open for lunch and dinner; closed Tuesdays.

Grand chefs may mostly be men, but in Italy, the perfect little *trattoria*—the one with the best kind of home cooking—usually has a woman running the kitchen. One often jokes about the *nonna* (grandmother) in the kitchen teaching the *mama* all her old tricks. And yet, in Italy most rural *trattorie* are just that, created by a woman moved from her own kitchen to one for paying guests. The rest of the family provides service. Many a rural *trattorie* began in the poor years after the Second World War to help families make a better living than on a share-cropping farm. Some started as a bar, a bakery, or grocery. The little *trattoria* has since passed from grandmother to mother and daughter—or sometimes son. The best are still preparing food according to the *nonna*'s old recipes.

It was a special delight to discover Il Pettirosso, where a spry gray-bobbed grandmother of eighty-plus years is still working her old favorites for crowds of diners every day. Il Pettirosso sits just outside the old walls of Palaia, a large and bright restaurant with a terrace of equal size shaded by two great box-shaped oak trees. The terrace looks down on the impressive old Pieve di San Martino. Luciana Manganelli has been the chef here since she opened the restaurant in 1962; her son Paolo and granddaughter Francesca serve. Francesca's little boy runs around, with various aunts and cousins to tend him. Workers and local business people come for a fixed price lunch. During summer months the 150-seat restaurant is full in the evenings as well.

The menu is perfectly simple, perfectly Tuscan, more in the Florentine style than any other. *Antipasti* are the usual mixed bag: slices of prosciutto and cold cuts, liver toasts, prosciutto with melon, or a salad of sliced tomato and mozzarella. The traditional taste of old-fashioned Tuscan cooking begins with the *primi*, the first courses. In the fall, there are fresh *tagliolini* in either *funghi* or topped with truffles, both made with just oil and a touch of garlic and parsley. Luciana is especially proud of her *pappardelle della caccia*, wide noodles with a *ragù* of wild boar.

The beef is the famous Chianina, grilled on an open wood fire. I prefer the *tagliata*, slices of thick steaks covered with either fresh arugula and slivers of Parmesan, or with another delectable stew of local wild mushrooms. Luciana's own favorite is her traditional *cinghiale con olive*, a bit chewy but filled with pungent flavor.

Desserts are again a particularly well done version of most Tuscan menus: *cantucci* (biscuits) with *vin santo*, *panna cotta*, a fruit salad or, what Luciana thinks she does best, an irresistible *zuppa inglese*, a very typical Italian dessert fashioned after English trifle.

RECIPES FROM IL PETTIROSSO

Wild Boar in Olive Sauce
CINGHIALE CON OLIVE

❁

Serves 6-8

2 pounds wild boar, cut into bite-sized pieces
2 cloves garlic
1 onion
1 small bunch parsley leaves
2 sprigs rosemary leaves
¼ cup extra virgin olive oil
Salt and freshly ground pepper
1 teaspoon mixed spices including ground cinnamon, nutmeg, and allspice
½ cup meat broth

1 cup red wine
About 24 small Tuscan-type marinated black olives, with their pits

Place the meat in a bowl and cover with cold water. Allow to rest for an hour. Finely chop together the garlic, onion, parsley, and rosemary and saute in the olive oil. When the sauté begins to take on color, pick the pieces of meat out of the water without draining and add them to the pan. Add salt and freshly ground pepper, and then the spices and the broth. Cook over a low heat until the broth has evaporated. Add the red wine. Allow to reduce, and add half a cup of water. Cook over low heat until the meat is cooked through and tender.

Meanwhile, drain the olives and drop into a pan of boiling water for 10 minutes. Drain, add the olives to the stew, and serve.

Italian English Trifle
ZUPPA INGLESE

Serves 10

This is one of the desserts you'll find everywhere in Tuscany. Best to make the sauce on top of a *bain marie* to be sure it does not curdle. Alchermes is an old liqueur of mixed spices developed by the Medici. If not available, Grand Marnier or Curacao may be substituted.

12 egg yolks
2½ cups sugar
1 cup flour
2 vanilla beans
2 quarts milk
Juice of ½ lemon
1½ packages Savoyard biscuits or ladyfingers
Alchermes liqueur (or Grand Marnier or Curacao)
Bitter cocoa for sprinkling

Beat together the egg yolks, sugar, and flour. Slice open the vanilla beans, scrape out the seeds, and add them along with the milk to the egg/sugar/flour mixture. Place in the top of a *bain marie*. Cook over a low flame, mixing all the while with a wooden spoon. When the mixture thickens enough to coat the back of the spoon, add the juice of ½ lemon and remove the mixture from the flame.

Quickly dip the biscuits in the liqueur and lay them side by side in a large baking dish. Pour the thickened cream over the biscuits, and sprinkle with cocoa. Refrigerate for at least 4 hours before serving.

PECCIOLI

LA GREPPIA

Piazza del Carmine, Peccioli • Tel. 0587-672-011
*Reservations recommended; there are only seven tables. Open for lunch
and dinner; closed Tuesdays. Priced moderately expensive.*

Egisto Cavallini opened this elegant little wine bar/restaurant some years ago with his wife Daniela after twenty years of wandering through restaurants in Switzerland and Florence. He works alone in his little kitchen, devising innovative dishes based on produce from the area. The restaurant's seven tables are placed in small coves; the decoration includes a collection of local pottery, and every table is set with heavy stone platters as place mats.

It's a sophisticated menu, with dishes served a tad pretentiously on large designer plates. Interesting *antipasti* include rounds of truffle-flavored *tonino* cheese on bread baked to a browned melting softness, a baked *pecorino* served in a casserole, large shrimp wrapped in a warm thin slice of *lardo di Colonnata*, and, best of all, a dish of stewed beans and *funghi porcini* served with red bitter *radicchio* salad leaves. *Primi*, especially the *risotto*, are excellent. A *risotto* of small apple pieces together with tiny shrimp with a hint of Calvados is definitely worth trying, as is one with *radicchio*. The perfect *pasta al pomodoro* flows out of a crusty basket made from melted grated Parmesan cheese.

Meat courses include the usual roasts, with eleven different ways of saucing a fillet of beef. There's also a breast of duck, with a sauce of prunes and *vin santo*.

Beans with Wild Mushrooms
FAGIOLI CON FUNGHI

✺

Serves 6

2½ cups *cannellini* beans, soaked overnight
1 small bunch sage leaves
5 tablespoons extra virgin olive oil
4 cloves garlic
½ pound frozen *porcini* mushrooms, defrosted and coarsely chopped or a
   handful of dried *porcini*, soaked in ½ cup warm water
1 bunch parsley leaves, finely chopped
Salt and freshly ground pepper

Put the soaked beans to cook slowly in a large pot of water together with the sage, 1 tablespoon of oil, and 1 garlic clove. Cook until tender and reserve in their water.

Chop the 3 remaining garlic cloves, and, in a pan large enough to hold the beans as well, sauté them in the remaining 4 of tablespoons oil. Add the *funghi* (if you are using dried *porcini*, add the soaking water with the grit filtered out), the parsley, and salt and pepper to taste. Cook, reducing the mushroom water, for about 5 minutes, until the mushrooms and chopped garlic are tender.

With a slotted spoon, remove the beans and add to the mushrooms. Mix well, add a few tablespoons of the water in which the beans cooked, and cook together, reducing the juices to a creamy sauce. Serve warm or at room temperature.

Risotto with Apples and Shrimp
RISOTTO CON MELE E GAMBERI

❂

Serves 6

Dill is a strange addition here, not at all indigenous to Tuscan soil. Egisto orders it from a local supplier, but I leave it out, replacing it with chopped parsley for color. Red peppercorns come from a Mediterranean tree.

1¼ pounds whole fresh shrimp
Salt
2 red onions
2 green Granny Smith apples, peeled and cored
2 tablespoons extra virgin olive oil
2 cups *risotto* rice
2 small shot glass of Calvados
A handful of red peppercorns
1 large sprig dill, chopped
1 tablespoon cream

Peel and remove the heads and veins from the shrimp and reserve. Place the shrimp in a bowl, and cook the heads and peels in about 6 cups of salted water for 20 minutes. Drain, and keep at a low boil for cooking the *risotto*.

Chop the onions and quarter the apple. Slice each apple quarter into about 4 pieces. In a deep pot large enough to hold the *risotto*, sauté the onions and apples in the olive oil for about 5 minutes. Add the shrimp and cook for another minute, mixing.

Add the rice, mix and cook for another 5 minutes, stirring all the while. Pour in the Calvados. Allow to bubble and evaporate for several more minutes. Begin to add the simmering fish stock, just enough to cover with each addition as the rice absorbs the liquid. After about 10 minutes, add the red peppercorns and the dill. Continue to cook, adding broth, until the rice is *al dente*. Add the cream, and allow to rest for a few minutes before serving.

CHAPTER 9

Marina di Pisa to Upper Maremma

I F YOU ARE TAKEN, AS I AM, WITH RATHER DOWDY
SEASIDE RESORTS, MARINA DI PISA IS THE PERFECT
place to begin to wander down the Tuscan coast and follow the old Etruscan road into the hills of the Upper Maremma. Marina di Pisa lies at the
point where the Arno flows into the Mediterranean. It retains a Fellini-like
quality of seaside postwar Italy, with few fashionable boutiques and lots of
fishermen hanging their lines from worn piers. It exudes its aura of simple
straight hearty tastes and more reasonable prices than most resorts along
the shore. It also happens to have a fine fish restaurant right at the mouth of
the Arno, La Taverna dei Gabbiani.

The north bank of the river is completely taken up by the vast regional
park of San Rossore, filled with elegant giant Mediterranean umbrella
pines, oaks, all kinds of scrub, and the grand villa that was once the palatial
summer home of the kings of Italy and now serves the president as his official guest house.

The road along the southern bank of the Arno from Pisa goes directly
to Marina di Pisa. The road is lined with an appealing combination of fishing
shacks, little boats, and vegetable gardens. At a little more than the halfway
point, you'll spot a sign on the left, to San Pietro a Grado. It's a church not
to miss. The wonderfully harmonious dual-apsed Romanesque basilica rises
in the middle of a large green meadow. Here is the place where St. Peter
is said to have preached his first sermon upon reaching the Italian shore.
First-century archaeological remains that you see inside lend credence to the
story. The interior is as graceful as the façade and the short descriptions of
important relics give a good idea of the evolution of the basilica.

As you arrive in nearby Marina di Pisa, the road curves into the middle
of town. Side roads to the right lead to the esplanade along the seafront. At
the north end is the Arno meeting the sea, and, just opposite, La Taverna
dei Gabbiani (see page 245). The drive south from there along the seashore

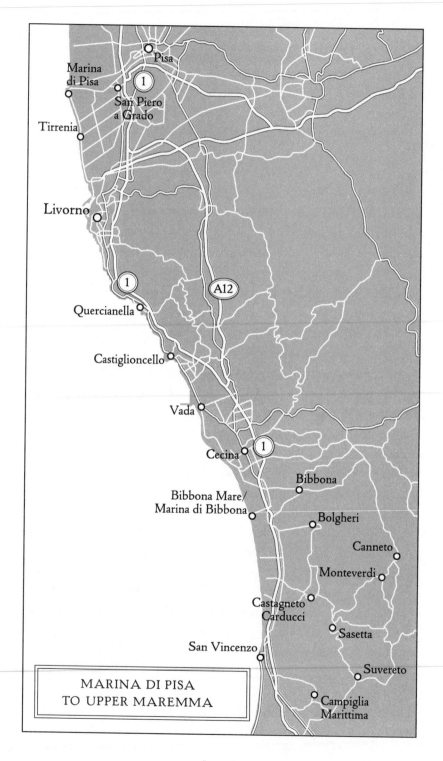

Marina
di Pisa

Pisa

San Piero
a Grado

Tirrenia

Livorno

Quercianella

A12

Castiglioncello

Vada

Cecina

Bibbona

Bibbona Mare/
Marina di Bibbona

Bolgheri

Canneto

Monteverdi

Castagneto
Carducci

Sasetta

San Vincenzo

Suvereto

MARINA DI PISA
TO UPPER MAREMMA

Campiglia
Marittima

brings you to another seaside resort, Tirrenia, and on to the outskirts of Livorno, a thriving seaport founded by the Medici in the fifteenth century to give some competition to unruly Pisa, which was continually needling the controlling Florentines. The enterprising Medicis, anxious to quickly populate the new port, invited all comers to settle there, among them Jews and Arabs fleeing the Spanish Inquisition. Livorno provided not only a safe haven for refugees, but also a convenient market for the rich booty of pirates in the Mediterranean.

To this day, the food of Livorno reflects its foreign heritage. Couscous arrived here from North Africa. Tuscan food writer Aldo Santini tells us that the ubiquitous tomato—so essential to the Italian kitchen—first arrived in this part of the Mediterranean with Jews fleeing Spain in the fifteenth century. The strange New World fruit—Mexican, actually—was having difficulty being accepted in Spain (and in England, where it also arrived with returning colonizers). True or not, it's a nice story.

Skirt the bustling port city and follow the old Roman road Aurelia that meanders along one of the more beautiful rivieras of Italy, through the lovely resorts of Quercianella and Castiglioncello. It is a coastline of pine- and oak-covered hills dipping down to the sea. Brilliant yellow broom begins to flower in late spring, the best time to travel here, and carries on through the summer. Swimming is right off the rocks. The coastline becomes flat at Vada and sandy beaches begin again, but the pine and brush forests continue along the coast to Cecina, Bibbona, Donoratico, and on. At Bibbona Mare, the seaside resort of Bibbona, you'll find one of the finest seafood restaurants along the coast, La Pineta di Luciano Zazzari (see page 250). Just past Cecina, a turn inland takes you to Bolgheri, the beginning of Upper Maremma and the so-called Route of the Etruscans, where vineyards and scrub amble up into ancient hill towns, ruins, and antiquities.

Bolgheri lies at the end of a majestic five-kilometer drive lined by hundreds of tall slender cypress trees, almost like "young giants," as the Nobel Prize winning (1905) Tuscan poet Giosue Carducci called them in an awed paean entitled, *Davanti San Guido*. The poem begins,

I cipressi che a Bolgheri alti e schietti
Van da San guido in duplice filar,
Quasi in corsa giganti giovenetti

Mi balzarono incontro e mi guardar.

(Bolgheri's high cypresses, in double file
from San Guido like young giants leaping
as they come to greet me....)

D.H. Lawrence described them as the dark shadows of an Etruscan past. The narrow avenue ends at the Gherardesca castle, a gracious castle extending over the portal into the little town. It used to be the feudal estate of one of Tuscany's great families, the Gherardesca. At one time, the family owned pretty much all of the land up and down the Tyrrhenian coast. Some of the best wines of Italy have been developed here in recent years, including the noted Sassicaia.

Many of the fields, vineyards, and impressive outbuildings and stables of the Gherardesca estates are still here to be admired as you approach Bolgheri from the seacoast. Bolgheri itself is little more than a few piazzas and narrow lanes. It is a pleasant stop, with several nice little restaurants, a shop with regional produce, and an inviting wine bar/specialties shop called Enoteca Tognoni that offers a good variety of the local game sausages and honeys and the best wines of the area. Honeys (from bees suckled on rosemary, heather, lavender, sunflower, *mille fiori*, and orange), bottled vegetables in oil (*funghi*, eggplant, artichokes, and dried tomatoes, to name a few), specialty pastas, and *biscotti*, delicious to taste and look at and worth purchasing. Among the several restaurants is La Taverna del Pittore (see page 256) sitting under a pleasant citrus vine at the back of the *enoteca*.

Leaving Bolgheri back down the tree-lined drive, a left turn after about a kilometer brings you slowly up to Castagneto Carducci (the Carducci added in the last century in homage to the poet), through olive groves and vineyards, past farmhouses that today are mostly second homes of smart well-to-do Florentines and Milanese.

Castagneto Carducci is a pretty tourist town overlooking the coast below. Wander through the lovely stone lanes, stop in at the little church of Santissimo Crosifisso, where you'll find a wondrous, much venerated fifteenth-century wooden crucifix. The few times I've been there, I found a continuous stream of rather elegant elderly local women come to have an intimate tête-à-tête with the old Christ. There's also a vast sea vista. On clear days one can see the islands of Elba, Corsica, Capraia, and Giglio.

From Castagneto Carducci a narrow road continues toward Sasetta, through the protected forest of the Poggio Neri. Even on the brightest June day, the most traffic you'll encounter on this road is the occasional tractor or perhaps a pack of young cyclists. The forest breaks every now and again on to open views of the surrounding countryside. Oaks and chestnuts line the road, along with cork trees, which you can identify by the large rectangles left where hunks of bark have been carved out of the trunks. The road looks trickier on the map than it actually is, and leads through fine countryside.

Two kilometers before Sasetta there is a left turn toward Monteverdi, a leisurely detour of about twenty kilometers that will take you to Canneto as well, a tiny walled enclave that hasn't changed a whit—except perhaps in the livelihood of its inhabitants—in the more than one thousand years of its life.

Before arriving at Canneto, have a look at one of the more ambitious food shops of the area, just at the entrance to Monteverdi Marittimo. You'll see advertising signs heralding Mucci before you come to town. Don't be turned off. When you get there you'll find an inauspicious little doorway announcing an *alimentari*. It's worth the visit. The day I visited, Carlo Staccioli, who runs the shop with his brother Andrea, led me into the back room where I found a scene from another age, audaciously familiar-looking to anyone with a farm in Tuscany. Sides of hairy boar were hanging from the walls. Sausages and hams crowded the little room. I was easily persuaded to try the various house-cured meats. They were fragrantly different. The excellent *prosciutto nostrale* (i.e., their own) is marinated in red wine and smeared with roughly ground black pepper and the back fat of the pig before being hung to dry. It was unlike any I've tasted elsewhere. The fennel-flavored sausage—*finocchiona*—was also special. I followed Carlo down a few stairs into an Etruscan grotto where the odor of aging cheeses was overwhelming. The cheeses lined the shelves around the room. I especially noted two, my favorite *marzolino*, the *pecorino* made from the first milk after spring grazing begins, aging in the ashes of burned olive leaves, and the older *pecorino stagionato di grotto* that had already spent eighteen months in a terracotta amphora before arriving at the Mucci cellar.

On the way out I pinched a large shiny black olive from an open basket. It was amazingly good. Carlo told me these were olives prepared in an old Tuscan manner, dried in the sun before going into their marinade of spices.

A few kilometers on is the old town of Canneto. Enter (by foot only) through the rather important looking two-gated portal and you find a little Romanesque church on your right. That's the top of town. Opposite the church you can walk down one of two narrow little streets, until after about two-hundred meters they join at the other end in another gate. You can hardly call it a town. It was constructed by shepherds to protect themselves and their flocks from intruders. Each of the houses enclosed a barn as well. The shepherds came home with their sheep and goats in the evening and herded them into the barns. The two heavy gates leading into the village were shut tight ensuring everyone a good night's sleep. Just outside the old city is the *trattoria* Osteria del Ghiotto (see page 254), which prides itself on cooking the fine game of the region in tasty traditional ways.

Rather than returning to Sasetta on the road you've traveled, follow a smaller road on the outskirts of Canneto that points you to Suvereto. After several kilometers you'll see a sign pointing to Sasetta. Take the road and soon you'll find yourself back on the road you left just before Sasetta. Stop for a minute at the historic center of the town, once an ancient feudal castle that also passed to the Gherardesca family in the fifteenth century. The little *borgo* sits perched on a cliff overlooking the Val di Cornia leading to the sea. On the second Sunday of October you'll find a delicious *sagra* in Sasetta, dedicated to *polenta* and a hearty fall soup.

The next medieval town through the forest is Suvereto, an imposing fortress town with an old ruin of an Aldobrandeschi castle. This winding road is the best way to approach. Circle the old city wall to the main portal where you immediately peer into an inviting street up into the walled town. Suvereto is the oldest of hill towns in this area, dating back to the Roman era. Its name probably comes from the cork (*sughero*) trees that must have given the town its livelihood even in Roman times. Just outside the main portal is one of the more interesting Romanesque churches of the entire Livorno province. San Giusto dates back to the tenth century; the church you see today has been there since the twelfth. The simple exterior has a handsome entrance topped by a small clover-shaped stone lunette. Inside you'll find an ancient baptismal font surrounded by a glittering chapel of pale blue and silver mosaic.

There are several little churches to discover within the walls, a convent dating back to the thirteenth century and some wonderful ancient lanes. In one small square — in a truly magical setting — is a fine restaurant, Eno-Olitica d'Ombrone (see page 259). Saturday is market day just under the wall. A lively folklore festival for three Sundays in a row, the last in November and the first two in December, celebrates the wild boar. (For a full program, call the Tourist Office at 0565-829-304, or email evs@suvereto.net)

Past Suvereto, further down toward the sea, is another small town worth a visit, Campiglia Marittima, with Ristorante Pizzica (see page 263), which overlooks the dramatically placed Church of San Giovanni rising on a lone platform atop the town cemetery just below. Beyond is the entire bay.

Along the way toward San Vincenzo is the archaeological park of San Silvestro, where an eleventh-century mining village has been uncovered. Etruscan tombs dot the park. Walking through it is a rigorous experience that will work up the appetite for the next hearty meal. Reservations to visit the park are necessary on weekdays. It is open to all on weekends and holidays, but check for seasonal times. (Tel. 0565-838-680.) Returning to the seacoast at San Vincenzo, you'll find an unpretentious little fish restaurant in a *bagno* right on the sea, Bagno Nettuno (see page 266).

The Etruscans are the ancient progenitors of Tuscany; even though they occupied much of the Italian peninsula only Tuscany has inherited the name, the main Etruscan ruins, the most important Etruscan works of art, and some food traditions as well. Ruins dot the countryside, including an important one in Venturina along the way from Suvereto to the sea.

The coast is best visited in May or late September, when fewer travelers and vacationers crowd the beaches, and a cool breeze freshens the air. In late spring, the wild flowers burst forth everywhere. The soft sea breeze is euphoric. September is time for wine gathering, with the smells of autumn and magnificent dark-green visions of ancient olive trees bursting with fruit. I find the coast enticing in its mild winter as well.

SPECIALTIES OF MARINA DI PISA
TO UPPER MAREMMA

The Tuscan coastline is famous for the splendid fish from a still unpolluted sea, and for the wild game that abounds in little-known wild corners. Fish and game play an important role in the menus that you will find along the way.

From the seas along the mostly sandy coastline from Livorno south to Porto San Stefano come the best fresh fish of Italy, still prepared today in much the same way as in earlier years. But be aware that fish farms have recently sprung up and many popular fish are raised in salt ponds near the sea. The difference between them is in the eating: organic versus controlled. Purists will always check with the waiter to ascertain that the fish comes directly from the sea. At better restaurants one usually does not have to ask.

By far, the most popular fish, served grilled, roasted, or baked under a coat of salt, are the two delicate, fleshy princes of the sea: *branzino* (sea bass) and *orata* (gilt-head bream). (I give the names in Italian as they are on menus, and their British and, in some cases, French name, if possible. Many of these are unique to Mediterranean waters and have no equivalents in North America.) Less expensive, a mite bonier, but also delicate are *marmora* (striped bream), *dentice* (dentex), or *sarago* (sheepshead bream). They're all prepared in much the same ways as *branzino* and *orata*.

A favorite meaty fish, always a main ingredient in stews and soups — but also roasted in the oven together with slivers of potatoes, small tomatoes, and onions — is the bright red monster called *scorfano* (scorpion fish, or better known as the French *rascasse*). Like another fine-tasting red fish, *cappone* (red gunard), *scorfano* really looks like a crusty red beast. Roasted, it has an absolutely unbeatable juicy quality. The *cappone* is a bit dryer. I once heard *scorfano* called "the chicken of the sea." Both *scorfano* and *cappone* — or at least one of them — are essential to *cacciucco*, the local fish stew that is every bit as varied as the French *bouillabaisse*. (More about *cacciucco* below.) A similar fish and as tasty is *gallinella* (tub gunard). Another fish usually on the menu in seafood restaurants, mostly served *al forno* — baked — is the oval flat *San Pietro* (John Dory), a delicately-flavored rockfish as monstrous looking as the *scorfano*, but with dull brown rather than bright red skin.

Another favored fish along the Livornese coast is the little *triglia* (red mullet), bony, but delicious. It is often filleted into a fine pasta sauce. Tiny *triglie*, called *fragolini*—are only a few centimeters long, and are deep-fried in their entirety. *Triglie alla Livornese*, another local specialty, is red mullet sautéed in tomato sauce. Gray mullet, an entirely different sort of fish, goes by either *cefalo* or *muggina*.

A really ugly, but marvelously tasty, fish is *rospo* (angler or monkfish). Its head is so big that only its tail, *coda di rospo*, is ever seen out of water, even in open markets. It too is stewed or baked. *Cernia* (grouper) is also popular, found mostly filleted and fried. *Palombo* (smooth hound) is known also as *vitello del mare* (veal of the sea), perhaps because it is usually sliced and served as a small steak.

Still another really fine fish you'll find in these waters, *pezzagnia* (lizard fish), comes up to fishable waters only in springtime to breed, and thus is found on menus only between April and June. If it's there, do order it. It's also called *occhiona* (big eye) because of its enormous round and bulging green eyes. It, too, is either grilled or oven-roasted.

Larger fish are also served in *cartuccio*, tightly wrapped in baking paper with a dressing of simply extra-virgin olive oil and lemon and then baked.

Cacciucco is the best-known seafood dish of the Tuscan coast. It's a truly wondrous melange of various combinations of all of the above fish with cuttlefish and crustaceans, too. Every seaside restaurant has its own version, but each boasts a distinct variety. It's an enormous bowl of separately stewed fish and shellfish atop garlic-rubbed toast in a rich broth that's made from a blend of smaller fish and the heads of the bigger fish.

Shellfish—*frutti di mare*—abound in these waters. Different sizes or shapes of similar-looking crustaceans go by different names. A glossary is certainly in order, especially among the various kinds of cuttlefish with their big baggy heads and tentacles. Probably the tastiest among the octopus and squid families are *moscardini*, tough little things usually stewed in *guazzetto rosso*, a tomato sauce. The meatiest are *seppie*, cut into rings and served with pasta. *Calamari* and *totani*, the least chewy of them all, are also very popular. *Polpo* is a small octopus, a favorite of Tuscans, boiled, chopped, and either stewed or, with the addition of celery, made into a delicious vinegary salad.

Cozze are mussels, *gamberi* and *gamberetti* shrimp. There are dozens of different shrimp. Most special is the *gambera rossa*, an enormous bright red shrimp that I think is special to this area. *Scampi, cicali*, and *astrice* are crayfish usually served with their claws intact. *Vongole, datteri*, and *arselle* are clams. *Aragosti* are the lobsters that show up in these waters. *Granchi* are crabs; the local variety is sweet tasting and juicy.

You'll find three kinds of *zuppa* on every menu along the seacoast: a *zuppa di mare* includes all types of shellfish and squid, a *zuppa di cozze* only mussels, and a *zuppa di vongole* made with large or small clams.

As one leaves the coast for the hills, game replaces fish as the main specialty, especially in the Upper Maremma. The area is filled with natural parks and its woodland abounds with wildlife: boar, hare, deer, and game birds. Much is made of the available meat, from sausages to pasta sauces.

Antipasti include various sliced sausages made of *cinghiale* (wild boar) and other game flavored with the juniper berry that grows in abundance in the nearby woods. *Beccaccia al crostone* is a stew of woodcock served as *crostini*. Pasta dishes include *pappardelle al cinghiale* (wide noodles in a boar sauce) and the same *pappardelle* with a sauce of *lepre* (wild hare). Main courses can be *cinghiale* in *salsa* (marinated and stewed boar in red wine and tomatoes) or in *tegame* (simmered in its own juice.) Hare and boar are also cooked in *salmi*, i.e., stewed for a long period with herbs and spices. *Fagiano al diavolo* (pheasant in the devil's manner) is flavored with sage and cooked in white wine. *Tordi* (thrush) are usually cooked with sage and white wine.

One notable dish, neither fish nor game, is found all along this coast and in the hills too: *acquacotta*, or "cooked water," originated in the Mount Amiata area of the Maremma, but in one version or another it is now found throughout Tuscany. A simple, modest, hearty, tasty dish, *acquacotta* may well be one of the triumphs of Tuscan cooking. Don't leave the region without tasting it. Basically a simple onion broth, *acquacotta* in these parts has the soothing addition of seasonal vegetables, wild herbs, and local *pecorino*, making it almost a *minestrone*. It can be topped with hard boiled eggs as well.

The upper Maremma is also noted for its rich farmland and spring vegetables, notably the pointed little purple artichokes called *morello*, as well as asparagus and early tomatoes.

MARINA DI PISA

Via Tulio Crosio 1, Marina di Pisa • Tel. 050-34180

Open for dinner and sometimes for lunch—usually in summer—except on Mondays, and a reservation is suggested. Call to make sure about lunch as well. Can be pricey as fish restaurants are, but it is possible to eat well for less, too.

La Taverna dei Gabbiani lies at the mouth of the Arno, on the site of the demolished villa from where Gabriele D'Annunzio wooed Eleanora Duse.

Dino Giaconi and his brother Mario run this warm and inviting seafood restaurant. They grew up on this edge of the sea where the family ran a *stabilimento di bagno* on the beach just a few meters away from the restaurant. *Bagni* are concessions along the beach that rent out cabins, easy chairs, and showers, usually with a bar and restaurant attached. You can rent space by the day, or for longer periods. At theirs, Dino's grandfather cooked. All over Italy, entire families settle every year for a few summer weeks at some beach. Many choose a *bagno* for its food.

Dino is an inventive chef who knows and loves his fish. He'll show them off at the slightest hint, with almost a caress. His daily catch is full of shiny, bright-eyed specimens just emerged from the sea. His tubs of *frutti di mare* are varied; *calamari, scampi, cozze, vongole, granchi*. Dino recites his menu verbally as it changes with the daily catch. *Cacciucco* must be ordered beforehand. His *cacciucco* is a meticulous, long process that combines both fish and shellfish, cooked slowly in separate batches and collected in a rich tomato broth that is a meal in itself. (When you make your reservation, mention you'd like the *cacciucco*. It is not something they prepare every day.)

Nothing goes to waste…skins and bones, back to the sea, to the *gabbiani* (gulls) that inhabit the rocks just outside the restaurant.

One wonderfully light *antipasto* at this *taverna* is *mantecata* (or mash), usually of *branzino* or *orata*. It's a mousse made with a yolkless mayonnaise and just a touch of extra virgin olive oil to enhance the subtle flesh. Another is a tiny sea snail in a light wine sauce. You pick the snails out of their shells with a toothpick. They are delectable little tidbits. There's a brush growing along the seashore that the fisherman use to catch these little underwater creatures. The brush is dipped into the water and left there for the snails to cling to. The fishermen pluck them out of the water on the brush twice each day. The catch is quickly cooked.

As often in small Italian restaurants, the *antipasti* and *primi*—pasta, rice, and soup—are the most tempting at La Taverna dei Gabbiani. There are lots to choose from, among them *torta di acchiughe e cipolle*, a tart of onions and anchovies and the *mantecata* which is served on rounds of thin toasts.

Pasta here is prepared in a way common all along the coast. The pasta—usually *spaghetti* or homemade *tagliatelle*—is not thrown into boiling water. Rather it's cooked, almost like a *risotto*, directly in the sauce. It's a bit of a trick, especially with long *spaghetti* or *tagliatelle*; best to work with soft fresh *tagliatelle*. For harder, dry pasta, I'd recommend the home cook giving it a minute or two to soften in boiling water before adding it to the saucepan. At Taverna dei Gabbiani, however, the long pasta goes directly into a *soffrito* of olive oil, chopped onion, carrots, and celery. White wine goes in next. As it evaporates, the fish and boiling water are added. Water is added slowly, allowing the pasta to absorb each dose. Mixing with two wooden spoons goes on continually. As the pasta absorbs the liquid, the sauce absorbs the starch in the pasta. The result is creamy, well-flavored pasta. Pasta combinations at Gabbiani, according to season, include asparagus with shrimp, short *penne* with clams and fresh *porcini* mushrooms, combinations of *calimari* and red pepper, or mussels with fresh artichokes. A blackened *risotto*, made with *seppie* and their ink, is another specialty.

Fish Mousse

MANTECATA DI PESCE

●

Serves 6

1 fresh Mediterranean sea bass, weighing at least 2 pounds
Salt

FOR THE MAYONNAISE:

3 egg whites
Salt and freshly ground pepper
1⅓ cups vegetable or peanut oil, plus additional olive oil for dripping
12 slices of baguette bread, thinly sliced

Bring salted water to boil in a pan large enough to hold the entire fish.
Throw in the fish and cook for about 15 minutes, until the fish is cooked
through but still firm. Drain, and, before it cools, skin, bone and remove
the fleshy meat to a bowl. Break up with your hands into almost a paste,
and allow to cool to room temperature.

Make the mayonnaise by placing the egg whites in a food processor,
adding a pinch of salt, and turning on the machine, slowly, adding the vegetable oil in a thin stream. When the mixture thickens, turn off the machine.

Mix the mayonnaise into the fish with a fork, gently and carefully, amal-
gamating them well. Grind a good bit of pepper into the mixture. Put on
a flat plate and drip some fresh olive oil over it. Toast thin slices of the
baguette, drip some olive oil over each, and serve with the mousse, allowing
each diner to spread his own.

Anchovy and Onion Tart

TORTA DI ACCIUGHE E CIPOLLE

Serves 6

1 sheet frozen puff or other light crisp pastry

1 cup Béchamel, made from 1 tablespoon butter, 1 tablespoon flour, and
    1 cup milk

1¼ pounds fresh anchovies

2 large onions, thinly sliced

Salt and freshly ground pepper

A pinch of nutmeg

¼ cup olive oil

½ cup white wine

¼ cup brandy

2 eggs, well beaten

Preheat the oven to 350 degrees.

Roll out the pastry into a thin sheet to fit a large buttered pizza pan of about 24 inches in diameter. Prick holes in the pastry and bake for 5 minutes. Remove the pastry and set it aside, but keep the oven on at the same temperature.

Prepare the Béchamel by melting the butter, mixing in the flour, and slowly adding the milk. Bring to a boil, mixing all the while, then lower the heat and simmer until the sauce becomes creamy and thick. Set aside.

Prepare the anchovies by first slicing off the heads. Then open and remove the bone, an easy operation when you begin at the tail and gently pull it out. Chop the fillets into bite-sized pieces and reserve.

Cook the onions, barely covered with water, until they are soft and the water has completely evaporated. Put the onions in a bowl, and add salt and pepper to taste, and a good pinch of nutmeg. Add the oil, the chopped anchovies, the wine, a splash of brandy, and the beaten eggs. Mix in the Béchamel and season.

Spread the mixture smoothly over the pastry and bake for half an hour until the tart is well set. Serve warm.

Spaghettini with Asparagus and Shrimp
SPAGHETTINI CON ASPARAGI E GAMBERI

※

Serves 6

Dino cooks the thin pasta entirely in the sauce. The home cook would do better to soften it first and then finish it in the sauce. This recipe results in a creamy, rich, almost sweet pasta.

1 pound large shrimp
½ cup olive oil
3 shallots, chopped
½ cup dry white wine
3 large ripe tomatoes
1 small bunch parsley leaves, chopped
1 pound *spaghettini* or other thin long pasta
1 pound asparagus, steamed or boiled until cooked but still firm, and
    chopped into bite-sized pieces
Salt and freshly ground pepper

Peel the shrimp, remove the black vein. Prepare a stock with the shells and heads by putting them in a pan with 2 cups of water and boiling for about 10 minutes. Drain, reserving the water and keep it at a simmer. Chop the shrimp into bite-sized pieces.

Pour some boiling water over the tomatoes, peel, remove the seeds and chop coarsely. In a large pan, big enough to hold the pasta with the sauce, sauté the chopped shallots in the oil, add the shrimp and sauté for 3 minutes. Pour in the white wine. As it boils, add the tomatoes and parsley and cook for another five minutes. Add a good amount of salt and freshly ground pepper and lower the heat.

Drop the pasta into a large pot of boiling salted water, and as soon as it begins to boil again, turn off the heat. Drain the pasta, and add to the pot holding the shrimp. Almost cover with the reserved shrimp water, and begin to mix and cook, adding more water as the pasta absorbs. Add the chopped asparagus at the last minute, with some more salt and freshly ground pepper to taste. Serve immediately.

BIBBONA MARE

———— ❦ ————

LA PINETA

Via dei Cavalleggeri Nord 27, Marina di Bibbona • Tel. 0586-60016

La Pineta is open all year except October, for both lunch and dinner. Closed Monday and for lunch Tuesday. Reservations are absolutely necessary; for summer evenings four or five days in advance. Lunch is easier. Fairly expensive.

This seafood restaurant — a local favorite — is located on the beach of Bibbona Mare, just south of Cecina. La Pineta (or Zazzeri, after the owner, as most regular clients call the restaurant) is at the open end of a pine grove, looking out over the nearby islands of Capraia and Elba. The restaurant might well go unnoticed as just another beach shack, except for its reputation as the finest seafood restaurant around. La Pineta is a special treat, a bit pricey, but worthwhile.

Owner and chef Luciano Zazzeri, a trim elegant man, was a fisherman before he came ashore to open a simple little fish *trattoria*. He talks about fish with the restraint of an art dealer who knows he's got a Botticelli in hand; a kind of self-schooled sensibility that says, "Let the fish sell itself. Don't mess with it too much." He has the same attitude to all his other ingredients. His seafood, and his other produce — much of it comes from his father's *orto* (vegetable garden) — have turned La Pineta into a restaurant of simple elegance.

The warm *antipasti* are subtle combinations; a cabbage leaf stuffed with *ricotta* and fresh anchovies, salad of warm *calamari* in a creamy sauce of olives, pine nuts and white wine or a *sformato* of *ricotta* dressed with the big red *gamberi rossi* of the area. Asked what makes his *calamari* so good, Luciano will tell you, it's the place they come from and the way they are brought in. He buys directly from fishermen colleagues, and often goes out to fish with them as well.

Zazzeri treats vegetables with the same care. Tomatoes must never be cooked for too long or their sweetness may turn acerbic. Sweet white onions or red Tropea of Puglia go into the *soffritto* that's the base of *pasta alle triglie*, a delicacy of fresh pasta with small hunks of red mullet. Zazzeri doesn't believe in garlic or other strong tastes; it's the fish that counts. Few herbs other than parsley get used, but it's lots of parsley.

An oven-crisped flatbread made of fine couscous accompanies the *zuppetta di mare*. *Cacciucco* here is lighter than at most restaurants; the broth is thinner. Ingredients depend upon the catch of the day.

Desserts at La Pineta are good. There's a heavenly Napoleon with cream and caramel, and lots of others.

RECIPES FROM LA PINETA

Ricotta Mousse with Giant Shrimp
SFORMATO DI RICOTTA CON GAMBERI ROSSI

Serves 4

At La Pineta the mousse is made in individual cups, turned out on the tomato sauce and topped with the shrimp. At home, I make it in a round baking dish, top it with the tomatoes and surround it with the shrimp. It's delicious either way.

2 medium zucchini, chopped coarsely
1 shallot, chopped coarsely
3 tablespoons extra virgin olive oil
10½ ounces (about 1½ cups) *ricotta*
3 egg whites
Salt and freshly ground pepper
15 small cherry tomatoes
9 large red shrimp or scampi
2 ripe tomatoes, sliced (for garnish)

Preheat the oven to 350 degrees.

Sauté the zucchini and shallot in 2 tablespoons of olive oil for about 10 minutes, until they begin to soften and brown. Remove from heat. Beat the *ricotta* and egg whites together in a food processor for about 5 minutes. Remove to a bowl and add salt and pepper. Mix in the sautéed zucchini. Butter a round baking dish that will allow the *sformato* to rise (it will immediately fall again, so not to worry) and pour in the *ricotta* mixture. Bake for about half an hour, until the top begins to golden and the risen *sformato* is firm.

[251]

Quarter the cherry tomatoes and cook them quickly in the other tablespoon of olive oil. Squash them gently with a fork, and allow to rest.

Peel the shell from the body of each shrimp, leaving the tail and head. Steam them for about 3 or 4 minutes until they are just cooked. Put the *sformata* in its baking dish in the center of a large platter, top with the tomato sauce and surround with the shrimp. Serve warm.

Fresh Pasta with Red Mullet
STRACCETTI CON LE TRIGLIE

✺

Serves 4

Straccetti are thin fresh homemade pasta; *tagliarini* works well too.

6 red mullets of about ¾ pound each, cleaned
1 clove garlic
1 small hot pepper, seeded and minced
2 tablespoons extra virgin olive oil, plus more for dripping
1 cup water
Salt
1 pound *tagliarini*
5 cherry tomatoes, quartered
1 small bunch parsley, chopped

Put the mullets, garlic, pepper, oil, and water into a saucepan large enough to hold the pasta as well, and cook for about 7 minutes, or until almost cooked. Remove the fish and garlic. Fillet the fish carefully and return the fillets to the sauce.

Cook the pasta for 2 minutes in lots of boiling salted water. Remove and add the pasta to the fish. Mix well and continue to cook until the pasta is just *al dente*. Add the tomatoes, parsley, a dripping of oil, and serve.

Fresh Fish in "Crazy Water"

GALLINELLA ALL'ACQUA PAZZA

❋

Serves 6

Serve this either on top of, or accompanied by, a good amount of country bread. The water may be called crazy, but it's delicious.

2½ pounds fresh *gallinello* or other white fleshy fish, filleted
Olive oil
20 small ripe cherry tomatoes, halved
2 red onions, sliced thinly
½ cup water
½ cup white wine
15 *taggiasca* olives (mixed green and black), pitted
Salt and freshly ground pepper

Preheat the oven to 325 degrees.

Lay the fillets in a single layer in a baking dish, salt and pepper them, and drip some olive oil over each. Spread with the tomatoes and onions, cover with aluminum foil, and bake for 20 minutes.

Remove the fish from the oven, remove the foil just to add the wine and a scant ½ cup of water, cover again with the foil, and return to the oven. Cook for another 10 minutes. Remove the foil, add the olives and another dripping of olive oil. (This time don't recover with the foil) Cook for another 10 minutes, check the fish to see they are cooked, and serve with good rustic bread.

CANNETO

OSTERIA DEL GHIOTTO

Via di Lardersi (just under Canneto's old *borgo*), Canneto

Tel. 0565-784-435

It's moderately priced and small, only seven tables, so best to reserve in cool weather. In warmer months, an outdoor terrace gives more space. Open during the winter for lunch and dinner. Closing day is Tuesday. Also closed in February, and 20 days in November. During the summer, open only in evenings.

Nadia Ferri is a ferocious little woman who's been turning her own produce into delicious meals for most of her life. In 1998, with her son Cristiano Ferri and daughter-in-law Sandra, cooking became a full-time passion. This little *osteria* in the hills of Upper Maremma boasts an authenticity not easily found today. Nothing is served here that has not been acquired from local farmers and hunters and turned into traditional fare. If you like game and authentic old dishes, there's no better place to find it than Osteria del Ghiotto.

There's no menu, what you get is what's been found during the early morning rounds. Cristiano will tell you what's fresh and what Nadia has done with it, be it wood thrush, wild pigeon, or several sorts of wild mushrooms. Vegetables — they are the freshest — and poultry come from local farmer friends. From November through January Nadia helps her local *norcino* (pork butcher) prepare the various pork sausages and other preserved meat products that the restaurant serves until they run out in late spring. Later she tries to get similar products from friends. She helps the *norcino* flavor the *prosciutto* and *spalla* (pork shoulder), the bacon (*rigatino*) and the blood sausage (*melangata*). The liver is put into flavored fat and wrapped in caul to make *fegatello*. The roasts are made into *arista*, thinly sliced, rolled tightly with herbs, and preserved in fresh extra virgin olive oil. Other preserved bits of the pork are stuffed into the lower leg to make *zampone* and *contenna di maiale*, traditional stuffed trotters boiled with other meats for *bollito misto* and served at the New Year with lentils.

The wild boar served here is truly wild. It is brought in by hunters, as is hare. Rabbits and chickens are free range, arriving daily from nearby farms. Spring features wild asparagus and the small, locally grown purple artichokes called *morello*. Nadia preserves them in fresh olive oil. Not to be missed are the homemade *tortelloni*, heartily stuffed with a delicious filling of *ricotta* and Swiss chard.

It's tough to get a recipe from Nadia; when you ask how much of this or that goes into a dish, she only shrugs and says, *"quanto basta"* (when it's enough) or *"un bel po"* (a good amount). The safest is the one below.

RECIPE FROM OSTERIA DEL GHIOTTO

Artichokes Marinated in Olive Oil
CARCIOFI SOTT'OLIO

❀

Makes 1 quart

1 dozen (or more) baby artichokes (little pointed purple *morella*, if possible)
Salt
A mixture of ¾ white wine vinegar and ¼ white wine to cover for cooking
A handful of peppercorns
3 or 4 bay leaves
Extra virgin olive oil to cover

Trim the artichokes down to the light green leaves around the hearts and cook, with some salt, in the vinegar/wine mixture for 4 minutes. Remove. Drain and dry well with kitchen toweling.

Place in a jar, add a handful of peppercorns and some bay leaves, and cover with olive oil. Leave for a few days before eating. It is not necessary to refrigerate. The traditional way is to cut the artichokes in half and salt them as you eat.

BOLGHERI

LA TAVERNA DEL PITTORE
Largo Nonna Lucia 4, Bolgheri • Tel. 0565-762-184
*Open year round except the month of November. Closed Monday. Open
only for dinner from June 15 to September 15; otherwise open for lunch
and dinner. Prices are moderate.*

A wild orange tree rambles over the outdoor tables in front of La Taverna
del Pittore. Its perfume engulfs the entire place. The restaurant, owned by
the young Gofredo d'Andrea, has two lovely little rooms inside, with walls
covered by the work of local artists. The previous owner of the house was
himself an artist; his evocative landscapes are included among those
crowding the walls.

In addition to offering the traditional fare of the Maremma, Gofredo
and his chef Daniela Macchioni add some innovative dishes to the menu.
The local version of puffed fried bread—called *zonzelle*—comes as *antipasto*, warm and covered with a thin melting slice of *lardo di Colonnata*.
Delicious potato *gnocchi* are bathed in a sauce of melted *gorgonzola* and
taleggio cheeses, highlighted by large juicey grapes. *Puntarelle*, a crunchy
rough field green found in winter months along this mild coastline, is lightly
dressed with a creamy anchovy sauce, a dish you'll find more easily in Rome
than in Tuscany. *Lasagna* comes in two varieties: one with a creamy young
artichoke sauce, the other with *funghi porcini*.

You'll also find the meat specialties of the region, *salvaggino*, or produce
of the hunt—wild hare, boar, and other game—and Maremma beefsteaks
and cutlets. *Maltagliati*, or "badly cut," are only one of the several freshly
made pastas. They are covered with a fragrant duck sauce. *Tagliolini* (thin
fresh pasta) has a pigeon and eggplant sauce, the wide *pappardelle* come
with either boar or hare.

The house treat is a sweet, a Bolgheri specialty, the *cialdone della nonna
farcito*: a cone-shaped homemade waffle bursting with whipped cream and
covered with either a wild berry or chocolate sauce.

Pappardelle with Hare Sauce
PAPPARDELLE ALLA LEPRE

✦

Serves 6

This popular Tuscan dish can be made with rabbit as well. If you have hare, save the saddle for another use and make this sauce only with the meat from the legs, and, if you want, chopped pieces of the liver.

1 onion, chopped
1 rib celery, chopped
1 clove garlic, chopped
1 small bunch parsley leaves, chopped
3 tablespoons extra virgin olive oil
2 ounces *pancetta*, cubed
Boned leg meat of 1 hare, cut into strips
Leaves of 2 sprigs fresh thyme
1 tablespoon flour
½ cup red wine
1 cup hot chicken stock
Salt and freshly ground pepper
1¼ pounds *pappardelle*
1 cup Parmesan, grated

Melt the chopped onion, celery, garlic, and parsley in the olive oil, add the *pancetta*, and cook for a few minutes. Add the hare pieces and the thyme and cook until the hare is browned on all sides. Sprinkle the flour over the hare, mix well, cook for another minute, and add the wine, mixing well. Allow the wine to evaporate and add the chicken stock. Cover and cook over a low flame for about an hour, until the meat is cooked throughout, and the sauce is a nice thick consistency. Add salt and lots of freshly ground pepper.

Cook the *pappardelle* in a big pan of boiling salted water. Drain, pour the sauce over the pasta, and mix in half the Parmesan. Serve with the remaining cheese at table.

Artichoke Lasagna

LASAGNA AI CARCIOFI

❋

Serves 6-8

8 globe artichokes or 10 baby spring artichokes

2 lemons

¼ cup butter

Salt and freshly ground pepper

Béchamel sauce made from ¼ cup butter, 3 tablespoons flour, 4 cups milk,

Salt and freshly ground pepper

2 cups Parmesan, grated

¼ cup finely chopped mozzarella (1 large ball, about ½ pound)

1 pound fresh green *lasagna* noodles

Preheat the oven to 400 degrees.

Prepare a bowl of acidulated water by squeezing the juice of one lemon to the water.

To prepare the artichokes, snap off the outer leaves down to the tender inner leaves. Slice off the tops and quarter the artichokes, rubbing the cut edges with half a lemon to prevent them from discoloring. Cut out the fuzzy inner choke and thinly slice each quarter. Drop into the bowl of acidulated water. Repeat with all the artichokes.

Drain the artichokes and put them into a large flat pan. Add the butter and water just to cover. Cook over a medium-high fire until the water has totally evaporated and the artichokes are tender. Salt well and transfer to a large bowl. Mix with ¾ quarters of the Béchamel. Taste, add the juice of the remaining half lemon, and more salt and pepper if necessary.

Put the cheeses in two separate bowls. Fill another large bowl with cold water. Fill yet another pan with water, add some salt, and bring to a boil. Butter a baking pan large enough to hold the finished dish.

To assemble, butter a large baking pan. Drop enough pasta to cover the bottom of the baking dish into the boiling water. After a minute, remove the pasta with a slotted spoon and drop into a bowl of cold water to cool. When the pasta is cool, remove and layer the bottom of the baking dish with the noodles. Spread ⅓ of the artichoke cream over, then ¼ of each of the cheeses.

Repeat the process to make two more layers. Put another layer of pasta leaves on top, and cover with the remaining Béchamel and cheeses. Add some more salt, and grind some pepper over the top. (Up to this point, the *lasagna* can be prepared some hours before serving.)

Bake for about half an hour, until a golden-brown crust has formed. Allow to rest a bit before serving.

SUVERETO

ENO-OLITECA OMBRONE

Piazza dei Giudici, Suvereto • Tel. 0565-829-336

Lunch and dinner daily; closed Monday and Tuesday lunch. Closed January 7 through February 25. Reservations recommended, especially summer evenings. Moderately priced, to expensive.

This little jewel of a restaurant is located in one of the most delightful settings imaginable, an old olive mill connected by an ancient wall to the arched twelfth-century municipal hall of Suvereto. The dining terrace is enclosed by both. In the evenings the old *palazzo* is illuminated, enhancing even more the harmonious quality of the surroundings.

Graziella (Lella) Durante-Bini had little experience in the kitchen when she married into a family that had been restaurateurs for five generations. She did the logical thing, went to the local Cordon Bleu school and ended up teaching at various Tuscan cooking schools for 20 years. Even today, as she works overtime in the kitchen of Ombrone, she manages a cooking course out of season, twice a week at the restaurant. She likes to play a little with traditional dishes; as a result, Ombrone offers interesting variations on age-old Tuscan fare, what Lella calls "Cucina Toscana lightly revisited."

Her husband Giancarlo Bini knows as much as anyone about traditional Tuscan products. He is a collector of information, fine olive oils and wine, exotic teas and rare coffees, chocolates and liquors, as well as old tools of the mill. They are all there on display, to savor and to view.

The best way to open a meal at Ombrone is with a tasting of some of Giancarlo's oils on a *fett'unta*, toasted farm bread steeped in fresh olive oil. Here you get a sampling of four or five choice ones.

Fresh herbs, snipped at the last minute, are notable in both *antipasti* and first courses. Galantina of *calamaretto* (little squid) is served with wild herbs; *pomodoro con riso* (fresh tomatoes on rice) is remarkable for its delicate flavoring of different garden herbs. Lettuce soup, with a touch of anchovies, is a spring starter; in the winter local *farro* is combined with split peas. Fine Sienese pork is wrapped in a tuna sauce, a tasty half pigeon in a mix of honey and balsamic vinegar.

Before attempting the rich chocolate dessert or baked pear, have a tasting of the *pecorino*—either fresh or slightly aged—with a choice of sweet-sour marmalades and honey. It's the best old Tuscan way of finishing a meal, especially in those parts where sheep graze and lots of *pecorino* gets made. Ombrone's sharp pepper marmalade is especially interesting.

RECIPES FROM RISTORANTE ENO-OLITECA OMBRONE

Lettuce Soup
ZUPPA DI LATTUGA GRATINATA

Serves 8

4 heads lettuce
2 onions, finely sliced
1 clove garlic, chopped
3 tablespoons butter
5 tablespoons extra virgin olive oil
6 anchovy fillets preserved under salt, washed and soaked for an hour
6 cups vegetable broth
Salt and freshly ground pepper
1 bunch parsley leaves, chopped
1 small bunch basil leaves, chopped
8 slices toasted rustic bread
1½ cups grated *pecorino* or Parmesan

Preheat the oven to 400 degrees.

Cut the hard core from the bottom of the lettuce, remove any old leaves, and divide each head into six wedges. Slice each wedge into ½-inch widths.

Wash and spin dry. In a large soup pot, sauté the onion and garlic in the butter and olive oil. Drain the anchovies, add them to the pot, and allow to melt. Add the lettuce, and when it becomes limp, add the broth. Add the parsley and basil, and cook gently, covered, for another 15 minutes. Remove from heat, and add salt and lots of freshly ground pepper. Toast the bread and, if you like, rub each slice with half of a garlic clove. Place 4 of the slices on the bottom of a baking dish, cover with half the soup and a little less than half the cheese. Cover with the remaining slices of bread, the rest of the soup, and sprinkle the remaining cheese on top. Heat in the oven for 10 minutes. Serve hot, or warm.

Pigeon in Balsamic Vinegar and Honey
PICCIONE CON MIELE ED ACETO BALSAMICO

Serves 4

2 small pigeons or guinea hens, halved
1 clove garlic, finely chopped
Leaves of 2 sprigs rosemary, finely chopped
2 sprigs sage leaves, finely chopped
2 tablespoons extra virgin olive oil
¾ cup white wine
½ cup broth
2 tablespoons balsamic vinegar
2 tablespoons honey
Salt

Wash and dry the pigeon or guinea hens. Salt them well. Heat the garlic, rosemary, and sage leaves together with the olive oil in a pan with a cover that is large enough to hold the fowl as well. When the oil begins to bubble, add the fowl and brown well on all sides. Splash the white wine over the contents of the pan and allow to evaporate almost completely.

Add the broth, cover, and cook over a slow fire until the fowl is almost cooked, about an hour. Remove the cover, pour over the vinegar and cook over a medium heat until the liquid has a sauce-like quality. Before serving, drip the honey over each of the birds and serve with the sauce.

Hot Pepper Marmalade
MARMELLATA DI PEPERONCINI

Makes about 3 cups

2 pounds small hot red peppers
3 sweet red peppers
1½ pounds sugar
Juice of 1 lemon
1 vanilla bean, split lengthwise
4 cups white wine

Clean all the peppers of seeds and ribs. (Be careful with the hot ones; don't rub your eyes!) Put the peppers in a pan with the sugar, the lemon juice, half the wine, and the vanilla bean. Allow to sit for 4 hours. Place on the fire and add the remaining wine. Mix well and cook for an hour over moderate heat, mixing often. It should be reduced to a marmalade consistency.

Serve with fresh *pecorino* or other fresh yellow goat cheese.

Farro and Split Peas
MINESTRA DI FARRO E PISELLI

Serves 4

Ombrone uses a local *farro* for this dish; I prefer the fat *farro* of the Garfagnana which doesn't have to be soaked. The final dish does not have to be as dry as a *risotto*; it should have a bit of sauce around it when served.

1 cup dried split peas, soaked
1 large onion, chopped
5 tablespoons extra virgin olive oil
1 cup *farro*
1 head lettuce, sliced and chopped
4 cups hot vegetable broth
Salt and freshly ground pepper
½ cup Parmesan, grated
2½ ounces prosciutto, chopped
1 teaspoon balsamic vinegar

Soak the peas for about 3 hours. Sauté the onion for about 3 minutes in 3 tablespoons olive oil, add the *farro* and the peas, and sauté for another few minutes. Add ¾ of the lettuce, and cook over a low flame for another few minutes until the lettuce completely wilts. Add the vegetable broth, and cook over a minimal heat—barely simmering in order not to break up the peas—for about 50 minutes, until the peas are soft. If the broth gets totally absorbed and the mixture begins to dry out, add a little more broth. Add salt and pepper to taste at the end of the cooking. Mix in the Parmesan.

In another sauté pan, sauté the prosciutto in the remaining oil and splash in the balsamic vinegar. When the vinegar evaporates, add the mixture to the *farro* and peas and serve with more cheese at the table.

CAMPIGLIA MARITTIMA

RISTORANTE PIZZICA

Piazza della Vittoria 2, Campiglia Marittima • Tel. 0565-838-383
Lunch and dinner. Closed Mondays and, for vacation, fifteen days in September. Prices are moderate.

On the road from Suvereto to the coast at San Vincenzo, just under the old gate of Campiglia Marittima, you'll find the open terrace of Pizzica directly facing the twelfth-century Romanesque Church of San Giovanni. Beyond is the sea, with the curved bay of the Argentario, and, on a good day, a view of the nearby islands. In the evenings, the church is illuminated, giving it the aura of a stage set. To get the best view, reserve a table on the right of the enclosed terrace; otherwise the great pine tree growing directly in front might block your view.

Renza Venturelli serves the simple food of the region, enhanced by a modern innovation here and there. She has taken over the restaurant from her parents; her mother still cooks alongside Renza. Her grandfather Giuseppe opened the restaurant back in the 1950s, doing all the *casalinga* or home-cooking himself.

A good way to start a meal is with their *antipasto Pizzica*, a mixture of almost pudding-like, soft-cured local *raviggiolo*, sheep cheese served with a warmed spiced eggplant dressing. The homemade *gnocchi alla pastore* is little more than *gnocchi* on a bed of shaved, smoked, and aged *ricotta* with a touch of butter. The *pappardelle* in *salsa di cinghiale* (wild boar sauce) features juniper berries that grow in the nearby forests. There's also a thick grilled pork chop served with a sauce of green apples cooked with a bit of cognac and cream.

A special sweet *focaccia* (flatbread), locally known as *schiaccia* ("squashed"), is the specialty of Campiglia Marittima. Made with lard shortening, it is especially light and is served with *vin santo*, the sweet dessert wine of the area to end a meal.

RECIPES FROM RISTORANTE PIZZICA

Eggplant and Cheese Antipasto
ANTIPASTO PIZZICA

Serves 6

Pizzica serves the eggplant with the pudding-like *raviggiolo* cheese. I prefer it with the sweeter and more easily obtainable fresh *ricotta*.

2 shiny medium-sized eggplants, peeled and cut into small cubes
6 tablespoons extra virgin olive oil
2 cloves garlic, smashed or chopped
6 tablespoons water
Salt
1 hot chili pepper, chopped
10 ounces (about 1½ cups) *raviggiolo* or *ricotta* cheese

Put the oil and garlic into a large frying pan. When the oil begins to bubble around the garlic, add 6 tablespoons of water and the eggplant. Add plenty of salt and the chili pepper to taste. Remove to a serving bowl and serve warm accompanied by the cheese and lots of fresh or toasted farm bread.

Pork Chops with Apples
COSTOLETTE DI MAIALE ALLE MELE

✦

Serves 6

3 slightly tart green apples, such as Granny Smith, peeled, cored, and sliced
  into half-inch widths
3 tablespoons extra virgin olive oil
2 tablespoons cognac
3 tablespoons cream
6 thick pork chops
Salt and freshly ground pepper

Heat 2 tablespoons of oil in a sauté pan and sauté the apples until just soft
and browned. Throw in the cognac and allow to evaporate for a minute.
Add the cream, cook for another minute, and remove from heat.

Salt and pepper the pork chops and brush with the remaining olive oil.
Either grill or fry the pork chops, and serve with the apples and their sauce.

Campiglia Shortbread
SCHIACCIA CAMPIGLIESE

✦

½ cup sugar
½ cup flour
⅓ cup lard or shortening, at room temperature
1 egg
½ cup coarsely chopped walnuts or pine nuts
Butter or shortening for greasing the pan

Preheat the oven to 325 degrees.

Put the sugar and flour into a bowl and mix well. Work the lard in with
your fingers until the dough is grainy. Beat the egg and incorporate it into
the dough. Mix in the nuts.

Grease an 8-inch pie tin, and press the dough flat into it. Bake until the
top is golden and the *schiaccia* firm, about 45 minutes. While still warm,
cut into squares. At Pizzica the squares are dipped into small glasses of *vin
santo* at the end of a meal.

SAN VINCENZO

———— ❧❀❧ ————

BAGNO NETTUNO

On the beach at Via Costa 3, San Vincenzo • Tel. 0565-701-095

Open from a week before Easter through October, lunchtime and in the evenings. Reservations are recommended. Inexpensive to moderately priced.

The little seaside *bagno* restaurant Nettuno, is at the end of a short dead end street on the beach in San Vincenzo. To find it as you drive along the main street from the north, look for a little turn to the right called Via Costa which stops dead about 30 meters on. A boardwalk to the left leads to Nettuno. (It is just around the corner from the more elegant and renowned restaurant Gambero Rosso).

Elio Frassoni, owner and chef, is from Lombardy, but Nettuno is very much a Tuscan restaurant. Rosemary and garlic pervade, put to their tastiest best. The sounds of the sea, the light breeze, and soft splashing of waves provide the background music. *Crostini di mare*, a mixture of warm seafood, is served on crisp toast. The *ravioli di pesce* are stuffed delicately with *ricotta* cheese, *cernia* (grouper), and *scampi*; the smooth sauce is made of puréed shrimp and tomato. A zuppa of mussels and clams is served atop a tomato *bruschetta*. The restaurant's *cacciucco* must be ordered in advance for a minimum of four people.

Main course fish are served simply, either grilled in the pan or *alla piastra*, on a hot brick with little more than a stuffing of rosemary and garlic, salt and extra-virgin olive oil. Elio likes to make a bigger fish *alla Toscana*, gently baked in the oven in a sauce of tomatoes and black olives.

Mussels in Tomato Stew
COZZE ALLA MARINARA

Serves 4

2 pounds mussels
3 cloves garlic, chopped
1 small onion, chopped
1 small bunch parsley leaves, chopped
3 tablespoons olive oil
1 wineglass white wine
1 pound tomatoes, skinned and squeezed of juices and chopped, or the
    contents of 1 large (1 lb. 12 oz.) can Italian tomatoes, drained of juice
Freshly ground black pepper
2 sprigs thyme leaves
1 small hot pepper, chopped
4 slices day-old rustic Tuscan bread, toasted

Soak the mussels for at least an hour in a big pan of cold water. Scrub clean
and remove the beards. Discard any mussels that are broken or open.

While the mussels are soaking, prepare the sauce: Sauté the chopped
garlic, onion, and parsley leaves in the oil for five minutes. Add the wine,
allow to evaporate and add the tomatoes. If using tinned tomatoes, squeeze
them in one by one, breaking them up as you squeeze. Add lots of freshly
ground pepper, the thyme leaves and hot pepper. Cook gently, reducing the
sauce to a thick stew. (The mussels will add water and salt.)

Add the mussels and cook over a high heat, shaking the pan, until all
the mussels open. With a slotted spoon, remove the mussels to a serving
dish and pour the sauce over. Place a slice of toasted bread in each of four
soup bowls and divide the mussels over.

CHAPTER 10

The Maremma and Western Slopes of Mount Amiata

AS YOU LOOK UP TO MOUNT AMIATA FROM ANY-
WHERE IN SOUTHERN TUSCANY, IT SEEMS LESS
a dominating mountain than a long voluptuous island in the sky. The soft
summit of beech trees accentuates the roundness. It's hard to imagine that
a mere 180,000 years ago, it was a fuming volcano spewing down brim and
fire to form huge rocks that today support dramatic hill towns.

The mountain is etched on the horizon of much of central Tuscany.
You look at it in the morning to know what kind of day it's going to be.
An old proverb tells us that *"Quando l'Amiata mette il capello, devi aprire
l'ombrello"* (When Amiata wears a cap, open the umbrella).

Amiata is mostly attached to the lower Maremma, which lies directly
under it in the west. It's to the south of the area explored in Chapter Nine
and west of Chapter Seven's itinerary. I like best to approach the mountain
from the Grosseto coastline. From here, the road climbs gently through the
brush up to the chestnut forests and dramatic hill towns snuggling on the
tips of former volcanic peaks.

Before I came to know better, I'd always thought of this lower
Maremma as Tuscany's badlands, a Wild West sort of place where cowboys
rode off on fabled Maremma horses to round up their sheep, accompanied by long-haired white Maremma sheepdogs. It used to be an unhappy
malaria-infested place, memorialized in a popular folk song, *Maremma
Amara* (Bitter Maremma), a poignant, lilting melody about a dying bird.

A good bit of the flat Maremma remains an extension of the seaside
macchie, or scrub. But alongside the scrub and brush are great avenues of
gracious umbrella-shaped Mediterranean pines, majestic cypresses, and birch
trees. Vineyards and olive groves extend as far as the wooded foothills of the
mountain. Amiata itself is laden with hefty, centuries-old chestnut trees that
by November give the area one of its most useful nourishments.

Mount Amiata was once a real volcano; dormant for millennia, it is still filled with minerals, hot springs, and lots of strange looking rock formations. Many of these formations form the base of the clustered hill towns that dot the mountain landscape. Almost as prevalent are huge fortresses and castles. Most were built by the Aldobrandeschi family who came down from northern Lombardy sometime in the eleventh and twelfth centuries. They left massive castles in almost every town you'll see.

A good way to get through the southern Maremma to Mount Amiata is to leave the Livorno/Grosseto *superstrada* at Braccagni, and travel from there to a little trafficked road that takes you past Sticciano through Stazione Roccostrada to Paganico.

At Paganico, the real trip up to Mount Amiata begins. I recommend the road to Montenero, past Montegiovi to Castel del Piano and up to Seggiano. From Seggiano you can take the road to the summit of Mount Amiata, a lovely narrow forest road that every now and again allows the landscape through. At the top is Vetta Amiata with an enormous iron cross, and a small ski resort just below.

From the summit of Mount Amiata, head down to Abbadia San Salvatore, an old mercury mining town with the oldest and most beautiful abbey of the area. From San Salvatore, go on to Piancastagnaio, Bagnolo, and the amazing castle town of Santa Fiora. Monte Labbro, a soft mountain that many claim has a special spiritual aura, lies just beyond. From there it's a short drive to Arcidosso, the principal town of the Amiata area. The trip back to the coast will take you from Arcidosso through Cinigiano and Sasso d'Ombrone, down to the Maremma coast north of Grosseto.

Each stop along the way has its own special moment, its spectacular view, its verdant forest, a particular church, or a hill town of lovely old lanes. The tiny old town of Montenero, once an Aldobrandeschi estate, has

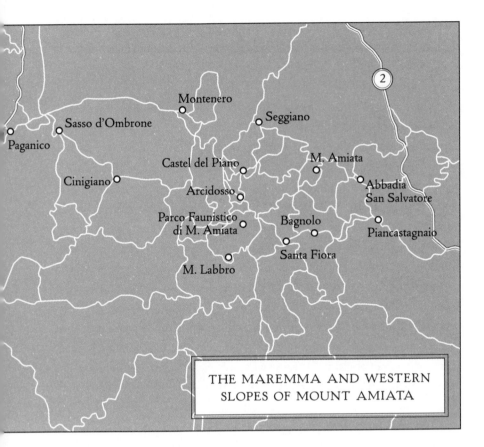

THE MAREMMA AND WESTERN
SLOPES OF MOUNT AMIATA

no major fortress, but boasts a handsome little graveled piazza with a fountain in its center. It's closed on three sides with small houses and palaces, a little wine museum, and an especially good restaurant called Antica Fattoria del Grottaione. Next to the restaurant you can visit the wine and oil cellars of Perazzeta, a major wine producer of the area (Via della Piazza, Tel. 0564-954-158). Montenero is one of the main stops along the Strade del Vino of Montecucco, a Mount Amiata wine zone that received its DOC designation as a distinguished wine area a few years ago.

Alessandro Bocci, owner of the Perazzeta wine cellars, is a native of Montenero (his sister owns the grocery next door; there's an open panel in the wall between them to pass wine on demand). Behind the square is Giorgio Franci's *frantoio*, the most prestigious oil press of the area (Via A. Grandi 5, Tel. 0564-954-000). It's a modern press that works overtime from the first of November through the winter months. Olives arrive by the ton, the aroma and noise mingle, and you can have an oil tasting in the dining room above the press. From Montenero there's a good view of Amiata, the Val d'Orcia below, and on a clear day, the distant rounded hills of the Crete Senese.

The main road continues to Castel del Piano. From there the next worthy stop is Seggiano, yet another town where you immediately feel the rekindling of old traditions in food and wine. You come upon this beige beehive of a town quite suddenly; it's an impressive view. Just before town, a turn to the right brings you to an interesting modern addition to the landscape: the sculpture garden of Daniel Spoerri. Over a large area of mostly meadow and olive trees, Spoerri — a Swiss artist — has placed some eighty sculptures of his own and works by other, mostly Swiss, sculptors. My favorite, by Olivier Estoppey, is a flock of 160 remarkably agile geese running from three bulky trumpeters announcing Judgment Day. There's a fine view from here of Seggiano and the massive Castello di Potentino just under the town. You'll also find a small restaurant at Spoerri's sculpture garden serving basic traditional food. Visits to the sculpture garden as well as the restaurant must be reserved in advance. (Il Giardino di Daniel Spoerri, Tel. 0564-950-457; Fax 0564-950-026; closed Monday, entrance fee 7 euros)

The medieval center of Seggiano is evocative with its small ancient alleyways, portals, and stairways. The town is becoming better known for its very special olive oil. It comes from an olive tree called *olivastra* that produces a light fragrant oil already known in Roman times. The oil is now enjoying a revival, thanks in part to the foreigners who have moved into the area. The *olivastra* grows only here, benefiting apparently from a combination of micro-climate and volcanic earth. You can also find a fine little cheese-making enterprise just at the entrance to Seggiano, the Caseificio Seggiano. It makes a variety of excellent *pecorino* (sheep) cheeses, from light fresh *ricotta* to a fine seasoned *pecorino* aged in the well of a cave.

Castello di Potentino, in the valley just under Seggiano, dates back to Etruscan times. Its earliest documentation is 1042. Today it is filled with fine old English furniture. It belongs to Hugh Greene, a brother of English author Graham, and his family, wife Julia and daughter Carlotta. They have planted vast new vineyards and olive groves. "It's really we women who are doing it," Carlotta told me. I came across her just as she was emerging from the olive groves with a small band of what she calls her "eco-slaves," young college kids who come from all over to live at the *castello* and work a few weeks or months at organic farming for which they receive bed and board. They had been picking olives the entire morning. We joined her and her helpmates for a hearty minestrone and cheese before they ventured out again. Carlotta, a writer, is an old acquaintance. She was the same willowy woman we'd first met as Charlotte in Jerusalem where she'd been researching a book on the Bedouin.

The huge stone castle was a complete ruin when they bought it. Carlotta and her mother have painstakingly restored it during the past eight years and she's more or less given up on serious writing and turned to serious wine making. Their wine is now one of the finest of the Montecucco DOC area as is their *olivastra* olive oil. The castle and its wine-making facilities are open to the public; there are also a few rooms for rent. To visit, reservations are necessary (Tel. 0564-950-326; Fax 0564-950014; email: castellodipotentino@virgilio.it).

The road back to Castel del Piano from Seggiano soon has a left turn that will take you through the forests directly up to the summit of Mount Amiata. From there another road takes you down to Abbadia San Salvatore, an old town that still has rusting equipment lying around from its better days as a mercury mining center. Here the imperative visit is to the great abbey itself, enclosed in a small square behind a medieval portal. Make sure not to miss it. You'll be stunned as you enter. Few churches are as evocative of the early Middle Ages. It's the oldest church in the area, begun by the Lombards in the eighth century, with a gold embellished alterpiece and magnificent dry-stone walls. The church is on two levels, with a monumental staircase leading up to the altar. The real marvel lies below in the crypt. Turn the light on (as you come down the few stairs the switch is on your right). You enter a chamber of slender, gently lit, ancient stone columns, each with its own decoration and capital. Fantastic animals and primitive human icons decorate each, with geometric designs and floral motifs. There's an interesting medieval town center near the Abbazia that's worth visiting as well.

Nearby Piancastagnaio a medieval hill town with a rich cultural past, dominated by a perfectly restored, overwhelming *rocca*, a castle that squats like an overlord on top of the town. From its tower, you can look down at the medieval houses as they tumble down the hillside, Humpty-Dumpties pushed off their high wall. The castle was originally built by the Aldobrandeschi family in the twelfth century. In the fourteenth the Sienese took it, and a century later, the Florentines. It still boasts the Medici family crest over its main door. The town takes its name from the chestnut woods all around it and celebrates the ubiquitous nut every November 1, All Saints Day, with Il Crastatone, a festival that features all the dishes derived from chestnuts. There are a great many. There's also a fine restaurant, just outside the castle wall, Ristorante Anna (see page 282). Near Piancastagnaio, on the way to Bagnolo, is a small cluster of houses called Tre Case; there you'll find a huge oak tree that Saint Francis is said to have rested by. It's one of the largest in Italy, designated as a "monumental plant."

Bagnolo is a drive-through town, but with a special mill that still stone-grinds chestnut and corn flours and a *forno* that bakes its bread in the old-fashioned way as well. An old-fashioned flatbread that still gets eaten here is made only in Bagnolo: a *schiacciatta di friccioli*, its top sprinkled with fried pork drippings.

Don't miss the remarkable little town of Santa Fiora nearby. It boasts the *pieve* of Sante Fiora e Lucilla, a church filled with sublime fifteenth-century della Robbia bas-reliefs including one that takes its inspiration from Piero della Francesca's beloved fresco of the Resurrection on the wall of the civic museum in San Sepolcro. You enter the town from the top, through the open entrance portal of what was once a Strozzi palace, a large chilly room-like gate that actually has a fireplace at its center. At the other side of the entrance, you exit into an inordinately large rectangular piazza fronted by an older structure of the thirteenth century, the castle of the previous ruling family, the Aldobrandeschi.

The Aldobrandeschi also built the lovely church of Sante Fiora e Lucilla. It lies at the end of Via Carolina, a narrow street running down from the right edge of the piazza. Among the other della Robbias in the church are a baptism of Christ and a Last Supper. The Resurrection is on the pulpit, complete with sleeping soldiers at the feet of the Christ. Along the same narrow Via Carolina is the restaurant Il Barilotto (see page 285), a pleasant lunch stop.

In one of the characteristic old streets around the center, the Via del Fondaccio, many of the tiny houses are still encrusted with medieval symbols on their lintels, mostly those of the hunt that was always so much a part of life here. If you get to the little church of St. Augustine, you'll find a small wooden Madonna and child said to be by Jacopo della Quercia. In all there is an amazing amount to see in this little town, including evidence of a small ghetto and synagogue dating from the sixteenth century when Jews fleeing Spain found refuge and civic privilege in much of the Maremma.

Just under the old town of Santa Fiora is a small hand-wrought water basin called *Le Pescherie*, or Fishing Hole, dug by the Aldobrandeschi in the thirteenth century to grow trout, undoubtedly one of the first fish farms around. Later the ruling Sforza turned it into a park, and it's still enjoyed today as such. Driving past *Le Pescherie*, there is a turn up onto the serene Monte Labbro, with an aura that people around here maintain is pure inspiration and spirit. It boasts therapeutic spring waters, pastures of grazing sheep, and some dramatic volcanic rock formations.

Davide Lazzaretti began the first Italian commune here in the mid-1800s as a protest against new taxation on tenant farmers. His was a spiritual endeavor too, and began with, at first, the backing of the church. He became too much of a messianic figure, however, and ended being killed by the *carabinieri* while leading a peaceful march through Arcidosso. He was buried in Santa Fiora, the only community that would accept his body. He's still a much revered figure in these parts; there is a monument to him on Monte Labbro.

The Parco Faunistico on Monte Labbro is a wild animal refuge with its own very special little restaurant. Antonella Sabatini has prepared lunches and dinners here in the Podere dei Nobili for many years (Tel. 0564-966-867; the park is closed Mondays). The restaurant is now run by her son-in-law and daughter, but she is still responsible for the varied menu that includes dishes featuring all the wild herbs of Monte Labbro. Antonella also raises her own vegetables and domestic animals for the restaurant. She serves pastas stuffed with various aromatic herbs, roast chicken with thyme, wild mint, oregano, and wild chives, or a turkey breast rolled with various wild salads. Antonella knows all the edible *funghi* on the mountain, and makes use of all of them. She also includes dandelions, poppies, and other weeds that grow in the fields in dishes at the restaurant.

She has a special way of preparing chickpeas, an old Maremma tradition, she told me. The chickpeas go into a large pot, ashes from the hot fire are siphoned in on top of them and boiling water poured over. In this way, they soak for at least six hours; she drains and washes them, rubs them dry, and the skin comes right off. All this happens before the chickpeas are put to cook slowly in more simmering water. They turn out unbelievably tender, skinless, and tasty.

Antonella has no freezer, nothing is from the tin. Her food is freshly made every day, the menu gets decided when she sees what is available, so it's best to call ahead.

Another restaurant to savor, a treat not to miss, is an inauspicious little inn between Monte Fiore and Arcidosso, at a crossroad with another road leading to Monte Amiata. Ristorante Aiuole (see page 289) is about seven kilometers from either town.

Arcidosso, just under Monte Labbro, is the biggest town of Mount Amiata, the capital of the area. It's mostly a modern commercial and cultural center, but its profile against the sky is a noble one. The old *centro storico* is a warren of ancient streets meandering from an old stone portal through narrow streets that bring you to yet another Aldobrandeschi castle. The *castello* dominates its profile from afar.

The way back down from Arcidosso takes you through to Sasso d'Ombrone and the harmonious hill towns of Cinigiano and Monticello. It's a lovely ride through fields of grazing sheep and even some Maremma horses.

SPECIALITIES OF THE AREA

There's an old saying on Mount Amiata that the daily diet here consisted of *"pan di legna e vin di nuvoli."* *Pan di legna* (bread of the woods) is the chestnut, the basis of so many dishes here. *Vin di nuvoli* (wine of the clouds) is the clear pure water of the mountain springs.

Today's delicious soup called *acquacotta*, "cooked water," is the historical beneficiary of the *vin di nuvoli* of the Amiata. This little soup comes in variants all over Tuscany. One of the best versions is here where it was born of little more than fresh onions, good olive oil, dried bread, and fresh spring water, to provide woodsmen their daily lunch in the forest. The livelihood of the mountain people came mostly from harvesting the woods. The *boscaiolo*, or woodsman, collected and turned the cut timber into carbon. Amiato, like so much of Tuscany, was poor country. When the *boscaioli* went off to chop wood, they carried their lunch with them: an onion or two and bread. Water came from the clean, pure springs all over the mountains. Leonella Quattrini, who now owns the Ristorante Aiuole near Arcidosso—a memorable restaurant—remembers her grandfather, a woodsman on Monte Labbro, taking his onions, oil, and bread from the larder each morning as he went out to chop and bring back the wood.

This was the original *acquacotta*, onions sliced and cooked in a bit of water, flavored undoubtedly with a good bit of salt, and poured over the bread. The soup has developed from there; today every cook has his own version with a variety of seasonal ingredients—Swiss chard, wild mushrooms in the fall, in summer zucchini and other flavors, carrots and celery, tomatoes, and so on. For Sunday lunch, or celebrations, an egg is dropped in at the last minute. Like so many other nourishing soups of Tuscany, *acquacotta* is still served over a slice of yesterday's bread.

Chestnuts provided much of the mountains' basic nourishment, understandable when you realize that a little more than two pounds of chestnuts provides the body with more than 1000 calories. In and around Santa Fiora and Piancastagnaio you'll see securely fenced, century old, well tended chestnut groves that produce *marroni*, unusually large dark brown nuts, from pruned large-trunked full plants. The smaller chestnuts—from less nurtured trees—are dried for several months, then peeled and finely ground into "sweet" flour that in turn is made into *polenta dolce*, a staple of the kitchen in these parts. Fiorella dei Santis, a *castagnetta* in Santa Fiora, showed us around her grove one day. Her family, she noted proudly, has been nurturing the grove for almost seventy-five years. Some of the trunks have diameters of well over three feet. From October through December Fiorella spends her entire day in the grove collecting, separating, and packing the chestnuts for their different uses. Wholesalers come every day with their trucks to collect the heavy burlap bags and take them to markets all over Italy. Other licensed collectors gather their chestnuts in the forests; no one without a license is allowed.

Chestnut flour is best after mid-December, the moment when stone grinding begins. Hearty chestnut *polenta* is served with simple game *ragù*, fresh *ricotta* cheese, or sausages. There's also a chestnut bread—*fiandulone*—flavored with rosemary, and a purée made from boiled chestnuts, *la pichiona*. The nuts are also prepared here like those sold on city streets, roasted on the ashes of an open fire in a long-handled hole-punched pan.

The forests are rich with wild mushrooms, *funghi porcini* and others. They sprout profusely under the chestnut trees. I was sitting in a cafe, having a coffee in Cinigiana, and fell into conversation with a group of rugged old men about the hills and their riches. It was fall. The talk naturally turned to *funghi*. One old chap told me of his youth in the woods collecting *funghi* for the noonday soup. He'd go off every day during the season from late September through early November. The mushrooms came home fresh and fragrant in their baskets, his mother cleaned and sliced them, heated some fresh olive oil, threw in some garlic, a few hot peppers, the *funghi*, some chopped parsley, and a little water. A goodly amount of salt finished off the dish as a final act of love. With a slice of the roughest sort of homemade bread to sop it up, it was a daily feast.

During their season, *porcini* go into many main courses, as do numerous other wild mushrooms: the little yellow *giallarelli* or *finferli*, the orange-topped *ovoli*, and, in springtime, a mushroom that some think is the finest around, the *prugnolo*. In one delicious *zuppa di funghi*, a variety of mushrooms are first sautéed and then puréed. Hunks of pungent *porcini* and some water go in at the last minute.

Olive oil is another of the area's singular products. The *olivastra seg-*

gianese, the tree I mentioned above, produces one of the sweetest, most fragrant oils I've ever tasted. It is not a well-known oil, but the small production travels far. Carlotta Greene, at Castello di Pontentino in Seggiano, exports it to England. In Seggiano itself, the first Sunday of December is devoted to a festival celebrating its pressing. Another notable oil here comes from Piancastagnaio, where volcanic ash has formed the particularly fertile soil.

Wild life is extensive. From mid-September on you may wake to sounds of a battlefield. Nothing explosive, just a lot of shooting. Birds, wild hare, and wild boar are all fair game. You find them on every menu during the winter months, delivered to local restaurants and *trattorie* by the hunters themselves.

Ricotta is the prime local cheese. It is eaten fresh with chestnut bread or turned into pasta fillings and tasty desserts. Another well-regarded product of the Maremma hills is honey taken from various mountain plants. It goes well with the various sheep's cheeses produced from the flocks one often sees here grazing on the mountain meadows.

Truffles — both black and white — are newcomers to the diet of Mount Amiata, eaten mostly in restaurants. In the past they were not sought; they were thought to require too much work. Today they flavor cheeses and sauces.

MONTENERO

ANTICA FATTORIA DEL GROTTAIONE
Via della Piazza, Montenero d'Orcia • Tel. and Fax 0564-954-020
Open for lunch and dinner, closed Mondays. Prices inexpensive to moderate.

The little square in Montenero is like a big courtyard. Antica Fattoria del Grottaione is located on the left. It's part of the old *fattoria* or administration building of a once large estate. The restaurant shares an old building with the Perazzeta wine and oil warehouse next door. The entire complex has been well restored. The restaurant with its arched rubbed-brick ceilings is a beautifully designed and inviting place. Summer dining is on the rear terrace with a view over the rich farmlands of the Val d'Orcia. Flavio Biserni opened the restaurant only a few years ago, after some years in Arcidosso. He is inventive and works hard at new versions of traditional dishes. Autumn brings chestnuts and game: Flavio offers fine *tortelli di castagne* (discs of pasta stuffed with chestnut puree) served with a *ragù* of *capriolo*, a much-hunted roe buck. Another dish I especially liked was *polenta con bietole di vigna e salsa di zucca*, *polenta* made with a special chard that grows in the vineyards between the vines. It has a slight winey taste. After it's cooked the chard *polenta* is cut into little squares to be covered with a pumpkin sauce. *Zuppa di spinaci e ricotta* is an old Maremma shepherd dish served here in a new entirely soothing version.

Flavio's house wine is the local wine of Montecucco, from Perazzeta next door. It is the basis for his *brasato di cinghiale*, wild boar stewed in wine. Another worthy main course is *baccala al contadino*, salt cod in a vegetable tomato sauce. It's all in the good tradition of Maremma's rural kitchen.

Swiss Chard Polenta with Squash and Pine Nut Sauce

POLENTA CON BIETOLE E SALSA DI ZUCCA

Serves 6

1 bunch Swiss chard leaves, with ribs removed

3 tablespoons extra virgin olive oil

A sprinkling of salt, plus an additional 1 teaspoon

1½ cups quick-cooking *polenta*

About 6 cups water

1 heaping tablespoon butter

2 garlic cloves

1 pound peeled and cubed squash or pumpkin

1½ cups chicken stock

1 sprig basil leaves, chopped

¼ cup pine nuts

Wash the chard, and put it, still wet, into a sauté pan with 1 tablespoon of oil and a good sprinkling of salt. When the chard has wilted, remove with its oil and remaining water and purée.

Put the puréed chard, the *polenta*, and 1 teaspoon of salt into a large pan with 1½ cups of water. Whisking constantly, bring to a boil, and add another 4½ cups water. Continue to cook over a medium flame, whisking all the time, until the *polenta* thickens, about 10 minutes. Add a heaping tablespoon of butter and whisk in. Remove from heat.

Turn out onto rectangular baking dish or large tart pan and spread smoothly. The polenta should not be more than an inch thick. Leave to cool and solidify, about 1 hour.

Meanwhile, make the sauce: Put the remaining 2 tablespoons of olive oil into a large saucepan with the garlic and squash cubes. Sauté for several minutes and add the chicken stock. Cook at a high heat until the squash is completely soft, and about 1 cup of liquid remains. Add the basil leaves and remove from heat. Lightly toast the pine nuts and reserve. Blend the squash with its remaining liquid and add the pine nuts.

Before serving, slice the hardened *polenta* into squares and warm in the oven (or fry if you like) before covering with the heated squash sauce.

Spinach and Ricotta Soup
ZUPPA DI SPINACI E RICOTTA

Serves 6

This delicious soup is not at all as acidic as it may sound. The water can be a light stock if you like. I prefer it with plain water.

1 pound onions (about 3 large), thinly sliced
1 tablespoon olive oil
5 pounds fresh spinach, washed and dried
1 small wine-glass red wine
1 pound fresh sheep *ricotta*, broken into small pieces
Salt and freshly ground pepper
6 slices day-old country bread, toasted

In a large soup pot, melt the onions in the olive oil over a low heat for about 20 minutes, stirring often, until the onion is completely soft. Add the spinach, bit by bit, until it all fits. As it melts down, throw in the red wine, and cook for half an hour over a low heat. Add the *ricotta*, and cover with boiling water. Add lots of salt and pepper and cook for another half hour. Place a toast in each soup bowl and pour the soup over.

PIANCASTAGNAIO

RISTORANTE ANNA
Viale Gramsci 486, Piancastagnaio • Tel. 0577-786-061
Best to reserve, especially for lunch. Open daily for lunch and dinner during the summer; closed Mondays in winter. Closed 15 days in September for yearly vacation. Prices are moderate.

Judging from the crowds that gather here daily for lunch, Ristorante Anna is a place for businessmen who like to eat well and for family celebrations. The surroundings, just outside the city wall, up a commercial street from the massive *castello*, are not very promising. Once inside, however, the feeling is one of a good country kitchen.

Giuseppe "Pino" Sprolli has been working with cook Anna Maria Petrucci for fifteen years developing a rich menu that changes with the seasons. In fall and winter, game, chestnut, and mushroom dishes dominate along with various hearty soups. Lighter fare comes with warmer weather; *zucchini lasagna*, made with both the vegetable and its flowers, is served with a simple tomato and basil sauce. *Gnocchi* come with a *pesto* of arugula.

Piancastagnaio in the province of Siena, just over the border that of Grosseto, and *pici*, the fresh pasta made south of Siena, makes its way onto Pino's menu. It is served with a simple garlic and oil dressing sprinkled with a good amount of fresh herbs.

The autumn/winter menu is hearty. The *funghi* soup with *farro* is a delicious mix of beans, *farro*, a bit of hot pepper, and precious wild *funghi* from the chestnut forests nearby. Freshly ground *polenta* comes with a sauce of meat *ragù* into which some *funghi* have been dropped.

The classic Tuscan dish, *fegatello*, today found in few restaurants, is a regular favorite at Ristorante Anna. It consists of hunks of pork liver cooked on a bed of fennel seeds. You usually find *fegatello* in meat markets resting in a bed of pork fat; here there's no visible fat, just a tender chunk of liver still lightly pink inside, permeated with fennel and rosemary. The stewed wild boar here is as good as you'll find anywhere.

Piancastagnaio is named after its ubiquitous nut, and chestnuts dominate dishes here. The best chestnut dessert in the area is at Ristorante Anna, a light chestnut cake topped with chestnut paste and whipped cream.

Arugula Pesto for Gnocchi
PESTO DI ARUGULA

Serves 6 generously

7 ounces arugula (about 3 bunches), with hard stems removed
1 bunch basil leaves
1 handful pine nuts
1 cup grated Parmesan cheese, plus additional cheese at table
1 clove garlic
1 teaspoon salt
1 cup extra virgin olive oil
1¼ pounds potato *gnocchi*

Put the first 6 ingredients into the food processor, turn it on, and slowly add the oil. Process until smooth. Mix well with the cooked *gnocchi* and serve with more cheese at table.

Pork Liver with Fennel Seeds
FEGATELLO

Serves 4

Ask your butcher for the liver and caul fat for this dish. You'll need enough caul fat to wrap the divided four pieces.

1 large pork liver, about 1½ pounds
Salt and freshly ground pepper
1 section caul fat
1 large handful fennel seeds
1 sprig rosemary
2 sprigs dried fennel stalks, if available
Olive oil

Preheat the oven to 350 degrees.

Cut the pork liver into four pieces. Salt and pepper each well. Divide the caul fat into four sections and wrap each piece of liver in the netting. Secure with a toothpick and lay into a baking dish over 1 or 2 sprigs of rosemary and dried fennel stalks. Throw a good handful of fennel seeds over the top and drip olive oil over each piece. Bake for about 15 minutes. The liver should not be overcooked, but still pink inside, and tender.

SANTA FIORA

IL BARILOTTO

Via Carolina 24, Santa Fiora • Tel. and Fax 0564-977089

Open for lunch and dinner. Closed Wednesday, and from November 20 through December 7, and from June 20 through July 1. Reservations recommended. Moderate prices.

You'll find this fine little restaurant along Via Carolina leading down from Santa Fiora's main Piazza Garibaldi to the Church of Sante Fiora e Lucilla. It specializes in traditional local food. The big season is fall, when game, wild mushrooms, and chestnuts dominate the menu. Pierangelo Croci, the owner, sees to it that it's good throughout the year. When local hunters no longer have game to bring him, he concentrates on local spring vegetables—artichokes, zucchini, and spring peas. Hearty soups mark the winter season; light, tomato-based pastas are fresh and fragrant during the summer. Other than stews and soups that take longer preparation, every dish is made "on the minute," when it's ordered.

Pierangelo's cook, Daniela, worked in Rome for years before she came to Santa Fiora and Il Barilotto's tiny kitchen. The restaurant, like so many in rural Tuscany, grew out of Pierangelo's father's grocery. His father first added a bar, then a little *osteria*, and, in 1927, received permission for a full restaurant. It's been growing ever since, situated wonderfully and serving good food.

Wild Mushroom Bruschetta
BRUSCHETTA DI FUNGHI

Serves 6

A mix of fresh field mushrooms with an added 1 ounce of dried *porcini* works well if fresh or frozen Italian *porcini* are not available. Soak the dried mushrooms for half an hour in warm water, squeeze out the water, and chop finely. Add them to the pan after the chopped field mushrooms.

¾ pound *funghi porcini* (can be frozen)
2 cloves garlic
1 small hot pepper
1 bunch parsley leaves
3 tablespoons extra virgin olive oil
Salt and freshly ground pepper
6 slices Tuscan bread, each about ½ inch wide, toasted

Clean the mushrooms. Chop both the caps and stems into tiny pieces. Mince the garlic, hot pepper, and parsley together.

Heat the oil together with the chopped garlic, pepper, and parsley mixture. When the oil begins to bubble, add the mushrooms, a good amount of salt and freshly ground pepper, and cook for about 10 minutes, until the mushrooms are soft and begin to release water. Divide the mushrooms over the toasted bread and serve.

Maremma "Cooked Water"
ACQUACOTTA MAREMMA

Serves 6

This typical Maremma dish has traveled all over Tuscany, altered as it goes. This is an embellishment of the original. Traditionally, an egg for each diner is added when *acquacotta* is served at festive Sunday lunch.

1 cup dried *borlotti* or cranberry beans
1 pound yellow onions, sliced
2 ribs celery, sliced
1 small hot pepper, chopped
2 tablespoons olive oil, plus additional at table
1½ pounds Swiss chard, finely chopped
4 tablespoons tomato paste
Salt and freshly ground pepper
2 cups boiling water
6 eggs (optional)
6 slices toasted Tuscan bread

Soak the beans overnight. Cook them slowly in water to cover by 1 inch. When soft, purée half the beans and mix with the remaining beans and their water. Set aside.

Over a very low fire, cook the onions, celery, and red pepper in the olive oil. Don't allow the onions to brown. About a half hour should do it.

Add the Swiss chard. Mix well and cook for another few minutes. Add the tomato concentrate to the bowl with the beans and their purée, and mix, then add this mixture to the soup pot. Add lots of salt and freshly ground pepper to taste. Add the water and cook for another half hour.

If serving eggs, drop them one by one into the soup pot, trying to keep them separate. Cover the pot until the eggs begin to become firm on top. To serve, place a slice of toast in each soup bowl. Scoop out an egg for each with a slotted spoon, place on the toast, and ladle soup to cover. Serve with fresh extra virgin olive oil to drip over at table.

Stewed Wild Boar
CINGHIALE ALLA MAREMMA

Serves 6

3 tablespoons olive oil
3 sprigs fresh rosemary
Leaves of 3 sprigs fresh sage
1¼ pounds wild boar, cubed
Salt and freshly ground pepper

1 cup hearty red wine
¾ pound fresh or tinned tomatoes, peeled and chopped
25 black olives, pitted

In a heavy pot large enough to hold all the ingredients, heat the olive oil together with 1 sprig each of the rosemary and the leaves from 1 sprig of sage. Brown the cubed meat on all sides. Add salt and pepper, and throw in the red wine. Allow to bubble and reduce to about half. Add the chopped tomatoes, lower the flame, and cook slowly, covered, for about 1½ hours, until the meat is cooked through and soft. Add the olives at the last minute. Taste and adjust for salt and pepper.

Chestnut Cream
CREMA DI CASTAGNE

Serves 4-6

1 pound peeled chestnuts (uncooked)
Milk
½ cup cream
½ cup sugar
¼ cup brandy
Whipped cream

Put the chestnuts in a saucepan and add milk to cover by an inch. Cook slowly until the milk has almost evaporated, about 15-20 minutes. The chestnuts should be soft enough to purée in a blender or a food mill.

Put the purée back into the saucepan with the cream, sugar, and brandy. Cook over a low heat until the sugar has melted. Mix well and pour into a serving dish to cool.

Serve with whipped cream at table.

ARCIDOSSO

RISTORANTE AIUOLE

Bivio Aiuole, at the base of Mount Amiata • Tel. 0564-967-300

Open for lunch and dinner. Closed Sunday evenings and Mondays, and the month of November. Moderately priced. Best to reserve.

Ristorante Aiuole, a delightful restaurant, is about seven kilometers from Arcidosso, on the road to Santa Fiora. It's at the very base of the road to Mount Amiata's summit; from Aiuole a road leads right to the top.

Ugo Quattrini is a large graceful man with a Mark Twain moustache bursting from his gentle face and eyes that twinkle when he talks about the food he serves in his restaurant. He is a man determined to maintain—and recreate—the culinary traditions of the Maremma mountains. The menu here was originally his mother's, carried on and further elaborated upon by her disciple, Anna Soldi, who currently runs the kitchen. It's like a family kitchen, just off the dining room. You can glimpse Ugo joining in to whip up something in a saucepan, or his petite, pretty wife Leonella—she normally sits at the cash register—quickly making a sauce for a particular pasta someone's ordered. Her father was a chef on grand Italian ocean liners like the *Michelangelo*; he still sometimes makes a grand meal for friends here. Otherwise Ugo advises and serves, comments and exchanges funny stories with diners most of whom seem to know one another.

His mother Rosanna opened the restaurant/hotel in the 1940s, on Ugo's fourteenth birthday, serving dishes that she'd been preparing all her life. Now it's his. There's no menu really—everything served is last minute, or prepared for the day. The restaurant fills for lunch with local diners, from the mayor to businessmen. Most of them eat exactly what Ugo suggests. At crowded moments, he hops into the kitchen to help. He claims Giancarlo Bini of Suvereto's Ombrone restaurant as his mentor, along with Giorgio Veronelli, the closest thing to a food maven in Italy.

Ugo not only knows food, but he can tell you about the whole area surrounding Arcidosso, an area he thinks of as mystically endowed. The various mountain springs, more than thirty of them, come in three qualities—"drunken water," "good water" and "strong water." They give special energy and mental health, he says. They also deflate any swollen stomach.

The first time I visited Aiuole, I asked Ugo to give me a tasting, a sampling of what he thought were his best dishes. We didn't know one another yet. He seated me at one end of the restaurant, and one by one placed fifteen dishes in front of me, announcing only the names. I didn't understand all the names, but finished them off with a zest I didn't know I possessed. We began with a *minestra*, a *farro* soup lightly touched with freshly ground pepper and the lovely *olivastra* oil. When I questioned the *farro*, assuming this was something transported from the Garfagnana (where it is plumper), he cited a local truism "where there was misery, there was *farro* and chestnut flour." Next came *gnudi*, a light and airy local specialty, a sort of large puff of *ricotta*, chard, and wild greens, served with a sprinkling of grated aged *pecorino* and, again, the oil. Another specialty of the house called *fiocchi di neve* (snow flakes) followed, large light balls of *ricotta* and mashed potato served with grated cheese and oil. Then arrived a large *tortelli* filled with *ricotta* and spinach and topped with a highly flavored, fragrant meat sauce. *Acquacotta*, with an addition of freshly harvested beans and a bit of tomato, came next, and then a *zuppa di funghi*. It wasn't *porcini* season. Ugo confessed that these were mushrooms he'd frozen in previous months. Such were his *primi*, the course that comes after *antipasto*, which, thankfully I'd not eaten. Now began his *secondi*, the main courses. A bit of rabbit in a caper and anchovy sauce was followed by a deliciously stuffed cabbage leaf, pork in tomato sauce, and a five-layer *melanzane parmigiana*.

Next, gratefully, was the final main course: wild boar in a chocolate sauce. I couldn't believe it had some tradition attached. Ugo explained that it was originally made here with the chocolate, raisins, and pine nuts left over from the traditional Easter eggs. I asked how such poverty could produce chocolate Easter eggs. It was a splurge, Ugo said, and the leftovers had to be used up. With all this I drank the house wine, a lovely Montalcino.

Samples of four desserts arrived on a single plate. They were, hard to believe, an almost weightless end to a long meal. The one I liked best was a dish of fresh *ricotta*, tasting almost like thick cream, topped by a delectable caramelized chestnut paste. Afterwards, Ugo and I sat down together to a glass of golden, almost orange, *grappa* that he told me, when I asked to buy a bottle, was forty years old and made from the fabled Sassacaia wine of Bolgheri.

"Naked" Ravioli
GNUDI

Serves 8

This is the filling for a *ravioli* that is made into a dumpling, without the pasta wraparound, thus the term "naked" *ravioli*, or as it's known in this area, *gnudi*. In the Casentino they are called *gnocchi di Casentino*. At Aiuole they are made without flour and light enough to melt in the mouth, not an easy task for the home cook. It's safer to put a bit of flour into the paste, allow it to rest overnight before forming the small balls. Fresh herbs and field greens such as nettles and young dandelions are added at Aiuole. Ugo serves them with dressing of fresh olive oil and Parmesan. They also go marvelously with a butter and cheese dressing or a simple tomato sauce.

2 pounds fresh spinach or Swiss chard combined with field greens (about
    3 cups), cooked and squeezed dry of water
1 pound *ricotta* cheese (about 2 cups)
3 eggs
1½ cups grated Parmesan or aged *pecorino* cheese
Salt and freshly ground pepper
Nutmeg
½ cup flour, and more as needed, plus additional for coating the *gnudi*
Extra virgin olive oil and more grated cheese as dressing

In a food processor, purée the cooked and dried greens with the *ricotta*. Add the eggs and grated cheese, salt, pepper, and a good grinding of nutmeg. Remove to a bowl, and sift in 3½ ounces of flour. Allow to rest overnight.

Use a teaspoon to scoop out all of the mixture. Roll each teaspoon of mixture into a small walnut-sized ball. Pour some flour onto a place and roll each of the balls in it. Place them on baking paper to rest for an hour. Drop into a large pot of well salted boiling water. When the *gnudi* rise to the top, lift them out gently with a slotted spoon onto a serving plate. Sprinkle with more cheese, drizzle with olive oil, and serve.

Stuffed Cabbage Leaves
CAVOLO RIPIENO

Serves 6

1 large white cabbage
1 pound pork sausage meat
3 tablespoons grated Parmesan
5 sprigs basil leaves, chopped
1 bunch parsley leaves, chopped
Salt and freshly ground pepper
Nutmeg
3 eggs
1½ cups tomato sauce

Preheat the oven to 350 degrees.

Bring a large pan of salted water to a boil, add the cabbage, and simmer it, covered, for half an hour. Remove to a colander and cool. When it's cool enough to handle, gently separate the leaves, cutting away the core from the bottom as you go to make it easier. The outside leaves will be almost impossible, but it gets easier as you reach the inner leaves. There should be at least 12 leaves, but the stuffing will probably fill even more. Reserve the core and the unusable leaves.

Mix the sausage meat well with the grated cheese, the chopped basil and parsley, some salt, and a good grinding of both pepper and nutmeg. In a food processor chop the unused core and leaves of the cabbage, and add to the sausage mixture. Gently beat the eggs and add, mixing well.

Pour half a cup of water into a baking pan large enough to hold all the stuffed leaves. Loosely fill and close each of the cabbage leaves and place one next to the other in the pan, seam side down. Pour the tomato sauce over the cabbage and bake for half an hour, basting if need be. Serve warm.

Rabbit in Caper/Anchovy Sauce

CONIGLIO CON SALSA DI CAPPERI ED ACCIUGHE

Serves 6

2 cloves garlic
2 sprigs rosemary
2 sprigs sage
2 tablespoons olive oil
1 large rabbit, cut into small pieces
The liver of the rabbit, cut in half
1 cup white wine
1 tablespoon capers preserved in vinegar
3 anchovy fillets

Chop together finely the garlic and leaves of 1 sprig each of the rosemary and sage. Heat with the oil in a pan large enough to hold the rabbit. As the oil around the garlic bubbles add the rabbit pieces and the liver. Sauté until the meat has lost its color.

Add the white wine and allow to evaporate by at least half. Remove the liver and purée with the capers and anchovy fillets. Put the mixture back into the pan, add half a scant cup of water and cook covered over a low flame until the rabbit is cooked through. At the end of the cooking, add the leaves of the remaining sprig of rosemary and sage. Serve with *polenta* or mashed potatoes.

AFTERWORD

We've lived in Tuscany now for more than thirty years. Almost as soon as we settled into our new old farmhouse, I remember being warned by foreign friends who'd been here longer than we that Italy was no longer what it once was. It is a lament we continue to hear often, with greater stringency as the years pass. My Italian friends continuously caution me that Italy is not the rosy picture I conjure. This almost goes without saying. But I hope this book will help to convince them that it's not as bad as all that, and with an open eye you still find the traditions that make this country so dear to so many of us.

Of course things change. The Esselunga supermarket arrived the same year we did...and for my first few summers here I think I was one of the few that ventured in. The communist party ran a cooperative chain of small supermarkets where local people bought staples occasionally, but here in red Tuscany they boycotted inroads of capitalism on the food front, and resisted anything but a recognizable freshness of produce. Even today as supermarkets and huge discount malls thrive—and even the coop has gone private—daily and weekly markets continue to be the center of domestic and social life in the small towns that make up most of the country.

Seemingly uncontrolled urban blight and industrial pollution pervade the valleys and city outskirts, traffic comes to a daily standstill on the *autostrada* leading into town, political life is a Byzantine miasma, the products of "progress" abound. But when we first arrived, our town had no ambulance service, no garbage collector—but for Emilio who came to pick up our trash bags once or twice a week and whom we rewarded with a bottle of *vin santo* and a tip twice a year—and a postman who came only when there was enough mail to deliver. Now we have a four-story health clinic and a fleet of ambulances, paid for and built with local voluntary funds, garbage vans and disposal bins (to where we must now deliver our trash), and mail service that brings us our daily English-language newspaper before noon.

When we first arrived so many old farmhouses were still abandoned, the beautiful hills were marred by overgrown vineyards and neglected olive groves. Houses were shuttered and bleak. In the evenings it was dark all around but for the dim light from neighboring hill towns.

Today we look out in the evening at brilliantly lit, restored old farm-houses, and well-tended olive groves and vineyards. Properties have been bought up by shopkeepers and business people from the densely populated valley below and by non-Italians like us. Farms are once again producing. I often think that we *stranieri*—foreigners—have done our bit to bring old traditions back to Tuscany. Few of our Italian neighbors still make their own wine, and they have leased their olive groves to others. We plod on, making our wine, picking our olives, tidying up the landscape, and at times even working the land ourselves.

But the village hasn't changed a whit, other than welcoming in new-comers of all hues and accents. The real population remains the same, 135 souls. It is a small well-tended village, gently nestling into a hill open to the valley on one side and the Apennine foothills on the other. Two gates at either end of a single winding street are all that remain of an ancient defen-sive wall. (One remnant of a defense tower sits under an entangled mass of green at the edge of our parking area.) The street is lined with red-roofed little stone houses, a few old *palazzi*, and one truly grand villa of the former feudal overlord that is now a Swiss *pension*. A little offshoot of the main road winds up steeply toward the church, past the old Benedictine convent that dominates the skyline. There were still seven ancient nuns living in *chiusura* (seclusion) when we arrived; now it's been abandoned for years. A few yards further up the little road spreads out into a small perfect piazza with its twelfth-century Romanesque church and bell tower, and the Palazzo Pretorio, its splendid front encrusted with coats of arms. The *palazzo* now houses the area archives and is the venue for occasional art shows, con-certs, and lectures. The piazza itself is the place for lots of events, including picture-taking of the many couples who choose this beautiful church and its setting for their biggest day.

We used to have a little *bottega* about midway through the village, the only shop for basics and a few fresh vegetables. Housewives picked up their daily needs here, exchanged gossip, and paid bills at the end of the month. The village children came every morning to fetch a *panino* or *schiacciata*, a snack to take off to school. Bread arrived from the next door *forno a legna* (wood-burning stove) during the morning hours; we ate it before it cooled. A butcher from the town below delivered meat to every home each day and took orders for the next day. The *forno* was just under the old gate (it still is, it's still good but no longer wood-burning) and a daily pick-up truck comes by in the morning to sell fresh vegetables, but the little *bottega* and daily deliveries of meat have succumbed to "progress." With prosperity arrived the usual crush of automobiles, two for most families.

Other than this, not a stone has been added to the village within the walls during the years we've been here. The *Belle Arte* commission in Florence has inflexible rules that govern every threatened change. No one can add a centimeter, or change the color of a façade, or cut a window where none has been before. New buildings are banned. The green zones remain green. Amazingly the breathtaking view from our terraces over the foothills towards the mountains is still essentially the same as it has been since the sixteenth century. The single threat on the horizon is a proposed car park—convenient for no one—to be carved from the olive groves on the far side of the hill under the church cemetery. Perhaps the *Belle Arte* commission will veto that as well. I hope so.

INDEX OF LOCATIONS

(Festivals, markets, museums, shops, and restaurants are listed under those subheadings)

INDEX OF RECIPES

Medieval Pork Roast with Juniper Berries and Pomegranate (*Arrosto di maiale medievale*) 153

Pappardelle with Hare Sauce (*Pappardelle alla lepre*) 257

Pork Chops with Apples (*Costolette di maiale alle mele*) 265

Pork Liver with Fennel Seeds (*Fegatello*) 284

Pork Tenderloin with Chestnuts (*Maiale con castagne*) 79

Rabbit in Caper/Anchovy Sauce (*Coniglio con salsa di capperi e acchiuge*) 293

Rabbit in Wine Vinegar (*Coniglio di Arrigo VII*) 204

Roast Leg of Lamb (*Agnello al forno*) 201

Stewed Wild Boar (*Cinghiale alla Maremma*) 287

Stuffed Cabbage Leaves (*Cavolo ripieno*) 292

Stuffed Pork Roast (*Portafogli alla fagiolino*) 126

Wild Boar in Olive Sauce (*Cinghiale con olive*) 228

Mousse

Fish Mousse (*Mentecata di pesce*) 247

Ricotta Mousse with Scampi (*Sformata di ricotta con gamberi rossi*) 251

Pasta

Artichoke *Lasagna* (*Lasagna ai carciofi*) 258

Farfalle with Red Beet Sauce (*Farfalle con barbabietola*) 131

Fresh Pasta with Red Mullet (*Straccetti con le triglie*) 252

Fusilli with Carrot and Bacon Sauce (*Fusilli con carote e pancetta*) 130

Pappardelle with Duck *Ragu* (*Pappardelle con salsa anatra*) 156

Pappardelle with Hare Sauce (*Pappardelle alla lepre*) 257

Pici with Thick, Garlicky Tomato Sauce (*Pici aglione*) 203

Potato *Tortelli* or *Ravioli* (*Tortelli di patate*) 171

Ravioli in Fresh Tomato Sauce (*Ravioli con salsa pomodoro*) 51

Scamorza Ravioli with Truffle Oil (*Ravioli di scamorza con olio di tartufi*) 146

Spaghettini with Asparagus and Shrimp (*Spaghettini con asparagi e gamberi*) 249

Summer Tomato Pasta (*Pasta pomodoro Estiva*) 129

Tagliatelle with Creamy Onion Sauce (*Tagliatelle con cipolle cremose*) 131

Testeroli with *Pesto* (*Testeroli con pesto*) 38

Polenta

Polenta "in Chains" (*Polenta incatentata*) 39

Swiss Chard *Polenta* with Squash and Pine Nut Sauce (*Polenta con bietole e salsa di zucca*) 281

Poultry

INDEX OF MAIN INGREDIENTS

ABOUT THE AUTHOR

Beth Elon and her husband, the political historian Amos Elon, have lived in Tuscany for more than thirty years. In that time, she restored a centuries-old farmhouse; reestablished its vineyard and olive groves (producing her own wine and olive oil); planted vegetable and herb gardens; cultivated the orchard; and learned to cook using the bounty of the local countryside—all with the help of her neighbors, who taught her how to do all of these things in the traditional Tuscan way.

Elon's previous books include *A Mediterranean Farm Kitchen* and *The Big Book of Pasta*.